Walter Van Tilburg Clark: Critiques

By Charlton Laird

Thunder on the River (1949)
The Miracle of Language (1953)
Modern English Handbook
with Robert M. Gorrell (1953; 6th ed., 1976)
Language in America (1970)
*And Gladly Teche: Notes on Instructing the Natives
in the Native Tongue* (1970)
Webster's New World Thesaurus (1971)
The Word (1981)

By Walter Van Tilburg Clark

The Ox-Bow Incident (1940)
The City of Trembling Leaves (1945)
The Track of the Cat (1949)
The Watchful Gods and Other Stories (1950)
The Journals of Alfred Doten, 1849–1903
edited by Walter Van Tilburg Clark (1973)

WALTER VAN TILBURG CLARK: CRITIQUES

EDITED BY

Charlton Laird

UNIVERSITY OF NEVADA PRESS

RENO, NEVADA • 1983

Library of Congress Cataloging in Publication Data
Main entry under title

Walter Van Tilburg Clark, critiques.

Includes bibliographical references and index.
1. Clark, Walter Van Tilburg, 1909–1971—Addresses,
essays, lectures. 2. Authors, American—20th century—
Biography—Addresses, essays, lectures. 3. Nevada in
literature—Addresses, essays, lectures. 4. West (U.S.)
in literature—Addresses, essays, lectures. I. Laird,
Charlton Grant, 1901–
PS3505.L376Z94 1983   813'.52   83–6789
ISBN 0–87417–077–X

University of Nevada Press, Reno, Nevada 89557 USA
© University of Nevada Press. All rights reserved
Book and jacket design by Dave Comstock
Printed in the United States of America

To Fred M. Anderson, M.D.,
who, like his friend Walter,
has done great good
for the community

Contents

Preface

The year 1971 recorded the death of Walter Van Tilburg Clark, Nevada's most distinguished literary figure and one of the leading interpreters of the American West. He had been closely linked to the Nevada campus and to northwestern Nevada; his father had been president of the university. Walter started his writing career as a student there and held two Nevada degrees. He became a faculty member in the Department of English and writer-in-residence—posts he held until his terminal illness.

His friends and colleagues were deeply moved at his death, and moved, also, to commemorate him. The present volume results from one of the projects initiated by them in his behalf. Dr. N. Edd Miller, then president of the university, was a prime mover, working with two committees: the Walter Clark Committee, chaired by Professor Robert D. Harvey, and the Hilliard Fund Committee, chaired by Professor Charlton Laird. The Hilliard Fund provided honoraria for a series of lectures on Clark, and Laird was named the first Hilliard Professor. Laird offered a seminar in Clark's work the following autumn from which in one way or another much of the content of this volume was engendered.

During the years that have intervened, many friends of Clark and some who never knew him have given generously toward creating the work here presented. Some contributions can be inferred from the table of contents. Clearly the most productive of the contributors has been Walter Clark's son Robert, who was able to flesh out his own astute criticism with a knowledge of his father and his father's writing that no one else could provide. Indispensable also were some of his other projects, not recognizable in the table of contents, such as the ordering of his father's papers. Likewise, Clark's daughter, Mrs. Barbara

Salmon, helped with editorial chores. Mr. Kenneth J. Carpenter, in charge of the Special Collections Department at the
University of Nevada Library, was zealous beyond the call of
his office in getting the Clark papers for the university, and seeing to their ordering and preservation. Lovers of Walter Clark's
work can be grateful to him that the only papers lost are those
that the author himself incinerated.

Credo

Walter Van Tilburg Clark

The following are excerpts from a letter written by Walter Van Tilburg Clark to his son Robert Morse Clark, dated February 1965, after the younger man had expressed doubts about his own efforts at writing.

Writing is not an occupation, it is a way of life, in a sense not altogether unlike that of a religious devotion. It is a means of *discovering* what one feels and believes about life more importantly than it is a means of expressing the feelings and beliefs discovered. Only a fool, or a propagandist in the worst sense, someone who hasn't the faintest understanding of what the personal discipline of writing really means, especially if he is still serving his apprenticeship, his novitiate, feels that he has a unique and burning message for the world. And it is beyond question that when he has delivered himself of that message, which he will do quickly and painlessly, like an elephant dropping a mouse (apologies to Mohammed . . .) it will prove to be something which has already been said at least 10,000 times, and which probably was not greatly worth the saying the last 9,999 of those times. . . . There are no new truths, in that simple sense. It is only that old truths take on new strength and meaning in changed circumstances when they have been rediscovered honestly and expensively out of one's own experience, that experience including, very much including, the sustained and repeated effort to write one's way into that truth as clearly, vitally and undogmatically as possible—the effort, in short, to *prove* that truth, not *preach* it, by compelling the reader to experience it himself. Which the boy with the burning message never does. Witness the scores of self-appointed saviors, beatnik "poets" and "fiction" writers in S. F. and elsewhere, from the author of *On the Road*—I forget his name—on down. . . . That book, and by exactly that title, was written twice before that particular fool was born—once by Jack London about the turn of the century, and again in the 1920s by a guy whose name also slips me at the moment—and this time it shouldn't. But anyway—he was an honest-to-God circus roustabout, hobo train-rider itinerant, tank-town prize fighter. And both books were much better than this last bit of fakery, not only because both authors really were "on the road," out of need, and really had some tough and important experiences they didn't deliberately cook up, but also because neither of them thought he was a savior. . . . Anyway—you know the stuff I mean. All the little self-appointed Christs and Buddhas mouthing shoddy paraphrases of their ancient masters with an air of ultimate discovery . . . and really revealing only their own pretentiousness, ignorance, blind egotism, bottomless self-pity and, of course, the fact that they have never taken the trouble to learn to write, or even to read, because no one who "really knows" is going to extinguish the God-given brilliance of his unique illumination by "making like a professor."

So . . . don't worry because you don't feel that you have anything important to say. Of course you don't—and the fact that you know you don't makes it certain that you *will* have if you keep trying to write as well as you can about particular actualities that interest and move you, trying to discover, as you write, why they interest and move you, until you find, in the true Jamesian sense, your "subject"—or rather, for that is what really happens—until your subject finds you. Which does not mean that all between now and then must go in the wastebasket. Plenty of good and publishable writing—writing well worth the reading—comes of any honest quest. Read Faulkner's first air-force and army stories, and even his *Sartoris;* he is beginning to find his home. They can't sit for a minute beside *The Sound and the Fury* or *Light in August* or *The Bear* . . . or compare the first stories of Henry James or even *The American* and *Daisy Miller* with the masterpiece *The Ambassadors*, or

Conrad's *Victory* with *The Heart of Darkness*. They don't look good in comparison. They are very much still in the quest stage. But they are alive, very much alive, and they deserve to be. . . .

It's not the kind of thing that one can make decisions about. And even if you never published, whether out of too modest misgivings, [or] belated learning and perfectionism like your old man's, or whatever, the writing would be well worth keeping up the rest of your life, because of what you would keep discovering by way of it about yourself and about everything else. I regret having *had* to throw away so much of what I have written, but I don't regret having written it. I learned much while I wrote even the worst of it.

PART I

Walter Clark
as Others Knew Him

Walter Clark, Reno, Nevada, about 1930. (Special Collections, Library, University of Nevada, Reno)

1

Literate Voice in Nevada

Charlton Laird

Many of the materials that appear in this book were generated through a seminar and a series of lectures at the University of Nevada, Reno, during the academic year 1973–74. Speakers were left free in their choice of subject, and it was hoped that at least one would provide a survey sufficiently general to serve as introduction. Inasmuch as none of the contributors was so presumptuous, the editor of this volume has felt obliged to attempt a preliminary sketch.

I n a land of few literate sounds, one informed voice raises echoes. Walter Van Tilburg Clark became such a voice. In the first quarter of the century, when young Walter was growing to maturity in Reno, his community, his state, even the Great Basin had little to do with the fine arts, with science or philosophy or the play of ideas, with anything suggesting cultured creativity. And the previous century had witnessed even less.

Exceptions were few. Mark Twain, by the accident of his having wanted to avoid fighting in a war and by virtue of a convenient relative, spent a few years in Nevada and wrote a rousing book of reminiscences, *Roughing It.* But Samuel Clemens had no alkali in his bones, and once away from the Great Basin he was never drawn back except on speaking tours. The Latter-day Saints, centered in Salt Lake City, cultivated music, but tended to be suspicious of anything so readily susceptible of heresy as are unsanctified words. At times random figures appeared, more like meteors than inhabitants; their orbits took them elsewhere. A few, including Dr. J. E. Church, stayed; a transplanted professor of the classics, he taught Latin and Greek but was delighted with the mountains and developed what became the basic technique for snow surveys everywhere. Indian art was extensive but mostly ignored by whites, who were generally inhospitable to anybody or anything foreign to them, which would have included other races and other sorts of minds, along with the native American.

Certain types of figures flourished. They included leaders of men—Brigham Young was among them—of homey, practical men. There were mining barons on the Comstock and ranching barons wherever cattle or sheep could find pasture. There were audible politicians, some more notable for triviality and corruption than for statesmanship, but a senator is a senator with senatorial power, whatever the untutored mores he might bring to Washington. Itinerants came and went, explorers such as John C. Frémont, scientists such as John Wesley Powell, a few painters and illustrators such as Frederick Remington. But of mature, indigenous self-expression the Old West provided little.

Today the arts, even rather esoteric arts such as ballet and opera, are a part of life in the West, so that Clark can now be seen to have been one of the leaders of a transitional generation. From the Mormon country came Vardis Fisher and Bernard De Voto; from the "high country" of Wyoming, Wallace Stegner; from Oregon, H. L. Davis, writers who turned to the world they knew and used it for serious literary expression, for the kind of writing possible only when skilled craftsmanship, keen intelligence, intimate knowledge, and artistic devotion can be combined in one person.

Clark differed from the others, who mostly had earthy origins. Davis's family pioneered eastern Oregon. Fisher grew up the child of dry farmers (see *Toilers of the Hills*), although he later earned a doctorate *magna cum laude* at the University of Chicago. Stegner was the son of a dirt farmer who sought better land throughout the West and into Canada, and found too little of it. Clark, on the other hand, grew to maturity knowing campus life better than life among the cowpokes. His father, president of a small university, was a recipient of the French

Legion of Honor for service to economics and education. His mother was a highly literate woman, a violinist and social worker. But among the distinguished men of his generation, Clark was the writer who turned most to ranching as it was known in the Old West and, along with it, to mining and sheepherding.

This duality in Clark, his inheritance of European culture as it found a home in the New World, and his love of people with workingman's hands—cowboys, muckers, unpretentious folk of all sorts—moves through his writing. He was himself a sophisticated person; he read widely and perceptively. He loved art and music, and could dabble in both. On the other hand, he worked at whatever job came along, including "helping a little on nearby ranches." And he liked nothing better than sliding onto a bar stool and drinking his beer where sweaty men were lounging, talking of little but the day's doings, and not very subtly of them.

Biographical Sketch

Clark's career as a writer of national and international distinction was brief but brilliant, lasting little more than a decade. But he was a creative person all his days, and this decade must be seen as part of a longer whole. His life can be segmented as follows. (For greater detail, see part 4 of this volume, chapters 17 and 18.)

1909–1932: Youth in the West. After an infancy in Maine and New York, Clark came to Reno at the age of eight, and attended the public schools, including the local university (both B.A. and M.A. in English). He did the usual sorts of things: indulging in sports, dating, and becoming excited about school activities. As one would expect from a young man of good family with commanding devotion, good physique, and native capacity, he generally distinguished himself. He was fond of hiking and camping in the mountains and by some favorite lakes. He hunted and fished, but soon discovered that he liked live animals better than dead ones, and was content to watch and listen. He came to know various parts of the West and many sorts of people living in it. He read omnivorously, and was intrigued by myth and lore, especially the Arthurian story. He began to get about a little; he even visited Robinson Jeffers, to whose poetry he had become devoted.

Meanwhile, he had been trying to write, especially verse. He scribbled almost constantly, throwing away most of what he produced, but occasionally having something printed in school magazines and the like. When he reordered his files in 1932, he burned a great heap of poems, which he estimated at "about four hundred." Among the publications from this period, which he later deprecated, *Ten Women in Gale's House* (1932), was privately published by his father. It is reminiscent of Clark's youthful idols, Jeffers and Edwin Arlington Robinson.

1932–1940: Maturity in the East. Clark was given a teaching assistantship in English at the University of Vermont, and took a second master's degree there. He was writing zealously: prose squibs, brief verse, and a number of rather long poems not published during his lifetime.[1] He married a Presbyterian minister's daughter, whom he had known at the University of Nevada and elsewhere, and the young couple lived precariously for a time—those were depression days—amid places and people that were later to be resurrected in a few of his shorter pieces. He started teaching at Cazenovia, New York, where he soon became very busy, with classes during the day, activities such as coaching in the evening (dramatics and basketball), and then writing, far into the night, sustained, as he put it, "by too much coffee and too many cigarettes." He published some verse here and there, notably in *Poetry*, then the best American journal devoted to verse, but he was turning more and more to prose fiction.

The crucial period may have been the winter of 1933–34, which Clark and his bride spent in an old farmhouse near Essex, New York, very much as Tim Hazard and Mary in *The City of Trembling Leaves* spend their honeymoon at Lake Tahoe, buried in snow. During subsequent years he worked at many pieces, most of which he burned. One extended manuscript has survived, a short novel entitled "Water," which may be as early as 1934–35. It won a prize but failed to find a publisher, probably because it read too much like his verse—stiff, mannered, and philosophical. It did, however, attract the attention of an agent, who asked if the author had anything else to publish. Robert Clark has written me that his father "then rummaged in a corner, as he put it, dusted off the completed draft of the Ox-Bow that he had tied up in a bundle, and sent it." The elder Clark says he had written it during Christmas and Easter vacations, probably in both 1937–38 and 1938–39. It was published in 1940 as The Ox-Bow Incident, was widely praised, and became a best-seller. At about the same time Clark published "Hook," which was featured on television, in Life, and elsewhere. Barely turned thirty, Clark had become a national literary figure.

1940–1950: The Golden Decade. Everybody wanted to print Clark, and he placed manuscripts in the best journals. He was now able to rewrite tales that had been done earlier in unsuccessful drafts, and he added new stories. He was included in the O'Brien selection of best short stories for five consecutive years, with a first prize. One story in The Saturday Evening Post brought him as much money as his advance on Ox-Bow, a novel that became a motion picture. The movie was a critical success but a box office failure—not the sort of western popular in those days. But Clark lived modestly, and he was now free to subordinate making a living to writing. The family stayed some months at an artists' and writers' colony at Indian Springs, north of Las Vegas, where Clark worked at a version of the autobiographical novel that was to become The City of Trembling Leaves (1945).

At Cazenovia and later at Rye, New York, he continued to punish himself, working incessantly. He lost fifty pounds, acquired a touch of tuberculosis, and was near collapse. He was a large-framed man who, when in good flesh, weighed nearly two hundred pounds. He took part of a year to recuperate in Taos, and then moved his family to a ranch in Washoe Valley, between Reno and Carson City.

There he wrote and revised The Track of the Cat, published in 1949. He also worked on "The Watchful Gods" (1950), along with a rewrite of "Water," two novellas never published, and various shorter pieces. His books were being translated and published abroad. By 1950, with three widely acclaimed novels and many briefer pieces, including some of the finest short stories in the language, he would have been on anybody's list of the most promising living American writers. In 1950 the Clarks moved to their favorite community, Virginia City.

1950–1962: The Confused Itinerant Years. During this period Clark had many homes and much public exposure. His reputation as a literary figure grew, but his literary production did not. He taught for a time in the Virginia City High School, and then in the Department of English at the University of Nevada, Reno, where he became convinced that some of his colleagues were being mistreated by the administration. He resigned in protest: he said he loved the university as his alma mater, but he could not continue to teach under an administration that had become fascistic. He hoped to bring pressure on the Board of Regents, but officially they ignored him. In subsequent years he held various teaching posts and a fellowship at Wesleyan University. In 1956, at San Francisco State University, he undertook to build up a program in creative writing that he hoped to make the best anywhere, and many would say he succeeded. He was in demand at writers' institutes and as a public speaker.

During this time *The Track of the Cat* became a movie, and Clark continued to write furiously, but he published little. He projected or started at least two dozen major works, some in as many as five extant drafts, all incomplete. He accused himself of having become a perfectionist, and said that his various teaching posts burned up the time and energy he needed for serious writing, so that nothing came from deep within him. One of his satiric pieces concerns a "man of letters" reduced to a catatonic state; though seeming about to write, he does not move, and questioned can answer only "words, words."

1962–1971: Suspended Animation. By 1962 the administration at the University of Nevada had been replaced by men who appreciated Clark's worth. Brought back as a writer-in-residence, he would be expected to continue his writing, starting with a book making use of journals recently acquired by the university: the diary and other papers of Alfred Doten, for half a century a writer and editor on the Comstock Lode. Clark

planned a sort of biographical volume that would tell the news-
man's story, but would be a mirror of the frontier as well. He
considered "Alf" a kaleidoscopic figure well worth reconstruct-
ing, but he hoped also to use Doten's multifarious doings to
catch the temper of the times and the savor of the land. He
probably intended a sort of fictionized biography that would
grow into an epic of the West.

For some known reasons, along with some probably unknown ones, he abandoned this project and agreed instead to
edit the diaries. The job intrigued him; he joked that he had
been possessed by the spirit of Alf. But Clark was no scholarly
editor at heart and he worked sporadically on the task. Except
for his teaching, which was never exacting during these years,
he spent the remainder of his life preparing the manuscript.
When he died, November 10, 1971, his son Robert finished
the editing and saw the work into press.[2]

Clark's closing years were apparently pleasant but frustrating. He liked his teaching, especially three National Defense
Education Act institutes he took part in, and he always insisted
he was a teacher first and a writer second.[3] He seemed to enjoy
his friendships on the campus and in Virginia City, where he
had bought an old house and was having it rebuilt as a permanent home. But he was disturbed, as he sometimes hinted. Had
he, at middle age, written himself out? He would occasionally
mention that stories were stirring within him—as he put it,
"As soon as I can get Alf off my back"; "When the house is
finished"; "When Barbara's health improves." In 1968 he had
an operation for cancer that was both a physical and emotional
shock. Then his wife died, also of cancer. When he was getting
nicely back to work, his doctors discovered that the cancer had
not been caught in time and had become inoperable. He had
a few months, perhaps a year, probably with much pain. He
spent it putting his affairs in order, trying to remain genial, as
he wasted away.

Why So Little?

Even a brief biographical sketch of Clark raises questions,
especially as to the last three periods. His youth and appren-

ticeship required nearly thirty years, not unusual considering the pitch of competence that the young writer had reached before he started publishing much. This period accounts in part for Clark's facility, for the amazing speed at which he produced when he could write comfortably. It suggests his abiding interest in thought and thought processes, his all-embracing humanity. The third period, which I have endeavored to emphasize by calling it "The Golden Decade," staggers the imagination if one tries to visualize the outpouring of genius during this brief time. It was made possible only because Clark had learned to write at a precipitate pace, had mastered his craft, and had stored up much that he wanted to say, especially in unsuccessful drafts that, though burned, were not forgotten, and constituted prewriting for a later, more successful version. And he now was able to buy himself time and freedom of mind.

Thereafter Clark lived twenty years, mostly in good health, but published nothing that would warrant a book such as the present one to be written about him. Why? His voice was subdued, but not from lack of trying. During the decade beginning about 1951 he seized upon dozens of good creative subjects, worked for hundreds of pages on some, and made repeated starts on others. He must eventually have come to wonder if something inside him precluded his ever again finishing a long, serious piece of writing. He even dropped such hints occasionally. That may have been one reason he accepted the offer to write a book about Alf Doten; he would be obligated to finish it, and he made a practice of meeting his obligations.

One can find extenuating circumstance. Clark took his teaching seriously, and worked unending hours with students. Many scholars and writers who finance their creative work by teaching give their students short shrift. Not Walter Clark. He lavished time on students, most of whom could never repay it with publishable creative work. Going from campus to campus, with varied assignments, he splintered his attention and squandered his time. That was apparently one reason he accepted the post at San Francisco State College; he could settle down and would have only creative writing to teach. But he also had administrative duties, which proved even more consumptive of

time, so that the five years in San Francisco were his least productive—except, of course, that he did much good for many
people.

And place was involved. It was important to Clark. Most of
his stories are set in a determinate locale—settings Clark knew
well from having lived there. The Scripps oceanographic station appears in "The Fish Who Could Close His Eyes." The
Clark summer home appears in "The Watchful Gods," in
"Hook," and elsewhere. Essex and West Nyack in New York
provided backgrounds, but more than anywhere else, Clark felt
that northwestern Nevada was his living and working home,
particularly old towns—Virginia City and Austin. He was
probably more than joking when he called Pyramid Lake and
the lake on Mount Rose "sacred shrines." Both reoccur in his
works, Pyramid especially, in "The Pretender," "The Rise and
the Passing of Bar," repeatedly in *The City,* and in his unpublished works, notably in the verse and in the pastel plates and
ink drawings that accompany many poems. But for some ten
years after 1952, Clark was mostly elsewhere, enticed for brief
periods by some special offer, or in effect banished because he
could not tolerate what he believed to be injustice. All these
must have been deterrents, but they were no more than that,
and Clark was neither a weak nor a timid man. He had overcome obstacles, plenty of them, and laughed at them. But for
whatever reason he could not laugh at his own silence, or do
enough to end it.

A partial explanation can be sought, also, in Clark's way of
rewriting Most serious composition today, including professional composition, is rewritten. Legend has it that Dickens,
and others of his day, wrote with the printer's devil sitting on
the front steps; when the author had dashed off some pages, the
boy would take the instalment to his master, who would set it
into type. If so, that day is gone; except ephemeral jour-
nalism—where lack of time may preclude rewriting—almost
everything is rewritten, much of it repeatedly. Granted that an
author is to rewrite, he may do it in two ways. He can scribble
something, or bat it out on his typewriter, or dictate it; when
he reads it over and finds it wanting, he can throw it away and

start over, benefiting from his previous ineptitudes. Or, he can accept the results of his attempt as a first draft, and can revise it, excising, condensing, inserting, expanding, rephrasing, rethinking, or whatever. He may do this rewriting at once, or he may keep his manuscript as a useful first step and redo it days, weeks, or even years later, and he may repeat this process.

Presumably, all writers revise in both ways, but the second is much the more widely used. A writer may do what is sometimes called "prewriting": mulling over a subject, reading, taking notes, outlining, and the like. Then he produces what he calls a "draft." He has no intention of throwing this away, even if he is not much pleased with it. It becomes the basis of what he calls a "rewrite." He may expect to do several rewrites before he gets what he and his publisher want, both before and after the work has progressed enough so that it has been accepted for publication.

Clark used both methods of revising, but he differed from most professional writers in that he relied much more than is usual on the first—on writing fast and throwing away—and correspondingly less on the second. He did revise in the restricted sense, in that he took a manuscript—especially one already accepted by the publisher—and worked it over line by line and word by word, condensing and sharpening. But frequently, for inadequate drafts, he relied on the wastebasket, the incinerator, or the file-and-forget method—and, fortunately, he used the third of these enough that we now know quite a bit about his ways of working. Often, especially in later life, he planned at least two drafts.

Feeling a story in him, he would write as fast as his pen could go, not bothering to draft sentences or even to punctuate, separating bits of detail with dashes, trying to get the skeleton traced. One thinks of a composer, jotting down melodic themes, expecting to provide bridges, variations, and orchestration later. He recognized that other writers had written in other ways, but he became convinced that for him, writing came best if it came fast. And if it did not come fast and easily, he had better drop the whole idea, or at least put it aside for weeks or even for years.

Thus during the 1950s, and on into the 1960s, Clark had

reason to hope that with the next start, with one of his new ideas or a rejuvenation of an old one, he would once more find himself "running with the stallion." The evidence implies he did not. He might have, had he lived "to get Alf off his back." But that was something else he did not do.

Clark's handling of his material was very much his own. He had an enduring concern for relatively few themes, and to these he returned, even after he had explored them and after years had elapsed. Other areas he shunned, perhaps because they did not intrigue him, perhaps because he felt uncomfortable when he was unsure of himself. He almost excluded one-half the human species: he seldom gives evidence of trying to think or feel from the point of view of a woman. Two of his novels, *Ox-Bow* and *Cat*, were first written with no women in them. "The Watchful Gods" has a girl worshiped in Buck's daydreams, but she was scarcely mentioned in the first draft. Several women appear in *The City*; women were part of the life of young Walter Clark who was transmogrified into Tim Hazard, and they are important in the development of a sense of "the nuclear" in Tim, but they are there because of Tim, not much for themselves. Similarly, Clark was out of sympathy with much of what was happening in his lifetime; he could never have written *A Tree Grows in Brooklyn* or an internationally based story like *Confessions of Felix Krull*.

On the other hand, Clark's few favorite themes seem to have been always with him, both the symbol-forming objects and the permeating basic concepts. Aspens twinkle all through *The City*, but they crop up in many other writings, in the verse especially. A hawk is the protagonist of "Hook," but hawks become symbols in scene after scene, especially in the later poetry. Bar, a wild stallion, is the dominant figure in the short story that bears his name, but "running with the stallion" becomes a permeating theme in *The City*, and such steeds as Bar course their way through some other pieces. That modern urban life is destructive of human kind permeates "The Rapids," and the same theme moves through "The Pretender," and appears in all the novels. In *The City* it becomes the basis of raucous humor in the tales of Stephen Granger.

Inevitably, almost anything might activate one of these

themes—a clear spring had something to do with starting "The Wind and the Snow of Winter," and another spring flows into "The Indian Well." Once a story was started it became an accretion point, or—to change the figure in order to suggest another sort of working in the creative process—it would serve as the tap to release the flow of all that had been storing up. If necessary, Clark would deliberately build background for his story. Presented with the necessity of bringing his hero around the Horn to California in the mid-nineteenth century, he studied sailing vessels and made a sketch of the kind he wanted. He would draw the house plan of the ranch home where action was to take place, and would prepare maps of an imaginary countryside he was conceiving. But on the whole, once he had the idea for a story, he relied on himself as a storehouse of detail—all sorts of detail, geographical, historical, dialectal, everything.

Accordingly, he believed that a large part of a writer's job was to become a storehouse. As a young teacher, following widely accepted precepts he had read, he recommended keeping a journal, but after he had become a professional writer himself he changed his prescription, and told students, "Look and remember; look and remember, that's the thing." He explained, that "[I] don't even like cameras. They get one so busy with the gadget itself that he doesn't really see what he should be looking at." He cautioned against even mental notes, convinced that a deliberate attempt to use one's experience as material for writing spoiled both the collecting and the writing. As he puts it, in "Autobiographical Information":

> My favorite diversion, by all odds, [is] socializing, just sitting around with a beer or more in all kinds of places talking to all kinds of people about all kinds of things. (It's a professional necessity for a writer, too, but it's no good to him if he takes it that way, watching people and listening to them, making mental notes and saying to himself, "This I must remember." He'll never get to know people in the ways that matter most if he treats them as specimens. Nobody likes to be a specimen. The thing is to be really a part of whatever is going on, without

a thought about "using" it. The memory will keep what matters.)[4]

This method of becoming a reservoir, entering as fully as possible into life of all sorts and trusting the memory to serve as a retrieval bank, served Clark well. His published work, scintillating with sharp detail, justifies it. It might not work so well for most people, even for most would-be writers. No doubt Clark was a born observer. He probably trained himself to see and hear. And he must have had something approaching total recall. I have tried to train myself to observe, but I noticed on a number of occasions, when we watched the same scene, he saw more than I did. And I marveled when he described the birds and the little animals around his place. A half dozen ground squirrels were not a family of rodents to him; they were six individuals, each with its own philosophy of life. Clark could describe each of them with an exactitude suggesting that the furry bit was scampering before him as he spoke.

This, then, seems to have been the way Clark worked. He got an idea, which was probably no more than a specific quirk for handling one of the themes that were always with him. He would plot the incident, considering technical matters such as point of view, straight narrative, or a compressed scene with throwbacks, and the like. If the piece was to be long, he might leave himself notes, write sketches of principal characters, and something about them. When he felt ready, when he trusted that the story was about to "come," he would write, scribbling very fast in that beautiful but almost illegible calligraphy that was his handwriting. He would hope to keep going, trusting that his memory would supply without hesitation or question anything he needed. If the piece was to be short, he would finish it in a sitting, in a few hours. If it was long, he would still expect to write it fast, to keep it pouring, even though with intervals for sleep. If the story did not "come," he would stop. He might file the manuscript with notes for a future attempt. More frequently, it seems, he simply burned the whole pile, and tried it again the next day with a different approach. Or he would forget it as a bad job—which forgetting would not preclude his trying something on the same theme weeks or months or years later.

This way of working did not reflect indolence, undue impatience, or an amateur faith in "inspiration." It was the way he created best, or so he came to believe. With sufficient provocation he would revise with patient, persistent care. But he used revision in the conventional sense, of examining a body of script word by word and sentence by sentence, mainly from drafts he had basically established. Few of his starts ever became so established, as either completed or uncompleted drafts. By the time he was mature as a writer he had observed that his best writing came fast, and thereafter needed only routine scrubbing up. Accordingly, if a draft did not come fast, and did not continue to drag him along so that he could not stop it, he became suspicious of it. The stove or the wastebasket got it. As a man he was profligate of words and as an artist a wastrel of time, but he had learned that for him there was little use in throwing good words after bad. Or at least he thought he had learned this. Others did not always agree with him. Looking at his rejected drafts now, I wonder, and I believe others would wonder, what is wrong with them that a routine rewrite would not remedy. Why did he stop? Perhaps we must assume he knew better than any of us can know what he wanted to do, and he had become convinced he was not doing it. Anyhow, wisely or unwisely, that seems to have been the way he tackled the job.

Clearly, such a technique will work better for short pieces than for long ones. It served well for the young Walter Clark, writing verse; and it served well for the mature writer of short stories. In this connection we might recall that the young Clark was inclined to poetry, and that although he stopped trying to publish it he never stopped writing it. We should bear this in mind also when we consider that some of Clark's best writing appears in his short stories, which could be scribbled in a few hours. But a novel such as *The City of Trembling Leaves* cannot be finished in one sitting, or even in one onset of zeal leading to a few weeks of feverish composition, interrupted for snacks left outside the door by Barbara. We should also consider the

implications of this technique when we ask ourselves why
Clark stopped producing works that he considered finished—
his starts during that time ran to relatively long works, even
to collections of works.

Literary Character

Clark's literary character will best appear in the more detailed treatments to come, but a forecast may be in order. At
least two broad qualities might be noted: Clark could be an engaging storyteller, and he thought he had something to say that
his fellow Americans needed to hear. The first probably accounts for most of his popularity among readers and for his
acclaim by critics, but the second, which we might call his message, is harder to pin down, though it must not be ignored. Although readers may resent this implicit moral, the fact is that
it permeates what Clark wrote and in part suggests why he
wrote it.

Most critics have observed this strong inclination in Clark—
that he thought he had something to say for our own good—
but few have made much of it. Bernard De Voto deplored it;
he said, in effect, that a western writer's job is to make us see
the West, and he should not fuzz the picture by dealing in symbols and the human psyche. Max Westbrook, on the other
hand, sees most of Clark's published work as stemming from
and pointing to an archetypal elucidation of human nature
after the pattern of the psychologist Carl Gustav Jung.[5] But one
should add, lest this statement be misinterpreted, that
Westbrook insists repeatedly that "Clark's mythology is always
his own, always a modern and Americanized version which is
more a creation than a reaction."[6] Most commentators, insofar
as they have occupied positions at all, have found places somewhere between these two.

Clark tended to avoid private discussions of what he believed
and what his writing meant. Asked if the colors of the horses
in Ox-Bow are symbolic of anything, he would be likely to reply
that if these colors are symbols for you, then they are symbols
for you. Partly, no doubt, he was avoiding embroilment with
argumentative persons whose interpretations might be firmly

held but not well grounded. He would also have been giving expression to his deeply held conviction that creative processes are at least partly unconscious. Thus, although writers may not express all they want to, their work may embody truths they had never intended to enunciate and did not know they were airing. For individual readers a piece of writing will have something to say—and this "something" will actually be there—that the author may not have known he or she said. Clark seldom discussed such matters privately, but occasionally he brought up the subject, and on one such occasion I was present.

The Watchful Gods and Other Stories had just been published, and I had complimented him on it. He was always a little embarrassed when anybody praised his work, and he was probably hunting for something to say that would be at once modest and not inconsiderate. "I thought it would be interesting to try to work it out for that age," he said, or something to that effect. He seemed to consider the book a study of some deep-seated truth that could be expected to appear in a human being, or at any rate in many human beings, and would be different for a boy of twelve than it had been earlier or would be later. Clearly he thought "it" was of great importance, and his tone, if I understood him, implied he thought he had previously expounded the antecedent of "it" for some other levels of age.

I thought I knew in a broad way what he meant by "it," certainly not at all what the snickering boys in *The City* meant by the same pronoun, but while I was trying to find ways to keep him talking, I could sense him stiffen. He soon changed the subject. I later learned that the publishers had been at least as uncertain as I, and that Clark had written them a long letter which reveals that he had intended to be even more philosophical and theological than I had guessed. The mature Clark meant his morality always to be muted, and for many readers his most attractive pieces are those in which the morals are muted most, as in "Hook" and "The Wind and the Snow of Winter."

Clark as artist, as against Clark as teacher, can be completely delightful. Of his novels he seems to have preferred *The City*, perhaps because it most extensively embodies his philosophic tenets, or because it intimately conjures up his own past. How-

ever, most readers drawn to it luxuriate in its wealth of charm-
ing narrative and description. This love of the land and land-
based people may be unusually strong in westerners. The tale
moves with the chatter of believable youngsters, and is instinct
with love of the land and of all the little live things in it. This
dwelling on the small pleasures of daily living may seem sentimental. Clark was aware that his writing bordered at times on
sentimentality, and tried to guard against it. But he was aware,
also, that serious writers—and serious critics—can be too
much afraid of being sentimental. He makes a character in *The
City* say, "Don't be afraid of sentiment. It's better to be a fool
once in a while than all the time" (p. 502). The love of all the
earth was very real with Clark—who was an honest writer if
there ever was one—as it is real with many lovers of Clark's
work. Given the choice, they would rather be overly sentimental than overly symbolistic, and they are not above ignoring the
symbols and the allegory, while luxuriating in the western living that they have felt but had never seen or heard so consciously as they find it in Clark.

Notes

1. See chapters 8 and 12, below.

2. *The Journals of Alfred Doten, 1849–1903*, Walter Van Tilburg
Clark, ed. (Reno: University of Nevada Press, 1973).

3. I never understood what he meant by these remarks. He was
modest about his writing. At the same time, he was conscientious
about his teaching, and he surely knew he was a superb teacher. He
may have meant to be no more than factually honest and perhaps fit-
tingly deprecatory of himself, because capable teachers are more common than great literary artists. But Clark had a subtle mind and his
was a complex personality. I have wondered if he was indulging in
dramatic irony here, that he was actually declaring, as he trusted his
hearers would never know, that he had become unable to write publishable fiction because the artist in him was being overwhelmed by
the pedagogue. For more on the question, see the various discussions
below, especially those in chapters 2 and 4.

4. See chap. 17, below.

5. Max Westbrook, *Walter Van Tilburg Clark* (New York:
Twayne, 1969); henceforth called *Clark*. See also chap. 7, below.

6. *Clark*, p. 103.

2

Walter Clark and Nevada

James W. Hulse

*James W. Hulse, professor of history at the University of Nevada,
Reno, knows Clark's Nevada as few others could. A native of the
state, son of a hard-rock miner, he knew the old mining towns that
Clark loved. He did undergraduate and graduate work at the university, supporting himself as a newspaper reporter, in which capacity
he covered the Stout affair, which led to Clark's resignation and to
his leaving both the University of Nevada and the state. After completing his doctorate at Stanford University, Hulse returned to his
alma mater, and wrote a history of it and a history of Nevada. His
most ambitious research published to date is* Revolutionists in London: A Study of Five Unorthodox Socialists *(Oxford: Claren-
don Press, 1970).*

T here is no better way to begin a treatise on the relationship between Walter Van Tilburg Clark and Nevada
than to plagiarize one of his own terse remarks: "I love Nevada
for its country; I do not have much respect for its chosen business and political attitude." In a sense, this says it all. But readers will be expecting a traditional academic treatment, and so
I have a pedagogical duty to explicate and modify these asser-
tions.

It was a very special aspect of Nevada that Clark loved, and
only that aspect had much importance for his writing. To
define its limitations and to make some suggestions about what
he included and excluded from his personal Nevada is the purpose of these remarks. That his three novels are set in this area

and the nearby Sierra Nevada, and that some of his best short stories draw on the Nevada landscape, is enough to validate the classification of Clark as a Nevada writer. It does not, however, say much about the selective process that operated within him when he was doing his creative writing. Nor does it automatically give Nevadans a right to claim that they "produced" or "inspired" him. We should at least be open to the suggestion that Clark may have become one of the fairly important writers of American fiction in our time in spite of—not because of—the fact that he spent about half his life here. It is just possible that some things about Nevada interfered with his development as a creative writer.

Let us circle around—as Walter might have said—toward this theory and look at it from different approaches. Sometimes it is useful to go up a side canyon and to make a couple of switchbacks in approaching a higher ridge; at times this can afford a better look at the ground.

One of the best clues we have to Walter Clark's writing techniques and the problems that plagued him the last twenty years of his life can be found in an article he prepared for the *Chrysalis Review*, published in the spring of 1962, just before he returned to Reno to become writer-in-residence at the University of Nevada.[1] The article was an amended version of an address delivered to a class in creative writing at San Francisco State University in 1959. He had been asked to speak to a class on the theme "Communication and Art," and he had assumed that a routine academic lecture was expected. Shortly before the appointed time, he learned that he was expected to speak as a creative writer, and the prospect terrified him. He began the lecture, and the essay that resulted from it, with a long apologetic introduction, explaining how terrified and insecure he had become about the assignment to speak on the creative process. Clark was not at his best when he lamented in this way, and he took some time coming to grips with his theme, which was that Clark-the-writer and Clark-the-professor were two different creatures, sharing the same body to be sure, but often in conflict with each other. The "little man inside"—*homunculus*—(shall we in this context call him the creative spirit?)

had been silent and ineffective for several years by then, and
the professor was trying to draw out the writer for the purposes
of preparing his lecture. Clark was trying to say something important about the creative process for an academic audience,
and he was simultaneously asking himself what had happened
to his own inspiration. Clark-the-creative-writer was much
better at dialogue than was Clark-the-professor at self-criti-
cism, so we can be grateful that he undertook to examine the
enigma of his own writing techniques in dialogue form, in a
conversation with himself over what had happened to the "little man inside."

Clark-the-writer says the little man, whom he also calls "the
ancient one," "the sad one," "the ancient beast," "the hairy ancestor," and the like, is in absentia because he has been pestered
and bothered too much by Clark-the-professor. The intellec-
tualizing, analyzing, and criticizing of the professor inhibits the
ancient one, who works through language rather than in it.
The professor has often promised the writer summers in which
to renew contact with homunculus, but too often the promises
have been broken. There is a long critical excursion into the
works of Henry James to supplement the main points, and then
the professor takes leave of the writer. The professor is the narrator, and he describes their final exchange:

> . . . It was no small relief, I confess, to be out of his strenuous
> presence. No sooner had I begun to relish my escape, how-
> ever, than his voice came loudly down behind me.
>
> "Hey, professor!"
>
> I paused, not altogether without a sense of irritation.
> "Well?"
>
> "For Lord's sake send him back as quick as you get done
> tomorrow, will you?"
>
> "Send who back?"
>
> "The little man inside, of course. Who else?"
>
> "Is he with me?" I inquired, and truly could not be sure.
>
> "Of course he is, and will be till you get over this panic."
>
> "And you feel the need of his services?" I inquired ironi-
> cally.

"You know (a modified expletive) well I can't get along without him. But that's not all, by a long shot."

"What else then?" I was no little amused myself by now, at
this naive confession, but I was once more a bit before myself.

"You've got him all mixed up himself, professor, with all this
stupid babble about language and the imaginative process. He
won't be any use to anybody if he sticks around with you much
longer."[2]

Clark was having fun here, but he was at the same time making a significant observation. The passage reveals, as thorough-
ly as anything he ever wrote, his frustration at being unable
after 1950 to do creative writing that met his own rigid literary
standards. He yearned for a renewal of those conditions that
had enabled him to produce his novels and most of the short
stories in a relatively brief span of time.

Let us turn back to an earlier section of the *Chrysalis* essay,
to the point at which he finally broke through his frustration
and decided he had to get away to a solitary place to find *homunculus* in order to prepare his lecture for the academic audience.
He loaded his notes, some fresh paper, a typewriter, a tape recorder, and a supply of beer and whiskey into his car and drove
off. The actual destination is unclear, but we are rather quickly
in that halfway zone between the observed facts and the subconscious imagination, that state of mind that we know well
from some of the characters in the novels and short stories. The
figurative destination is far more explicit than the geographical
one.

Clark-the-professor tells us he set out for "a small, imaginary
mining community far in his interior, a town which we shall
call . . . as he has called it before, Gold Rock." The professor
searches for the writer at the Lucky Boy saloon and finally locates him "in a large, old house at the outer end of the upper-
most street."[3] Anyone who has read much of Clark will of
course remember at once an old friend, the prospector Mike
Braneen in "The Wind and the Snow of Winter," trudging into
Gold Rock. The place is no more historical than the Ox-Bow

Valley or Aspen Creek Valley of *The Track of the Cat*, but for Clark-the-writer at his effective moments, these were more real than the historical places he knew, and *homunculus* could be contacted there, if anywhere.

Indulge the historian, for a moment, in his more mundane pedagogical methods. Let us divide Nevada history into three periods. First, there was the era of original pioneers and the mining booms, with the construction of the ditches to irrigate the valleys, the recurring discoveries of new ore bodies, and the railroad enthusiasm. Progress was the password, money was easy, and life was a struggle toward the summits. This period ended for Nevada about 1880, when the Big Bonanza was gone, the railroad had become a leech, and the arable land was all taken. Then the second phase of Nevada's history began, and for about sixty years most Nevadans lived with the memories of the bonanza era. There were some new mining camps and new railroads and new projects, of course, but for most of Nevada's people and for most of the time between about 1880 and 1940, the golden age was in the past and the legends predominated about how it had been in Virginia City, Austin, Pioche, or, somewhat later, Tonopah and Goldfield. Reno and Las Vegas, as Richard Lillard has said, were still villages in 1940. But in the early 1940s, the Nevada we now know—the third Nevada—began to emerge. That decade brought industries and military bases occasioned by the war, the acceleration of transportation, exploitation of Nevada's loose gambling regulations, and the rapid growth of population. The region came into the mainstream as a highly publicized tourist attraction.

It was the second phase of Nevada's experience that Clark sought out for his most important creative explorations. He showed little interest in the mining camps during the boom years and even less in those bonanza kings and other Comstock personalities whose stories have delighted most local history buffs. His kinship was with those who did not make it in Virginia City's palmy days, but who were riding the range, or prospecting, or otherwise waiting it out in that half-century interregnum between the bonanza era and the casino era. He had virtually nothing to say about the socio-commercial transformation that took place in Reno and Las Vegas since 1940. He did not like it, and it did not move him to write.

There was much in the second Nevada that gave his talent its wings. Tim Hazard's Reno and the nearby "chosen places," such as Pyramid Lake, Death Valley, Lake Tahoe, the Black Rock, the Toiyabes, and Mt. Rose were a kind of natural icon through which he was able to sense, from time to time, something about the ultimate meaning of existence. In such places and among the people he occasionally encountered there, bypassed by the newer social forces, homunculus came to life. That second Nevada was his artistic milieu and, perhaps, as it vanished, it became his prison.

One wonders whether the University of Nevada, as well as the city of Reno, had an impact on Clark's creative work. If so, it was a selective and not always a positive influence. The university years obviously gave him an opportunity to enrich his understanding of the English literary tradition. He was generous in his expressions of gratitude for A. E. Hill, the professor of English and director of his master's thesis.

That work, written in 1931, is a most interesting document. It dealt with the Tristram legend. Clark examined several renderings of the legend from Sir Thomas Malory to Edward Arlington Robinson, commented on each of them, and offered some strong opinions. Many of his literary standards were already set; he found the versions of the tale rendered by Swinburne and Tennyson insipid and cheap, but that of Robinson nearly perfect. Clark acknowledged himself to be a virtual worshiper of Robinson; he admired the restraint of the Robinsonian blank verse and the poet's success in developing realistic characters from the figures in the legend. "Words, with him, are not ideas," Clark wrote, "but meticulously exact conductors to ideas. He has a queerly farseeing ability to reproduce things as they are, as they must have been, making words what they should be, merely mediators between reality and reality recreated." (This same basic idea, more felicitously expressed, reappeared some thirty years later in the Chrysalis essay.) Then after explaining his approach to characterization, he offered his own version of the legend in verse.

It is a most unusual master's thesis, and apparently Professor Hill had difficulty getting it accepted by the graduate committee responsible for advanced degrees at that time. But it is evident that the foundations of Clark's creative talent had already been laid. He was thinking very seriously about character development, the uses to which language could be put, and the ways of exercising imaginative restraint in the telling of a tale.

Otherwise it is difficult to argue that the University of Nevada years assisted him in his art. On two, or perhaps three, occasions, his associations with this institution must have been distracting and troublesome. First, when he was an undergraduate, between 1927 and 1931, his father—the president of the University—went through a period of bitter quarrels with the regents, a legislative investigation, and administrative problems occasioned by the depression. I have no evidence of how the ugly politics of those years affected the little man developing inside Clark, but as an alert student he cannot have been unaware of them. He was away from Reno for most of the last six or seven years of his father's administration, but he certainly knew that the presidency was damaging his father's health. When asked to talk about those events for the university's oral history program many years later, he emphatically refused. Tim Hazard in the City does not attend the university. Reading the occasional pieces that Clark wrote for Artemisia and Desert Wolf in the early 1930s, it is difficult to see any promise of the author of The Ox-Bow Incident. Only the master's thesis, which allowed him to explore the world and the literature of Tristram, showed promise.

Clark was gone from Nevada in the late 1930s and early 1940s—his most productive period. Homunculus apparently did not suffer from a heavy teaching load in a New York high school and he was still working successfully through words in the late 1940s, during most of which time Clark was living in Washoe Valley, working on The Track of the Cat and The Watchful Gods and Other Stories, his last important creative works, published in 1949 and 1950, respectively.

He returned to the University of Nevada as a teacher of creative writing in 1952, just in time for the crisis occasioned by the presidency of Minard W. Stout and the efforts to restrict academic freedom. This would have been the second disruptive experience resulting from his association with the university. We have already taken note of his later judgment that being a professor of creative writing restricted his creativity. And this restraint, compounded by the actions of an autocratic administration, must have hurt his productivity. When he left in anger in 1953, he wrote an eloquent letter of resignation. He had obviously meant to stay there indefinitely, but his conscience would not allow him to remain at an institution whose governing board and administration had adopted authoritarian tactics.

Perhaps those who knew Clark most intimately can answer this question: Did Clark, in returning to Nevada to work on the Doten diaries, hope to be able to return to Gold Rock and to awaken *homunculus* again? Certainly he enjoyed "Alf" for a while and planned a volume based on his experiences. Doten's travels from New England to the California gold country and to Nevada provided an abundance of the kind of raw material that had served so well in the best of Clark's novels and short stories. But in the course of his services to Alf—and incidentally to the university, which had a large investment in the documents—Clark obviously did not find the ancient one. Could it have been that his university, at the very time it was trying to give him the leisure and the raw material with which to do more creative work, inadvertently handed him a greater chore than he was prepared to handle? The journals are massive; they cover daily entries for a period of more than fifty years and they required extensive paring and supplementary historical research. Walter was as meticulous an editor as he was a creative writer, and he gave most of his last two or three years to the project.

Robert Clark generously lent me his father's copy of Grant Smith's *The History of the Comstock Lode* into which he had tucked some notes on Nevada. Presumably Walter looked at this in connection with a planned history of the Comstock Lode for young people, and he must also have used it to supplement his information on Doten. These notes do not give any reason to believe that *homunculus* was aroused by the historical records. Walter outlined Comstock history in a very conventional way, and the penciled manuscript he began gives no hint of anything unusual or creative that might have resulted from a prolonged excursion into Nevada history.

In an autobiographical statement prepared in 1964, Walter listed his interests. One of them, he said, was history, ". . . particularly western history as told by those who were personally involved in it, by way of journals, memoirs, letters, newspaper pieces, etc. (Much history, as written by professional historians, bores me to death. Most of them write so badly that they can't bring anything alive for the reader . . . .") Most of us historians, if we are honest, will plead guilty on this count. But will Walter's indictment of the historians prove to be pertinent to his own work on Doten? Perhaps Walter himself became so immersed in the data on Alf—so preoccupied with preserving the historical record—that he tried to cover too much. He was the master of the short story and the short novel, with one or a few central figures and the actions of a few hours or a few days. He did not become master of Alf; in fact, as he often said jokingly, the opposite may have become true.

At any rate, the Doten diaries, having appeared at last after preparation by Walter and his son, are an excellent bloc of historical raw material, and critics will find that the work has been well done. But these are Doten's volumes, not Clark's, and the latter's values and insights as a creative writer have little place in them. It was Clark-the-professor who did this job, and he did not even have the time, or the strength, or the will to finish the introduction that he contemplated for so long. So the final return to Nevada, and to Alf, and to Virginia City was much like that sad pilgrimage of Mike Braneen to Gold Rock.

Where else does one go—besides the novels and short stories—for Walter's thoughts on Nevada? His chapter "Reno—The City State" in Ray West's book *Rocky Mountain Cities* is interesting as a complementary piece to *The City of Trembling Leaves,* but there is an uncharacteristic chamber-of-commerce tone to the last part of it.[4] Clark was not trying to

deal with the mysteries there; he was being an apologist and
a popular historian—strange roles for one who must have been
immersed in *The Track of the Cat* at the same time. This is a
refreshing piece, nostalgic, like much of his other work, but it
adds little to an understanding of his relationship with Nevada.

A far more important piece for those who want to work on
the relationship between Clark and Nevada is the one he published in *Holiday* in 1957, under the title "Nevada's Fateful Desert."[5] It begins with his comments on the Spanish padres who
may have seen southern Nevada two centuries ago. He has
them looking northward at the mysterious mountains, so variant in color at different times of the day, so fearsome yet so
magnetic. It ends with witnesses standing on the slopes of Mt.
Davidson at dawn, watching the light of an atomic blast in the
southeast, with the decaying buildings of Virginia City, the
surroundings of mountains and desert, and the imminent possibility of a nuclear event beyond the expectations of the scien-
tist—with all these joining together to remind one "of the in-
significance, brevity, and loneliness of man, and the tremendous indifference of nature."

Walter Clark's Nevada, then, was a vast place with rich possibilities for associating with the mysteries of life, but only part
of its historical and social landscape was applicable to his art,
and that part was disappearing. After his boyhood years, he
kept coming back, both physically and in his imagination,
seeking the material and the settings that would enable *homunculus* to make contact with those ultimate realities beyond the
realm of words that we might be able to sense with the help
of creative language. But the Nevada that served his imagination could not be separated from the other Nevada that contained a university with its politics and its academic requirements, bustling cities with values foreign to his interests, and
friends and colleagues who, perhaps from an excess of admira-
tion and affection, proved to be rivals to *homunculus*. Perhaps
he was, in the final analysis, too devoted to one aspect of
Nevada to go beyond the level he achieved in *The Ox-Bow Incident, The City of Trembling Leaves*, and *The Track of the Cat*.

Notes

1. Walter Van Tilburg Clark, "The Writer and the Professor: or, Where Is the Little Man Inside?," *Chrysalis Review*, 2 (Spring, 1962) 60–107.

2. Ibid., p. 107.

3. Ibid., pp. 72, 73.

4. Walter Van Tilburg Clark, "Reno: The City State," in Ray West, *Rocky Mountain Cities* (New York: Norton, 1949), pp. 29–53.

5. Walter Van Tilburg Clark, "Nevada's Fateful Desert," *Holiday*, 22 (Nov. 1957) 76–77, 100–103.

3

Walter Clark:
Complicated Simplicity

Herbert Wilner

When Clark was offering courses in creative writing at the Univer-
sity of Iowa, he was so much impressed by the work of one of his
graduate students, Herbert Wilner, that he asked the younger man
to help design and later to implement a writing curriculum at San
Francisco State University. Wilner accepted, and during Clark's
years in the Bay Area, and after Clark had returned to Nevada, the
two remained fast friends. Meanwhile, Wilner became a published
novelist and critic. He died shortly after revising this lecture for print.

Central Images

I t is not hard to find the central images in Walter Van Tilburg
Clark's work and life.

Humankind, in general, in its limited time and by its limited
views, puts itself in the center of all things. Nature does not.
In nature humankind is neither trivial nor everlastingly significant. Humankind simply bears the particular burden of consciousness, and they bear it best who come to understand it
most, to understand that between humankind's desire and nature's necessity there must be balance. The romanticism essential to the human spirit is limited by the necessities essential
to the nature of life. If human beings, believing in their own
supremacy, disturb the balance, they only delude themselves
with ideas of power and self-fulfillment.

A person need not be particularly articulate to understand

this. All that is needed is vision. In fact, in one of the great short stories of our language, Clark's "Hook," the reader is made to understand something of this complicated simplicity by watching the life not of a human being, but of a hawk. And nature in Clark is not, in its necessities, a condition of easy sentiment. Nature is hard. It is even a hard word to use, for we conventionally think of it in relation to literature as a revitalizing contemplation of flora and fauna, landscape and seasons.

When I say "nature" I mean the laws by which all living things share in a common process and a common ultimate fate. And these facts also belong to humankind's particular burden of consciousness. A vision of balance must be made to operate in human relationships with other persons as well as in life with and in nature. The one leads to justice; the other leads to order.

I have made a very abstract statement for Clark's work and life. It is strange and unsuitable. He was least of all, to those of us who knew him, an abstract man. I have also made it very simple because it is a very easy thing to say. To live it out, on the other hand, especially for someone very rich in and thus very burdened by consciousness, is hard. I think it was very hard for Clark himself. I want to dwell on this. I believe it will turn up things about him as a writer, a teacher, and as a representative American. The last phrase is almost useless today, but that is also to the point. It is hard to live out in one's own person, as I think Clark did, the vanishing qualities of a decent and difficult ideal when one's country and culture hustle to finish off that ideal.

Walter Clark is extraordinarily vivid to me one year after his death, and so I should admit at the beginning there is very little I can contribute in my sense of him as a person that would be governed by whatever is meant by "objective." He filled a part of my life as he fills it now with an impressive presence. Even as I then as well as now kept and keep a small collection of reservations and irritations, I say freely that I loved the man and admired his values, even as they sometimes crucified by demanding too much, especially from himself. I suppose that at the bottom of some of the feelings I had for him was the exotic hold he had on me that never eroded through all the twenty

years of my knowing him. I have in mind something more than
the fact that he was from the West and I from Brooklyn, and
that the deserts and solitudes in which he felt at home terrified
me. Perhaps I mean that in his person he seemed in touch with
a sense of time so full of flow and continuity that it appeared
very much older and less vulnerable to error than did my own
sense of the past. Yet he was himself a contemporary person,
even to the point of trivia. He had no formal religion, nor did
he, as I understood him, worship nature, as such.

I want to scatter some images of him from my recollection.
I once saw Clark at a service station as I was driving by. He
was standing at the side of the pump while his convertible
Volkswagen was being filled. The attendant was nearby, there
were cars around, and in the close distance the high redwoods
of the San Francisco suburb in which Clark then lived must
have broken the plane of the horizon he was looking toward.
He was staring into the distance. He was wearing a tan rain-
coat, his hands in the pockets, and with the added inches of
the cement platform of the gas pumps he appeared quite tall
and somewhat lean. His face was unsmiling, but quite cheerful.
He was quite alert, not at all daydreaming, and yet he seemed
to be looking at something that someone standing at his shoulder would not have seen. As I drove on and he fell out of my
sight—all this was a matter of seconds and he had not seen
me—I knew I had taken in an impression that would last. It
has. That was fifteen years ago. In that crowded and ordinary
spot Clark seemed to have been surrounded by space. It seemed
both an ambience he gave off and one that came to him.

I remember him in a variety of conversations that would
have appeared to produce the opposite effect, in which we were
closed off in a living room, or a campus office or corridor, and
my head drummed with the resonances of his voice. My "conversations" with him often took the form of listening to his
monologues, which were filled with anecdotes—what might
more technically be called yarns. His voice was deep, resonat-
ing, and it impressed with how much more power it kept in reserve than it used. He was someone you would say was soft-spo-
ken, but you would not want to be nearby when he yelled.

His conversational material with me was fairly predictable: athletics, Reno, Virginia City, Nevada in general, mining days, the Sierras, and sometimes—when the transition to it was easy—books and authors. His emphasis, apart from shop-talk, was on what happened to whom and where. His pace was easy, elaborative, and generally unspoiled by analytic observations along the way. Neither was it spoiled much by an interrupting question I might venture. But when I would begin to suspect he never even heard my question, he would, three or four minutes later, without losing his pace, give the answer to it, making it a part of his narrative.

His language was almost always colloquial and discursive. He would not, for instance, say of a man he talked about that he did this or that as a result of an "inferiority complex." He might say, "He scratched along most of the time at the bottom of his possibilities." It strikes me as rather odd now that when I read Twain, and sometimes Melville, I hear echoes of Clark's patterns of speech, though Clark, in his own writing, is more often more formal than either of them, more obviously involved in composition.

In the oral tale, after the preliminary sentences, when the characters began to move, and their place and situation took on their life, Clark, as he went on with the yarn, became an enlivened witness of what he himself was making. His eyes brightened, his hands began to move more, and the listener—at least myself as listener—was caught in the double snare of marveling at the substance of the yarn he told. He was a natural at stories, and they were sometimes, it seemed to me, full of natural stretchers. The bartender, for instance, was not just big, or the linebacker, or the miner. They were huge. And the facts were minutely specific: "The guy stood 6 foot 4½ inches and weighed 253 pounds." The figures were delivered with the authority of a medical report. There were times when I thought I was going to check out that height and weight stuff the next day. I never did. It would have gone against the spirit of the story. Worse than that, I might have found the information was exactly right, and I would not have known how to handle that.

These yarns were told with a kind of obsession, and, taken as a whole, were rather singular in character. The substance was usually male-oriented, and fairly often the climax came in the form of violence. If a bullying brute had arrived at his come-uppance, Clark could even relish for a while the gory details he made of the scene. And never, even at these moments, be-tray the fact—it lived in his eyes, in the little poke of a finger flicking ash from a cigarette—that he was by nature a gentle man.

I remember after-dinner times when these tales carried us to one, two, and sometimes three o'clock in the morning. In the beginning of my knowing him, I often wondered what kept him at it. Whence came the need for it? Then I began to understand the storytelling—if it is not excessively subtle to think so—as the other side of the need for silence. The silence and storytel-ling derived from the same part of the recognizably unified temperament. He was, I decided, an essentially silent man. It had nothing to do with melancholy, least of all with depres-sion. It bore relationship to his living feel for the flow of time, and to his sense of space, and to his knowledge of that universe of arrangements in which the human person bore within itself the rhythm and the consciousness of such mysteries. The mys-teries themselves, as they unfolded in the self, were unutterable in any direct speech between persons, even between friends. But when people got together, especially friends, the necessary silences and solitudes had to be broken, or what did they get together for? And from their stories—and not by admissions or confessions or psychiatric parlor-room revelations—one per-son after a while could make out the nature of the other. I de-cided the storytelling for Clark was very much his way of mak-ing contribution to communion as well as community. In short, a ritual.

And yet there was almost always the impenetrable ultimate space. I see him, for instance, in another image that perdures. Again he is standing. This is a faculty party. Everyone chatters. Clark has his back to a wall, but he does not touch it. He wears his corduroy jacket and the blue tennis shirt with the little figure of the alligator on the flap over the pocket. He drinks boilermakers, and though he nurses the beer, someone is always refilling the shot glass with bourbon. There was always someone to see to his bourbon. He is glowing pleasantly and swaying slightly on the balls of his feet, but his back never touches the wall. (He told me once, jokingly, that it was a signal system: at a large party that made sitting difficult, it was time to get on home when he swayed enough that his back did touch the wall.) A small circle of people crowd in on him, and he is sometimes listening to one or another of them, and sometimes telling one of his own stories. I see him from a distance across the room. He is eminently cheerful, very much with the party; and yet he is also for me rather prominently walled off by that air of space, so that he is simultaneously in touch and remote.

This quality of spatial enclosure had an effect on me in different and unaccountable ways. It gave him a sense of formidability mixed with shyness, of great dignity mixed with vulnerability. For instance, though he was entirely masculine, and his stories were almost always of men, I found myself inhibited with him from any kind of locker-room talk. Obscenities, which come easy to my speech if I have the right listener, seemed improper before him for reasons never quite explainable to me. His values had nothing to do with the puritanical, except for his ruthless sense of duty. He seemed aloof also from subjects that slipped from the comfortably personal to the uncomfortably private. I never spoke with him, as I could with other friends, about my own deepest sense of self, about my parents, or about any of those touchstone topics that begin to move you into Freudian territory. I was not worried about my privacy; I thought it was an invasion of his to make him listen. He himself never ventured into such disclosures with me.

He had an instinctive abhorrence of the exaggerated Freudian. He had no taste for clawing at the raw meat of personality, someone else's or his own. That is not to say that he had no interest in character or the psychology of behavior. How could he lack that and love so much to read fiction, teach it, write it? It is obvious that he would have admired the work of Melville and Conrad, but he also admired and taught the fiction of Dostoevski and Kafka. I believe rather that he thought the Freudian alone in daily life was a preoccupation with the mechanics of self that could only enlarge an appetite already excessive, would only remove persons further from the large sense of time and place that gave them their context and their balance.

He said to me once of a colleague who spent years with a psychiatrist, and years afterward in a paralyzing attention to the problems that had brought him to the psychiatrist, that the patient's troubles reminded him of the story of the centipede who had managed to keep himself thoughtlessly on the move despite his ungainly equipment until some creature more simply constructed raised the question, How do you coordinate all those legs? The centipede, unaware he had been coordinating anything special, turned over on his back and for the first time inspected all those legs. Indeed, it was phenomenal. He studied and studied it. Awed by the complexity of what it would take to coordinate all that, the centipede, of course, remained on his back, studying and studying himself. He never moved again.

Perhaps I have thus far and too exclusively made associations for Clark that present him in the simple terms of a man of the American West. He was certainly that, and to an almost incorruptible extreme. He loathed cities. There was not in him a bit of what we ordinarily mean by urbanity. He had never been to Europe, had no interest in going, had turned down State Department invitations to lecture there, all expenses paid. He was a strong-minded man who knew his nature was to dig in rather than spread out; knew for instance that even if he loved books he disliked libraries; knew that he liked paintings but disliked museums, disliked crowds, and could speak no foreign language. Why go to Europe, then, even if it was so available and fashionable to the American writer and academic, if it meant only what would have been for him the dismal experience of racing from city to city, from lecture halls to reception rooms to lecture halls? The threats of enclosure—by language, by people, by buildings—must have stifled all his curiosity. There was, he admitted to me, but one place that still aroused some possibility of the tourist in him: Alaska.

In his writing the very best of his work for me takes place

outdoors, continuing a unique American tradition that began with Cooper, included Melville and Twain, and was kept very much alive in the shrinking landscape of the twentieth century by Hemingway and Faulkner—and by Clark himself. His life, then, as well as his work, should have been as lucid and whole as the simplicities that we have all applied to the making and receiving of our western myths. And he was whole, and he was lucid, in his life as in his work; but it was all, as I suggested when I began, through complication and difficulty and cost. I said I would dwell on this. It is time I did. It is time I talked of Clark as a writer and teacher of writing.

Writer and Teacher of Writing

Clark loved to teach, had great skills for it, and made an art out of confronting a text or a manuscript as the intervening ground of communion between himself and students. I think he placed the role of teacher, at any level of schooling, above that of any other calling. Accordingly, as teacher, he demanded much of himself, gave much, and was angered, even a little puzzled, by colleagues who fell unforgivably short of these demands. He admired learning, but he deplored the teaching of literature that was merely informational. He believed in process as much as he did in purpose. He wanted students to have the profoundest comprehension of, say, Conrad's "Heart of Darkness," but the way toward such comprehension was in itself the means for an opening in the powers of perception. He wanted his students to *see*, and by that I think he meant every part of the whole connective vocabulary we keep for that rare quality: vision, perception, recognition, insight, outlook, point of view, and even, and not least, eyesight itself.

In supporting creative writing courses and programs, he advocated more than editorial service for extraordinarily talented students, and more than the providing of a place where several or many of them could make a literary community for a few important years in their lives. I know that at San Francisco State, where he gave so much of himself to build up the writing program, a main part of his assumptions was in the long view that saw students who had undertaken the

writing program as teachers themselves of writing and literature. His hope, then, was that they too, whatever became
of their writing, would convey as teachers, of youngsters or
adults, a living engagement with the process of reading and
writing that would contribute to perception and vision.

The work he himself did in this process amazed me. I wish
I could say it always thrilled me. I confess it sometimes de-
moralized me; for he set the example by which I felt I could
do no less. In large undergraduate writing classes that made
it impossible to hold individual conferences with all the students for every story they submitted, Clark would make his
comments on the manuscript itself. Aside from the usual cor-
rections about matters of composition, he wrote an overall
statement in response to the student's attempt at shaping
a short story. The statement, in Clark's very small and intense
and sometimes difficult script, would run close to a page.
It made specific observations about character development,
descriptive detail, clarity of situation, the rendering of place,
the problems of viewpoint—everything made so familiar by
the now old-fashioned anthologies in the Brooks and Warren
tradition, but all of it personally directed to the student's
own work.[1] And it must be said that the work was most
often bad, sometimes mediocre, occasionally promising, and
rarely finished. Think for a moment of the typical student
who submitted his feeble effort to Clark for the first time.
He must have been struck slightly dumb by the length and
intensity of the response he got. He knew it came not only
from a certain teacher he was fortunate enough to have, but
from a man who was himself a master in the writing of the
short story.

With older, more sophisticated, more talented students,
Clark spent hours in conference time. Often he worked with
them on novels, helping to conceptualize, to edit, to revise,
almost to copyread draft after draft until the mind might go
numb and the spirit shrivel from being so long and tediously
with the repeated reading of the same material. But he had
patience with the evidence of the slightest progress, and he
took heart if a student so much as crawled toward the goal.

He was even clerically efficient, almost compulsive, with the less rewarding but necessary pedagogic tasks. He kept precise gradebooks, recorded summaries of conferences, wrote detailed letters of recommendation, plugged for fellowships for students of talent and responsibility. He attended committee meetings, and even allowed himself at times to be pushed into administrative work by people he should have resented for not having spared him. After years and years of it no one spared him, and no one or nothing could.

What he put into his teaching and what he took from it not only cut time from his writing but, more fatefully, disconnected the impulses he had for his own fiction. It was more than time alone of which his teaching deprived him. He was, after all, throughout the rich period of his production in fiction, a rapid writer. He told me he had done the essential work on Ox-Bow through a Christmas and Easter vacation while he was teaching high school in upstate New York. He said he had written "Hook" in one sitting of about six hours. And throughout his years of college teaching he did have his similar vacation periods and summers. I have really to turn my images of him back to those conditions of space and time and silence and conversation to guess at what the teaching of creative writing did, at least in part, to stifle the fiction that was still imaginatively alive in him. His head had grown stuffed with the language of reading and writing. The essential mental vocabulary, the private and as yet unformed language that, in his qualities as a writer should have been waiting passively to come alive in the clusters of images that generated his own best writing, had grown familiar and worn with use.

Students, as well they might, marveled at what his knowledge and articulateness could give them. I marveled too. Meeting me once, for instance, in the corridor of our building, he glanced at the book I held in my hand and was going to use in the class I was headed for. It was Faulkner's As I Lay Dying. Clark nodded, smiled, shifted his weight a little and lingered with me a moment. I took it for the signs I was used to by now: a desire to say a few words mixed with the reticence, even shyness, that accompanied the openings of most of his conversations. I broke the ice. I admitted that I did not clearly understand the book. I did not think it was a clear book. I came about ten minutes late to that class; Clark, with no air of trying to tell me how the book ought to be read, spent the ten minutes tossing off his recollection of the sequences of images with which Faulkner had decorated the novel. I remember references he was able to make to a man's shoes, a woman's dress, a tree, pieces of description of the river in flood. None of this solved the book for me. I do remember being mildly surprised at Clark's recall. I asked him when he had last read the book. He said when he had taught it at Montana. I figured that to four or five years back. Then I thought of a discussion we had once had about James's *Turn of the Screw*, when I had been truly startled by Clark's explication, dependent entirely on his recollection of all the convoluted threads in that perpetrated obfuscation out of which James had made the story. So I said to him in the corridor when we talked of *As I Lay Dying*: "My God, you've got total recall on what you read." He responded with a tone of misgiving: "After all these years teaching it, there are pages of *Heart of Darkness* I can recite by heart."

If no more than a fragment of his faculty for linguistic recall operated on manuscripts he read, on the comments and discussions he produced out of them, one can imagine the enormous clearing of his head Clark had to practice before he could release an unfettered sentence for his own fiction; and what an effort after that to move on without literary self-consciousness, without the critical faculty's pouncing on the impulse of the developing image. "It keeps coming too much from the head," he remarked in one of the rare moments in which he spoke to me of his difficulties with his own writing. He complained of the innumerable opening chapters he wrote again and again, and threw away again and again. Despite the increasing severity of the strains put on him by teaching, he never quit believing that he would break through. The writing would come again. I imagine he believed he needed to find in his own resources—as though it were a matter of his physiology alone—the new rhythms for making the combinations work, the teaching and the writing. But as the years passed and the break did not come,

I imagine also—it would have been so natural to someone given to the feel of things, to the rhythm of sequences—that he began to develop his own set of anxieties about the act of writing, about the sources of the creative spirit left in him for the act. He might have become—at least in my imagination— a force deprived of its powers by an excessive confrontation with the mechanics of those powers.

I say none of this in despair. Least of all do I imply anything regretful, much less futile, in it. I am only dwelling on the difficulties, as I said I would, of a vision of life that is often too easily labeled, when it comes to Clark's writing, a romantic simplification, a provincial hangover from an old American West. And I bear in mind the other simplicity I hear, especially from writers, that his excessive devotion to teaching was a betrayal of priorities, that Clark's own talents as a writer should have come first, should have been protected by him with a little more of the Joycean cunning. I am trying, really and only, to present the picture of Clark that was a natural extension of what I see as the central image of his work, in which balance must be made to operate in one's own relationship with other persons, as well as in one's life with and in nature. It means, of course, that one's own necessities are constantly tried by someone else's necessities as well as by the limits of nature. There is nothing at all in it that comes under what is ordinarily meant by romantic. There is not even a way that has been given to us by any system of debits and credits to know how the balance works—or what it even accurately is.

I had, for example, visited with Clark in Virginia City in the early summer of 1971. He was by that time terminally ill. When I returned and went out one day to the campus at San Francisco State, I met a middle-aged woman who had been a former student of his and now worked in one of the college offices as an editorial consultant on faculty research. When we met, she usually inquired about Clark. She did this time also. I gave her the unhappy news. I was much too abrupt. Her lips trembled for a moment, then she burst into tears. She apologized. She tried to control herself, but she continued to cry. There was something she wanted to say, but I had to wait for her to be able to manage it. "He never knew," she said, "what his attention to people like me meant. He never knew how he changed my life." I do not think she meant Clark taught her how to read better, to write better, though I know for a fact he helped her in both. I believe she more entirely meant she had been somewhat stunned, and all for her future good, that a man she so deeply admired, by his work and through his presence, had valued her, had given as much of his time and energy to her as he would have to younger students whose talents made it obvious that they had a writer's career before them.

From the few years I spent with him at San Francisco State, I could make a long list of students who had admitted to me what knowing Clark had meant to them in more than the academic sense alone. The list would be much longer if it were to include students from Montana and Nevada and Iowa (where I should put myself on it), and those summer places to which he came for brief writers' conferences. Is there a way to balance such a list against the book or books it may have prevented him from writing? What value can be placed on something that never came to be written?

One must rather celebrate this fulfilled life—whatever the cost was to Clark himself—in which some books that permanently matter were indeed written, in which teaching that was dramatically significant was accomplished—and the life, unique in our day for what it renounced and what it affirmed, came out whole. I think he was committed to the belief—*bound to it*—that writers ought in their own life to live out to the limit of their possibilities the ideal images out of which their work was made. If this wording has a somewhat pretentious Conradian ring to it, it is perhaps because I see Clark—who was himself without pretension—as a Marlowesque[2] sort of person who would even set idealism aside for the more necessary requirements of a liveable decency.

Force and Restraint

I have no doubt that his work permanently matters. I mean more than *The Ox-Bow Incident* which, to my prejudices, is lower on the list of Clark's achievements than conventional association holds it. That book is too full of conversation and of the sense of a narrator's easy talkativeness to put me in mind of the deepest, richest sources of Clark's writing. I think the best of his work opened into and was sealed by a sense of space. I think it rendered its contemporary moment with great vividness, even as it echoed back into a time that was long before its contemporaneousness and lived ahead into a time that was both unforeseeable and unavoidable. Most of all, in what to me is the best of his work, I feel, as I read, the permanence of silence even as I pronounce to myself the rich, rhythmic cadence of his language.

For such reasons I remain convinced, for example, with each reading of The Track of the Cat that it contains about one hundred pages of continuous narrative that is among the most remarkable prose writing I know. The material is immensely difficult for a sustained piece of fiction. There is nothing in it but a single character, a man who hunts a big cat. And the cat, or panther, is mainly present only in the form of paw tracks in the snow. And the man hunts it in a mountain landscape that becomes increasingly difficult to describe as it grows more and more obscured by a blizzard. How, I ask myself at every reading, did the author keep this up for one hundred pages?

"That part just flowed," he told me once. "It was the other stuff that gave me a hard time."

The flow is deep, its pressure is high, and the visible sources for the created tension are in the images of a single man, a landscape, and a panther. The man, Curt Bridges, is arrogant, tough, mean-minded, and, in the outdoors, totally capable. The panther is large, has killed cattle and the man's brother, and by this time in the book carries the weight of symbol. The landscape is mountain country beginning to fill with wind-driven snow. The ingredients are by themselves ordinary, the material of chases and hunts. Extraordinary is the force by which Clark compels us to see for so long the variousness of little events even as we are mindful of the gathering toward the one ultimate event; to see the gradual diminishment of Curt's vision but not of the detail given to the reader as the arrogant

man has to shelter himself in a small cave from the blinding
snowstorm that obscures the vast territory over which he believed himself—with his cradled rifle—to be a god. More and
more intensely through these hundred pages the reader sees
with a doubled vision, as if one eye were at the microscope that
gave back all the lineaments, while the other gazed through the
telescope at the universe in which the details live.

The sound also. There is no one for Curt to speak to. When
he talks to himself we are only more mindful of the solitary
human voice for which there are no human ears. We can hear
the howling wind without too much strangeness; but in the pervasive human silence even the silently falling snow begins to
thump. I imagine that Clark, as he wrote this section of The
Track of the Cat, heard his silence even as Milton saw his darkness, and at the very end of the section, to put the exclamation
mark to what Clark so well understood as so humanly difficult
and universally permanent, we hear Curt—all his arrogance
gone, disintegrated now by the lack in himself of those laws of
balance he had never recognized—listening to an accompany-
ing scream as he falls from the cliff and tumbles through space
to his death. Only faintly does he understand this scream to be
his own sound. But the reader, appalled for so long by the
human silence, hears that shattering puny roar with terror, as
though it were the world's last sound, even as he or she recognizes that was exactly what such a reversible "hunt" was all
about: there is no last sound, and it will never be only human.

Much of what is so impressive for me in the prose comes from
Clark's response to this recognition. It ignites no fevers in him,
nor does it leave him passionless. Unlike Hemingway, for instance, Clark does not need a ritualized style to protect him
from the recognition, or to celebrate it. He simply and scrupul-
ously delivers out of a balanced vision not the things of nature
alone, or the supremacy of nature over humankind, but the relationships among the things in nature and the inescapable
laws that bind them. To catch each of these elements in a moment of extremity is nothing more than any fiction writer
needs—a source of dramatic pressure. Clark feels the pressure,
he never lets it go ("That part just flowed"), but he delivers out

of it—in diction—image and cadence, with a great deal of restraint. The wholeness and the power come out of the inter-
mingling of the forces and the restraint.

I have been making observations on only one-fourth of one
novel by Clark. I do not want to go into much more of it, but
I began with this section of *The Track of the Cat* because it seems
to me to be central to the best, the unique aspect of the work.
And it continues for me the themes deriving from Clark's vision, and the human and fictional difficulty of holding them.

I may be forcing a pattern, but of Clark's short stories I think
I hold the highest place for those sharing in the impulses and
qualities of that amazing section of *The Track of the Cat*: space,
time, solitariness, the laws of ultimate relationships, the preva-
lence of silence made bearable by the relief of language, images
of the near and distant field, and the impelling sense of the protagonist's motion toward fulfillment or frustration. Thus of the
ten stories in *The Watchful Gods,* including the novella of that
title, exactly half are carried through by the conditions just
mentioned, and of the other five several border on those conditions. With the exception of the novella itself, where I think
the narrative voice is oddly talkative and sporadically uncertain and lapsing at times into direct sentiments that diminish
the concreteness of observation, the remaining four stories of
that "pure" Clark make a commanding fictional statement for
his vision of the beauty and order and law of living things in
the struggle for balance. I mean "Hook," a story I think a masterpiece, "The Wind and the Snow of Winter," "The Rapids,"
and "The Indian Well."

I promised not to explicate, but I cannot refrain, in passing
among the stories, from a few words about "Why Don't You
Look Where You're Going?" The story is written with refreshing whimsy and playfulness. But it is written by Clark; it bears
the emblems of his mind. The vastness here is not his characteristic mountain or desert country, but the ocean. We begin
with an ocean liner at sea and a growing cluster of passengers
who start talking about some object observed by one and then
another of them in the distance on the empty sea. They speculate about what the object could be until they settle on the fact

that it really is a small sailboat managed by a single man, who is simply and inexplicably there, a speck in an ocean space, who should never have encountered anything at all in all that space. But by the end of the little story the gross ocean liner has nearly collided with him.

The Clark implications are clear enough. I want only to cite the brief opening paragraph because its image is so stunning. It so much sets the "law" of the story. It shows so well how Clark works out of image. It reads: "White as a sainted leviathan, but too huge for even God to have imagined it, the liner played eastward easily. It swam at a much greater speed than appeared, for it was alone in open ocean, and there were only the waves to pass." The first clause gives us Moby Dick, the second cancels it, and the third tells why. Playfully the second sentence prepares us to accept the solitary man in the little sailboat as a kind of Ahab, but in what will be a very congenial and un-maniacal version.

In Clark's own prejudices he favored *The City of Trembling Leaves* among his three novels. One need never have known its author to guess this novel is personal, intimately shaped out of the writer's experience, a *Bildungsroman* in which a youth of sensitivity and talent progresses toward a unified artistic view, gradually suppressing his yearning for unachievable romantic ideals as he moves toward a more limited and liveable sense of the necessary without surrendering the impulses of the ideals. The book seems to contradict all I have emphasized about Clark's work. It is extremely populous. It is full of dialogues. It is not in any obvious way male-oriented. It even carries the place of "city" in its title. But I cling to my prejudices. I admire most in the book those occasions when Timothy Hazard is alone, or accompanied by Rachel only, and there is little dialogue and very little of it speaks directly to the subjects of the novel. The young couple, for instance, might be on Mt. Rose, and what is between them is revealed by Clark's vivid attention to the place itself. At such moments, what Timothy can see, hear, smell, and touch heightens his life for me beyond all his own, or any other character's, conscious efforts at thinking about or talking of the nature of life.

Clark is that kind of writer. He works best when a place and an action to which he is sensitive intervene between the narrative voice and the character. The intervention relieves him from having to deal directly with the raw meat of personality, or from having his characters talk directly about the subjects of the novel.

Clark himself said it quite effectively once in a letter to a mutual friend that I had the opportunity to see. The subject was not writing but teaching. The friend had written and sent to Clark for his comment an article on the teaching of literature. It tended to emphasize the direct assault, the role of teacher as deliberately more than that of an interpreter of texts. The article went on to suggest that the unfolding of the teacher's own person could be the most useful and forceful part of the teaching process. Clark had some reservations about such methods. He thought the text between the student and the teacher was primary. He indirectly suggested his lack of appreciation for the cult of personality. He offered an illustration in a little parable that I can paraphrase from memory.

If I am with my friend, Clark said, and we share out of our friendship some reason for being together, and together we see a bird perched on the limb of a tree, and then we stop talking to each other and turn together to look at the bird, and in our watching it together we see the bird alight from the limb and take flight, and we both watch the flight and are aware that each of us is in his own way watching the same thing, we learn something valuable of each other for having been aware of how each of us watched the same beautiful thing.

The little tale covers more ground than teaching. I think it governed a good part of Clark's life, and I tried to hint at how it operated in what to me are the richest veins of his fiction. But I would say also that it was a very hard ore to mine for fiction. And I am back again to remarking on what was so hard for him in the central images of his vision, even to the point of what was useable in it for a large body of fiction. Traditionally the novel—no matter what is being sold in it—is something like a department store. It generally thrives on a great variety of counters; and the more customers and salesclerks the better.

To shift the image, the giants of the novel of the nineteenth century, those who made an industry out of the form, were principally those who were fascinated by the social webs of human entanglements, who saw men and women as central to their version of a novel even if they were not philosophically central to their vision of a universe. The names come easily: Balzac, Dickens, Thackeray, Dostoevski, Tolstoy, James; and for the more modern era: Proust, Mann, Lawrence, Faulkner. Clark was a superbly intelligent reader of this fiction. In his own work, however, I think he unloosed the most natural flow when he dealt with what was most natural to him. Character, as such, did not that much obsess him. Names of his fictional characters and the mind's associations with them are not what leap out for me in the contemplation of his fiction. Neither does the best of his work call to mind for me those domestic and indoor situations in which most characters in life as well as in fiction dramatize their personal entanglements as representations of social class and manner, and political views, and time present and time past in the historical as well as the personal sense. These conventional materials of fiction were not a part of the rhythms of Clark's own nature and vision.

Thus in pointing out that the sudden halt to Clark's writing had something to do with the complicated way in which he undertook his teaching, one might also have to admit that it was even more complicated than that. He had hard material for fiction; and he kept to a hard and honest view of it. One wonders how many novels could have come from it in the best of circumstances.

Whatever it was that cut the flow of Clark's fiction, we can all feel, whether we write or not, what it means to have that flow cut off. But I have not been looking at these difficulties to raise sentiments about them. What I most had in mind when I spoke at the beginning for how Clark embodied the vanishing qualities, as a representative American, of a decent ideal, was how integral, how whole, he always was whatever the internal pressures he had to manage in order to keep the balance between internal need and external necessities.

My reiteration of this theme of wholeness does not mean he

did not have his contradictions. A sensibility that compels
someone in the first place to write fiction begins in contradictions. Clark had his share. He had a moral abhorrence of violence, but he kept a boy's fascination for its details. This ambivalence toward ideas of violence is as much a part of the true
subject matter of *The Ox-Bow Incident* as law and justice are.
He had a lot of anger in him and a hot flashpoint; but I never
witnessed his loss of control over them. I have spoken about
how extraordinary a teacher he was, but he could be curt with
an arrogant student or one gone silly with an esthetic self-pity.

Clark had a large technical understanding of music—and he
used it in *The City of Trembling Leaves*—but to my knowledge
he preferred a tennis match to a concert, a football game on
television to records on a stereo. He loved Virginia City and
came finally to buy a house there. It finally became his permanent place despite summer tourists and the honky-tonk carni-
val air. And he knew and relished all the stories of the bonanza
days, even as he detested what the bonanza was all about—rip-
ping up the land for metal. He detested our car-happy culture,
but he liked to drive, loved his own cars, and gave them affec-
tionately personal names, as though they might have been
horses.

I am summoning up these final details, many of them trivial,
not just to tally the costs of his wholeness, but to defeat the
details themselves. He is a man I always knew and know now
more in essence than in detail. He is vivid in the details, but
permanent in the essence. He is like the meaning of a history
more than he is like the history itself.

I think it is also just to say—and it should be said—that in
his last years he increasingly moved away from all that began
to be intolerable to him in our chaotic atmosphere. Perhaps,
in that sense, Virginia City was as much a hideaway as it was
a place to live. But even turned away, he never quit. As most
of us know, he undertook for the University of Nevada Press,
and for what was inherently valuable in the work itself, the job
of editing the journals of Alf Doten. The task proved difficult,
and the publisher tells me that, for whatever reason, sometimes
months would go by without Clark's touching the diaries. His

letters to me during those years were obsessively concerned with the Doten work, and once in a while an edge of lament filled a sentence or invaded the tone. He never directly complained. He never even indirectly expressed regret for his undertaking. He told me once, but in a whimsical way as he talked of how Doten had overtaken his life, that he had written a personal check and inadvertently signed it with Alf Doten's name. Whimsically, also, he admitted that his own dreams were not only being filled with pictures of Alf Doten, but he was even beginning to dream some of the dreams Doten had recorded in his journals. An end to the work always promised to be nearer than it was, and through most of all this time he kept on teaching at the university. He finally got the Doten materials cut down by a third, to just under a million words. Meanwhile, he kept before him the imminence of his retirement, the completion of the Doten task, and after that a hopeful clearing of his desks, his mind, and the beginning of a rhythm that would get him back to the two or three novels he had kept conceptually alive in his mind through all those fictionally silent years.[3]

It did not happen. He underwent an operation for cancer, and made arrangements to retire. He seemed for a while to recover, but his last illness came, and it came hard. He was given once more and for the last time to reiterate how the private ideals necessary to the spirit of the individual stood at balance with the necessities essential to the nature of life itself. For as long as he could, he refused pain-killing medicines. They made him woozy and kept him from intervals when he could still read. Most of all, they deprived him of full consciousness, which to him was a deprivation of the will, and of experience.

It was a gray, cold, snow-and-ice day that saw his funeral in Reno. But at the cemetery in Virginia City, the sky cleared and the sun broke through. And at that precise moment, when my own feelings were beginning to show as too nakedly human, too visibly self-involved, there came, through a break in the clearing sky and over the ridge of a nearby hill, a flock of intervening birds. I looked up and watched them. I was told later they were probably starlings. I know little of the names of birds, but I knew enough at that moment—someone had taught me—to watch them. They made a beautiful swoop, and then departed, and left behind them, for me, a vast and meanful silence.

Notes

1. Robert Penn Warren and Cleanth Brooks, Jr., wrote a textbook that had much to do with redirecting the teaching of literature in American colleges. —Ed.

2. Wilner is presumably referring to a character in Conrad's *Lord Jim*, not to the playwright Marlow. —Ed.

3. When Wilner wrote, Clark's unpublished manuscripts were not available, and thus he had no way of knowing how much Clark had been writing during most of his "silent" years. —Ed.

4

Walter Clark's Frontier

Wallace Stegner

Wallace Stegner, author of fiction, biography, and criticism, is prob-ably the most admired living writer in and of the American West. Shortly before delivering the paper printed below, he had added Angle of Repose and All the Little Live Things to an already distinguished list. His personal association with Clark is surveyed in the present article, which thus becomes a testimonial to a literary friendship, as well as the estimate by one creative mind of another. The lecture, commissioned as part of a series on Clark, has been printed, with some excisions, in The Atlantic, 232 (1973) 94–98. *It is the property of the Hilliard Fund, and its printing by* The Atlan-tic *was authorized by the University of Nevada administration.*

Max Westbrook's little book on the writings of Walter
Van Tilburg Clark—a book whose perceptions I often
agree with though its metaphysical terminology and its Zen-
and-Jung dialectic leave me pretty confused—begins with an
anecdote told by Walt Clark himself.[1] He said he was once introduced to a lady in the East as the author of *The Ox-Bow Incident.* She was incredulous. "You wrote *that?* My God, I thought
you'd been dead for fifty years. You know, Owen Wister and
all those people."

It is an instructive story. For one thing, it demonstrates the
swiftness with which *The Ox-Bow Incident* made its way onto
the small shelf of western classics. It further suggests that a book
on that shelf is somehow embalmed: it has no contemporary
reality to the ordinary reader, it is not something written

by a modern writer or relevant to modern men and women, it escapes out of time, it acquires the remoteness and larger-than-life simplicities of myth and of certain kinds of folklore. And finally, as Westbrook points out (it is his principal reason for repeating the anecdote), the lady made a common but serious error in relating *The Ox-Bow Incident* to *The Virginian*. It is like *The Virginian* in only superficial ways. Its purpose is not the celebration or even the definition of the cowboy hero whom Wister and Remington, between them, self-consciously created.[2] To link it with Wister's belated chivalry is like comparing Conrad with Captain Marryat because both wrote about sailors. In fact, *The Ox-Bow Incident* is a novel that Henry James, that "historian of fine consciences," had more to do with than Wister did.

It is one of Westbrook's premises that Clark has been generally misread by the critics. I agree. It seems almost a statement of the standard condition of novelists of the West, who are a little like the old folks in the Becket play, continually rising up out of the garbage cans to say something, and continually having the lids crammed down on them again. We may want to speak to the nation or the world, but often, by the condescending assumptions of critics who cannot or will not read us, we are allowed to speak only to our own back alley or within the echoing hollow of our own garbage can. Walter Clark's western materials no more limit the depth and relevance of his fiction than the barbarous backwoods setting of *Huckleberry Finn* or the scruffiness of Yoknapatawpha County limit the validity of Mark Twain or Faulkner.

So Walter Clark was not simply a regional writer. Now that he is untimely dead, it is entirely appropriate that readers and seminars and groups should be discussing and analyzing how much more he was. But I add my bit to the discussion diffidently, for I am not a critic, and I do not want to contribute another misreading. Neither do I want to exploit his writings, as one would exploit some natural resource, for the making of a critical by-product. That is too much like cutting down redwoods to make Prestolite fireplace logs out of the sawdust. I only want to revisit him, and I welcome the opportunity to re-

mind myself of the things in him that I always admired and envied, and to see what a new look will reveal.

My responses are personal, not only because I knew and liked
Walter Clark, but because in many ways our careers have been
parallel. We were almost exact contemporaries—he was six
months younger than I—and we grew up in the same part of
the world, he from the age of eight in Reno, I from the age of
twelve in Salt Lake City. The Great Basin is a unifying force;
wherever you live in it, you flow toward every other part. Without knowing it, Walt and I shared much, even a passion for basketball and tennis. We may have played each other in one tournament or other, though if we did I do not remember. His name
would have meant nothing to me then; and anyway I tend to
forget people I played against forty or more years ago, especially
if they beat me, as he probably would have. But the cultural
geopolitics of the Great Basin was and is a reality even if it
never brought us together, and it eventually did let Walt and
me flow together into the same desert sink.

I had known him as a splendid novelist from *The Ox-Bow
Incident,* but it was not until I read *The City of Trembling Leaves*
that I recognized a blood brother. Shared responses to a shared
reality are more important in literary communication than are
shared ideas. If literature speaks to temperament, as Conrad
said, then it speaks to experience simultaneously. I recognized
myself in Tim Hazard and, I thought, in Tim's creator. We
spoke the same language; we held attitudes that even when
they differed were compatible. That sense of cultural affinity,
of a shared and recognized youth, led me to look Walt up the
next time I drove through Nevada, and my wife and I spent a
long afternoon and evening of beer and talk with him and Barbara in the Carson Valley.

That was the beginning of a valued but not close friendship.
I never saw as much of him as I should have liked; we were together a total of hardly ten days in more than twenty years.
Though I once hired him to teach at Stanford, I hired him to
replace me, and I was in Denmark all the time he was in Palo
Alto. We corresponded off and on, saw each other occasionally. But from that first meeting we were friends and more than

friends—allies, members of the same tribe, inheritors of the same western estate. Maybe the estate was meager, maybe we were the Diggers of literature, but the mysteries we pretended to were mutual, shared, ours. He taught me a lot about who I was. He was the kind of mirror which, because of isolation and the peculiar newness and poverty of my cultural traditions, I had never had a chance to look into.

I have just reread him, all except the early poems and a few ephemeral essays. It was a too-brief pleasure, for he was a novelist for only one decade, from *The Ox-Bow Incident* in 1940 to *The Track of the Cat* in 1949, and from posterity's point of view he wrote only four books. I should like to reflect a little on what his books mean to me, where they elude me, and how they are related to and how they differ from my own attempts in a similar direction. The cultural circumstances that breed likeness are not strong enough to breed identity. Though in many ways we were alike, in at least one major circumstance we were different, and that difference had something to do with a difference in the books we wrote.

We were alike in our response to country. We were Western-ers in what desert, mountains, weather, space, meant to us. He was something of a mystic, as I am not, and if Westbrook is to be believed, he had a conscious intention of dramatizing Jun-gian archetypes and finding objective correlatives for sacrality within a profane culture. That goes over my head. Certainly I never felt the watchful gods of nature in quite Walt's way—I was probably content with their objective correlatives—but al-most as much as he, I think, I felt an awe in the presence of unhumanized nature, I wanted to belong in the natural world and be part of it and be *right* with it, as in dozens of places Walt demonstrated that he did. Almost as much as he, but later in my life, I grew to hate the profane western culture, the economics and psychology of a rapacious society. I disliked it as reality and I distrusted it when it elevated itself into the west-ern myths that aggrandized arrogance, machismo, vigilante or sidearm justice, and the oversimplified good-guy/bad-guy moralities invented mainly by east-coast dudes fascinated by the romantic figure of the horseman, and happily utilized by a lot of horsemen and sidearm Galahads as self-justification. Those myths have made an impervious shield for all kinds of Westerners, drugstore as well as authentic cowboys, in the dangerous wilderness of moral responsibility. I think Walt and I both felt that, strongly. I sense a fellow moralist in him.

We were both, however, to some extent products of the western experience and culture, in both good and bad and neutral ways. We were both squarer, I imagine, than boys our age in so-called sophisticated places. We accepted the traditional western sexual mores, the division of women into good women and bad women, and a whole lot about the male obligations of protection, chivalry, and, when called for, adoration. We accepted the prevailing athleticism of our place and time, and wanted to excel in competitive sports. We did not think of competition as evil in itself; we wanted sound minds in sound bodies; we wanted to play the game as clean as a hound's tooth, and all that. Put to the test, we respected self-reliance, and when we made literary moves we made them in the spirit of exploration and pioneering. We wanted to go out into our native deserts and mountains and bring back gold; we wanted to help our infant civilization to places as high as we ourselves sometimes felt we went. Our literary quest was a version of the dream of the garden of the world; we wanted as much as any Mormon elder to make the desert blossom, though with different fruits. In a way that many deculturized and future-shocked moderns will never understand, there was a civilization-building impulse somewhere in our ambitions.

But I was far more completely a product of the young West than Walt Clark was. The civilized tradition of books, ideas, poetry, history, philosophy, all the instruments and residue of human self-examination, all the storage-and-retrieval possibilities of human experience, I knew only in school, and most imperfectly. It was all a foreign culture superimposed on my barbarism, and entirely foreign to my home, my family associations, my native conditioning. If at school I was part of the age of polished stone, and beginning to be literate, at home I was paleolithic and without the alphabet. No member of my family had ever finished high school, much less college: my father had

left school after the eighth grade, my mother after the sixth.
During our years in Salt Lake City, our household was at what
I tend to think of as the Amos and Andy level of culture, and
it had attained to that only after years at the Davy Crockett
level, on the crudest of frontiers where we saw people few and
seldom and books hardly at all. I have written about that cultural poverty in *Wolf Willow,* and it has no place here except
to indicate the way in which Walt Clark and I differed fundamentally and from the beginning. I was a western boy who
came hungrily toward civilization from the profound barbarism
of the frontier, and was confronted with the fairly common task
assigned would-be American writers—that of encompassing in
one lifetime, from scratch, the total achievement of the race.
Walt was luckier: he was a western boy who possessed civilization from childhood.

He grew up in a cultivated house, and his translation west-
ward at the age of eight was not a move toward deprivation.
His father was highly educated, the president of the University
of Nevada; his mother was a gifted musician. Books, music,
and ideas that I discovered late and by accident, or never
discovered at all, were Walt's from birth. He really *had* the
two worlds of civilization and the West, where I had only
the West, and became a kind of pretender, or at best seeker,
every morning when I left for school. My school life affected
my home life hardly at all, and it was a long time before
pure accident gave me the notion that it might be possible
for *me* to be a writer. Writers were people from elsewhere,
or long ago. And when I began writing, I began by simply
trying to report. It was another good while before I realized
that I was writing primarily toward a much more personal
life, up toward the higher intellectual ledges that I knew
about from school. It was a little like trying to make Alley
Oop, and Alley's dinosaurian concerns, relevant and significant to the National Academy. I had to discover, and in
part create, a history and an identity for myself, and then climb
from that foothold.

Walt knew very early the terms of his division. He was
light-years ahead of me in self-knowledge and awareness.

When he sat down to write about the West he was not, like me, limited to writing about scrub oak or sagebrush and wishing that they were the silver apples of the moon. He was self-consciously trying to graft the silver apples onto the sagebrush rootstock.

Wilderness: The Raw Material

Many western novels, both realistic and mythic, have been on the side of the wilderness against the vulgarizing tendencies of settlement. The result has been sometimes nostalgia, sometimes bitterness, depending on whether the novelist looks hardest at past or present. You may see one or the other, or both, in all sorts of books, from Willa Cather's A Lost Lady (or for that matter Cooper's The Pioneers, the ancestor of hundreds of western novels), to Larry McMurtry's The Last Picture Show. We began to regret the wilderness almost before we invaded it, and yearn for the past before we had one. For those who conceive the American dream romantically, its inevitable corruption is disgusting. "Lilies that fester smell far worse than weeds."

It is Walter Clark's distinction that he was never that simplistic, and became neither bitter nor nostalgic. He was on the side of the primal wilderness, but his wilderness was never Eden; its gods were both benign and destructive. He was opposed to the profane and exploitive and despiritualized culture of the settlement, but not to the point of repudiating it utterly, dropping out or copping out or shouting at it from a safe literary sniping post. He consistently tried to make the past, including the spiritually healthy but limited past of the displaced Indians, relate to the present. He repudiated the machismo that won, and half ruined, the West, but did not repudiate its energy. He wanted it reinforced with spirituality, art, respect for the earth, a knowledge of good and evil. He wanted it to become a true civilization, not a ruthless occupation disguised as a romantic myth.

In Clark's last novel The Track of the Cat, Curt and Curt's mother seem to represent a misguided exploitive harshness, a rigidity or sterility of mind and act, and the Paiute, Joe Sam, seems to represent a primitive nature mysticism victimized and debased. The drunken father is a casualty, as are, in their own ways, his children Arthur and Grace. Of the whole Bridges family, only the youngest son Hal has in him the possibilities of growth, reconciliation, and redemption. And there too, I realize on rereading the book, I recognized myself in Walt Clark's writing. Because I was a sort of Hal, without knowing I was. Rereading Walter Clark made me go back and glance through a book of my own, *The Big Rock Candy Mountain*, which I published a half dozen years before *The Track of the Cat*. On the very last page, in the last two paragraphs, I found my own more personal and more agonized statement of Walter's persistent theme. My character Bruce Mason, who is as close to myself as Tim Hazard is to Walt Clark, is ruminating at his father's funeral, after a quarter of a million words of turmoil, effort, bad guesses, mistakes, violence, and cross purposes:

> It was good to have been along and to have shared it. There were things he had learned that could not be taken away from him. Perhaps it took several generations to make a man, perhaps it took several combinations and re-creations of his mother's gentleness and resilience, his father's enormous energy and appetite for the new, a subtle blending of masculine and feminine, selfish and selfless, stubborn and yielding, before a proper man could be fashioned.
>
> He was the only one left to fulfill that contract and try to justify the labor and the harshness and the mistakes of his parents' lives, and that responsibility was so clearly his, was so great an obligation, that it made unimportant and unreal the sight of the motley collection of pallbearers staggering under the weight of his father's body, and the back door of the hearse closing quietly upon the casket and the flowers.

"You can't mean that ending," an eastern friend told me. But I did, and I think Walt Clark would have understood what I meant—something more than personal to me or my characters—something about the West's difficult becoming, something about its mistakes and crimes, something about its spiritual birthright sold for a mess of pottage, something about its hope. For he could not forget, and neither can I, that the

western experience is more than personal; it is part of the process of civilization-building. It was precisely that perception
that moved Willa Cather to describe her Bohemian farm girl
Antonía Shimerda as "a rich mine of life, like the founders of
early races."

I think the attitude is characteristically western. We feel
more affinity with Romulus and Remus than with Nero. We are
still busy founding Rome while in New York they fiddle to celebrate its burning.

Civilization: The Theme

Civilization is Walter Clark's theme; the West is only his raw
material. What else is the burden of The Ox-Bow Incident? That
novel is a long way from being a simple reversal of the vigilante
stereotype or an ironic questioning of vigilante justice. It is a
proving of the whole blind ethics of an essentially false, imperfectly formed, excessively masculine society, and of the way in
which individuals, out of personal inadequacy, out of mistaken
loyalties and priorities, out of a fear of seeming womanish, or
out of plain cowardice, let themselves be pushed into murder.
We live mainly by forms and patterns, the novel says. If the
forms are bad, we live badly. We have no problem telling where
good and evil dwell when we are dealing with the Virginian and
Trampas. But here you cannot tell them by the color of their
hats. Neither the lynchers nor the lynched are all good guys
or bad guys. Many of the lynchers would rather not be there
and have not known how to say so. The hanged men are a
greenhorn, an old senile man, and a Mexican no better than
he should be. The terrified greenhorn, once he has accepted
his situation, dies better than the Mexican, who was at first
bold and unafraid. Davies, who opposed from the beginning
the lynch mood of Tetley, failed to stop him because, quite simply, Tetley had more guts than he did. The preacher's morality
is not binding because it is imported, almost irrelevant. Evil has
courage, good is sometimes cowardly, reality gets bent by appearances.

The book does not end with the discovery that the hanged
men are innocent and that lynch law has been a profound mis-

take. It goes on examining *how* profound a mistake. The moral
ambiguities reverberate through the town. We begin to know
the good guys from the bad guys by the way they deal with their
own complicity in a tragic error. And the moral questioning,
the first stage of conscience, goes on in the mind of that most
Jamesian cowboy Art Croft, very much as it goes on in the consciousness of the nameless I/we narrator of *The Nigger of the
"Narcissus"* after the crew comes ashore.

The Ox-Bow Incident* was misread, as Westbrook says. It still
is. I hate to think so, but I suspect that its unchallenged place
on the shelf of western classics is due not to its being com-
prehended and appreciated, but to its being persistently misread as an example of the kind of mythic western that Walt
Clark was all but parodying. Look at the blurbs on the Signet
paperback, and at the summary of the book on the first inside
page. To Signet and Signet's readers it is a novel of excitement
and suspense and nervous trigger fingers. They do not read it
as the report of a failure of individual and social conscience and
nerve, an account of wrong sanctioned and forced by the false
ethics of a backward folk-culture. They do not read it as a la-
mentable episode of a civilization in the throes of being born.

Clark's adaptation of the western makes use of its machinery
but substitutes a complex and ambiguous moral problem for the
blacks and whites of the genre. His version of the *Kunstroman*
is equally desimplified. I call *The City of Trembling Leaves* a
Kunstroman rather than a spiritual autobiography because,
though there are unquestionably autobiographical elements in
it, Clark has taken evasive action—made Tim Hazard's pilgrimage also Walt Clark's. There is much internal evidence of
this, such as the preoccupation with the Tristram cycle, with
tennis, with the purifications to be found in the mountains, the
awareness of the watchful gods.

Never mind. Biography or autobiography, *The City of
Trembling Leaves* belongs in the pigeonhole with *A Portrait of
the Artist as a Young Man, Look Homeward Angel, Wilhelm Meis-
ter, The Hill of Dreams,* and some more somber books such as
Jude the Obscure, and especially some American portraits of the
artist such as *The Song of the Lark.* It chronicles the develop-

ment of a sensitive adolescent into an artist. It is preoccupied with the relationship between art and life, that obsessive theme of Thomas Mann's, and it explores that relationship not only through Tim's music and through the painting and sculpture of Lawrence Black, but also through the several variations on artistic adjustment made by Tim's musician friends in Carmel. It reveals a skinless sensibility in its mystical feeling for Pyramid Lake, the Sierra, and the desert. It weds Tim Hazard to the physical universe by a rite of passage and a symbolic skinny-dip straight out of Frazer's *Golden Bough*, or if you follow Westbrook, out of Jung. These are all fairly standard elements of a literary genre at least a hundred years old before Walt Clark took hold of it—a genre, one should note, much favored by self-obsessed romantics.

But if Tim Hazard is romantic, the book is not. It is steadily cauterized by irony. And the element of repudiation and compulsive self-exile, almost standard among spiritual autobiographies, is absolutely missing. Tim Hazard, this sensitive youth with musical aspirations and a high cultural potential, grows up in Reno and is never at war with it. It does not frustrate him. He hardly notices it, in fact. He is absorbed with school, and girls, and running, and tennis, and playing in dance bands. He accepts—and so did I—the standards of his time and place, and tries to star in what they value; or if he cannot accept them, he ignores them. His father and his brother are not his kind, but he does not think of them as his enemies or threats to his spirit. Reno in its double aspect of middle-class town and jackpot center is not for him the threat that Dublin was to Joyce, or Asheville and his mother's boarding house to Tom Wolfe, or Wellington, New Zealand, to Katherine Mansfield, or America to Ezra Pound.

Most important, the end of Tim Hazard's long struggle to be an artist is not flight or exile, as in so many lives and books, but reconciliation with his town and his past. Art, you might say, leads him not away from the limited western American town, but deeper into it. He adds music to Reno without obliterating the traces of Reno that are left in himself. He is not led, as his friend Lawrence Black is, to a self-destructive perfectionism, either. He does not think of himself as contaminated by moving from jazz bands to symphonies, from folk music to composition, and back again—by the divergencies of taste between himself and his town. Some things he outgrows, as he outgrows his adolescent adorations and excesses, but they have strengthened him rather than harmed him. And that makes *The City of Trembling Leaves* unique in its genre. Clark has not justified himself at the expense of his surroundings, if we may take Tim to represent Clark. He has tried to use them to grow from, and in.

One must admit flaws in the book. For me, at least, there is an excess of philosophical abstraction. In trying to marry ideas pertinent to a sophisticated culture to the daily life of a western town, Clark has sometimes let the ideas blur the town. In trying to present Tim's adolescent adorations sympathetically but ironically, and at the same time not be ironic about the ultimate seriousness of Tim's efforts to make a unity of his divided heritage, he is sometimes overlong and unduly detailed, as if he feared the realistic boy might get lost under the symbolic artist. It is, in fact, an almost impossible task he set himself, at this stage of the West's history, and it reminds me of another long, imperfect novel about an artist born in a little western town, Willa Cather's *The Song of the Lark*. Willa Cather assumed that the American artist must escape his or her birthplace and be a kind of stranger in the earth. When Clark lets Tim Hazard, after many failures, achieve his "Symphony of the Leaves," he has dared to suggest that there is a possible reconciliation among serious art, the ordinariness of a little western city, and the primal gods of the earth. It is something I should like to believe.

The City of Trembling Leaves appeared in 1945, the same year in which Clark's short story "The Wind and the Snow of Winter" received first prize in the O. Henry awards. The story is an absolutely first-rate achievement. But in terms of what it attempts, in the absolute importance of what it says, it is almost insignificant beside the ambitious novel that most reviewers dismissed as an autobiographical self-indulgence.

In *The Ox-Bow Incident* Walter Clark had suggested that the values of the frontier society were narrow, false, only half formed, and had planted a civilizing seed of conscience and doubt and unrest—and hence, of youth—in the mind of the sensitive cowpuncher who was one of the lynchers. In *The City of Trembling Leaves* he had suggested that a native western boy, given adequate motivation, might become an artist even in the unlikely arena of the Biggest Little City in the World, and make his commonplace origins serve his art.

In *The Track of the Cat* he came at his theme of civilization, of the evil of the exploitive and profane white culture, and the possibility of reconciliation between that culture's energies and the watchful primal gods of the earth, in quite another way. A lot of reviewers were irresistibly reminded of Melville's white whale, and the book had a mixed reception. On rereading it, I find myself willing to grant some of their objections, but not willing to grant that the flaws are fatal. *The Track of the Cat* may be in some ways Walter Clark's best book.

The realistic objections are valid enough. Mountain lions do not act that way, do not hunt men, probably could not break the neck of a two-year-old steer, much less a bull, much less two or three steers and a bull in one flurry. Only a lion given a heavy injection of literary evil would act that way, and some readers would have been less uneasy if Walt had made his symbolic beast an old rogue grizzly, the only animal possible to the Sierra Nevada that *could* break the neck of a steer, and *might* stalk his hunter. Once more, never mind: Keats said Cortez, Shakespeare put a seacoast on Bohemia. The beast is animate (and in good part imaginary) evil, and if the evil is made real to me, I am willing to suspend my disbelief in its objective correlative.

Some sticklers for realism, George R. Stewart for one, have objected that there is a fairly constant violation of the point of view—that Arthur, for instance, wakened by the bellowing of the attacked steers, would not be likely to hear it "like muted horns a little out of tune." Stewart would say that simile came out of Walt Clark, not out of Arthur Bridges.

Yes, sure. I would probably question that little technical impropriety myself in a student's story. But Walter Clark was no student, and what he had to say was important. His Arthur is endowed with some of the prophetic mysticism and second-sight of Joe Sam, the family's Paiute hired man. Moreover, it is only by peering over the shoulders of his characters and nudging us with his own voice that Clark is able to steer us among all the tensions of the story and suggest the conflicts between Curt and Joe Sam, Curt and Arthur, Gwen and the mother, the drunken father and all the others, love and hate, good and evil. And I keep remembering that one of Walt's abiding intentions was to naturalize subtlety, sensitivity, spirituality, modulated and even ambiguous ideas, in his realistic western setting. He chose not to be limited, like some phonographic naturalist, by the verbal and spiritual vocabulary of probability. So far as I am concerned, it is legitimate if he gets away with it. He does.

Especially in the early sections, *The Track of the Cat* is a slow, tense drama, melodramatically lighted. I have used it for years as a magnificent illustration of how to achieve suspense by eye-strain. The characters are never overexplained; they reveal themselves in speech and act, and if their creator's need to make them symbolic as well as real sometimes strains them toward some monomaniac excess, they are actually less strained in that way than some of the characters (the preacher, say, or Tetley in *The Ox-Bow Incident,* or the wonderful, manic musician Knute Fenderson in *The City of Trembling Leaves*). If we grant his panther a little legitimate heightening, we should not deny the same privilege to the human characters.

Symbolic, all of them, but for the most part persuasively real too. There is a real lion loose in the mountains, but the black painter of evil lives in the ranch house, in Curt, as dominating and arrogant as the worst of the *Ox-Bow* lynchers; and in Curt's mother, harshly pious, capable of suffering but invulnerable to understanding; and to some lesser extent in Curt's weak and evasive father. Their evil has already defeated the gentle brother, Arthur, long before Curt finds his broken-necked body in the snow. The same family evil—and I think we realize very soon that it is a social evil, a regional evil, a national evil, an evil of attitude like the cowardice and mob impulse in *The*

Ox-Bow Incident—has completely destroyed the sister, Grace. The only person capable of resisting it, the only one of them besides defeated Arthur who can make contact with the Paiute Cassandra and primitive survivor Joe Sam, is Hal, the youngest son. I have already admitted to identifying myself with Hal and feeling his role as my own. It is hard to resist the temptation to be a culture hero. But Hal's in-between position, his hopeful stance as combiner and reconciler, is the essential stance of Art Croft too, and of Tim Hazard, and of Walt Clark.

Perhaps strangely, I respond less to Curt's disintegration than to the slow, tense drama in the ranch house. I feel it as a necessity of the plot rather than as a realistic or even philosophical probability. My experience with the Curts of the world does not lead me to think they are ever touched by the primal gods, that they ever comprehend good and evil, that they are very often visited by poetic justice. For me, Curt at the end is out of Eugene O'Neill, the Great God Brown in chaps, a literary figure where the others, heightened or not, are authentic. But I will put up with both him and the black painter—excesses of the literary and symbolizing imagination—to know the believable, complex, human torments of that ranch family in a crisis.

All of Walter Clark's novels were written from ideas, I believe, especially from a preoccupation with problems of good and evil within the context of the real West. He was a little like Hawthorne in knowing all the time what he wanted to say. The characters he created to say it through, whether historical or contemporary, have most of the time a solidity and realism that are altogether admirable. If he had a weakness, it was that sometimes his ideas outran their objective correlatives, and he steered them, or talked about them, rather than letting them act. Not often. And when the symbolic, larger meanings emerge, as so often, directly from something as solid as a log, when we meet and recognize the substance before we are asked to look at the shadow, then I follow him with my hat in my hand. He was not quite, like Hawthorne, trying to develop a usable past, or not that alone; he was trying rather to marry sensitivity and philosophical ideas to the half-primitive western life he knew. He kept trying to do the impossible, and he never missed by far. From 1949 on, many of us were waiting for the book that would outdo the three splendid earlier books and cap the career. It never came. Why?

Some have guessed that teaching distracted him, and certainly he was a teacher incredibly generous with his time. But he was a teacher all his life—at Vermont, in the Cazenovia high school, at Montana, at San Francisco State, at Nevada, with shorter stints at Stanford, Connecticut Wesleyan, and perhaps other places. He wrote all his books between the demands of teaching, and I cannot believe that it was teaching that stopped him. More than that, he told me in the early 1960s that he wrote all the time, and kept throwing away what he wrote. That was long after *The Track of the Cat*.

So did he after all fall victim to the perfectionism that he specifically repudiated in his character Lawrence Black? It is possible. What he had written had been widely misunderstood. His clash of belief and attitude with Leslie Fiedler at Montana might have made him determined to say it in some way that even Fiedler could understand, and he might have become discouraged with the difficulty, first of saying it, and then of making it audible beyond the garbage can and the alley. Without knowing how he felt, I suspect that the dramatization of his difficulty, through the association with Fiedler and the challenge embodied in such essays as "The Montana Face," would have made him more self-critical. And yet he was always self-critical; I cannot conceive that mere difficulty would have silenced him or led him to destroy his work.[3]

What then? I wish I knew. But the fact that from 1962 onward he devoted much of his creative time to the editing of the papers of a pioneer named Alfred Doten suggests, if not an answer, some of the parts of an answer. To turn from fiction to history has been the tendency of scores of American writers who were reared on the thinly civilized frontiers. We have all done it, and it started nearly a hundred years ago, with Edward Eggleston in Indiana. Once we have written the books that deal with the early settlement years of our region, or with our own growing up to identity and awareness, we are likely to find neither the present nor the past rich enough to nourish the imagination. For one thing, the western past has been sanctified by myth, and so cut off. For another, both present and past are too new. The apparent maturity that comes with the creation of valid literature about a new region is apparent only. Culturally the first literature, even the finest, may be premature, the product of applying a seasoned and organic tradition to an unseasoned place and society. And the growing of a native tradition takes generations.

This is speculation only. I was speculating in those terms years ago, and about others besides Walt Clark. I had in mind myself, too. I looked at Bernard DeVoto, and Paul Horgan, and Bud Guthrie, and H. L. Davis, and a lot of good western writers, and I found them slipping away from fiction and into history, as if at a certain point in their careers they found that they had done what their circumstances permitted, and had now to start digging the foundations for the real cultural house that would come with time. In a sense, that is the history of American literature, not merely of western literature. The kind of cultural deprivation that Hawthorne and Henry James lamented is not fatal, as witness their own careers; neither is it fatal in the West, in a newer time, as witness the achievements of Walter Clark.

But without a more developed and cohesive society than the West, in its short life and against all the handicaps of revolutionary change and dispersion, has been able to grow—and without a native audience for its native arts—there may come a time in a writer's career when the clutch of the imagination will no longer take hold on the materials that are most one's own.

If those things are true, or partly true, then it is understandable that Walter Clark's career as novelist should have been short. The remarkable thing is that he rendered his own divided inheritance with such subtlety and skill. His books are on the permanent shelf, and I do not mean the shelf of mythic, easy, deluding westerns. His theme was civilization, and he recorded, indelibly, its first steps in a new country. He naturalized the struggle between good and evil in Nevada as surely as Robinson Jeffers naturalized tragedy on the Big Sur coast.

Notes

1. Max Westbrook, *Walter Van Tilburg Clark* (New York: Twayne, 1969).

2. See Ben Merchant Vorpahl, *My Dear Wister* (Palo Alto: American West Publ. Co., 1972).

3. Stegner is correct. We now know that Clark continued to write and that much of his work he did not destroy. But neither did he put much of it into publishable form. —Ed.

PART II

Studies of Major Published Works

Walter Clark, Wyoming, 1950. (Special Collections, Library, University of Nevada, Reno)

Introduction

Charlton Laird

*T*he *Ox-Bow Incident* served to introduce Walter Clark to
his audience, and has continued to be his most popular
and most widely known work, partly because the moving picture version, unsuccessful as a box office attraction, became
thereby widely shown on late-night television. Critics have
generally tended to prefer *The Track of the Cat* or almost any
of the short stories, a judgment in which Clark himself con-
curred, saying laughingly that posterity would probably know
him as "the author of *The Ox-Bow Incident* and the singer of
'Blood on the Saddle'," a sentimental ballad that Walter occasionally sang to the delight of his friends. *Ox-Bow* has retained
its popularity; if we may trust the surviving evidence, Clark was
asked to lecture on it more frequently than on all his later, more
ambitious works combined.

So far as I know, Clark left no extensive statement about *Ox-
Bow*. He did provide some generalities in response to requests
from the publisher of the Italian edition, but the questions must
not have been very searching.[1] In answer to one, Clark found
it necessary to explain what an ox-bow is, why he had preferred
Incident in the title, and that, "I was not trying to write a
[sociological] treatise. I was trying to write a novel." Perhaps
the best way to infer what Clark himself thought of *Ox-Bow*
is to examine the lecture notes he made for himself, some of
which survive.[2] By comparing the size and quality of the paper
used for the notes, the various inks and pencils, marginal iden-
tifications, and the like, I should say we have evidence of at
least ten lectures.[3] Most of the briefer sets of notes are inevitably repetitive, but one notices that no two are alike, either in
subject matter or in order. Obviously Clark was rethinking his
subject every time he delivered a lecture.

One of the most interesting sets of notes is that for an after-luncheon talk at San Francisco State University, April 22 (perhaps 1957). The announced subject must have been something like "Values in the Printed Ox-Bow Lost in the Movie Version." Clark points out that this question cannot be broached until we have considered what the author was trying to do. He said that his "major intention" was "to say something about the democratic process of justice in time of stress," and secondly, to suggest that, "it can happen here . . . indeed had happened." In developing the discussion, he mentioned that he included the black, Sparks, partly to remind the reader that plenty of innocent blacks had been lynched. One of the more obvious losses concerned the simplification of relationships among the characters; in the movie version, two of the cowhands, Art and Gil, were combined in order to provide a starring vehicle for Henry Fonda, but the play between the two cowpunchers was lost when they were simplified into one.

Another source of simplification involved Clark's sources. All actions and characters were fiction, he said, but they were drawn from historical incidents and characters—for example, the figure of the Confederate Army officer Tetley relied in part on Hitler and von Hindenburg. He seems to have been concerned about this point, perhaps because several critics had been. After a discussion he concludes, "So, yes, the Ox-Bow did in part spring from the feelings about what was happening in Europe."

On at least one other occasion Clark considered this problem in greater detail, along with something about the early versions of the novel. I happened to be present; a colleague had included Ox-Bow in a course in the modern American novel, and had asked Walter to respond to questions. He never refused students anything, and accordingly accepted. I managed to be free and slipped into a back seat. The talk was only well started when someone asked Clark why he chose the subject he did. I took no notes, but his answer went about as follows:

> You have to remember what the times were like. I had become irked at the way the West was treated in popular fiction and the moving pictures, with two-gun cowboys stuffed with Sun-

day-school virtues, and heroines who could go through a knock-down without getting a curl misplaced. I had read *Don Quixote*, in which Cervantes set out to satirize the silly romances of his day. I decided to write a Quixotesque "western" that I hoped in my youthful enthusiasm would make the whole thing look so silly that people would stop writing or reading such junk.

About the same thing happened to me that happened to Cervantes. My satire was pretty trivial, and I probably knew deep down it wouldn't make much difference, anyhow. And I was disturbed about what had happened in Italy with fascism there, and was growing in Germany with the Nazi horror, and I thought that was the great threat to the modern world, and specifically to American democracy. I saw the seeds of Naziism in our country, and maybe especially in the Old West—or if not, then in a simple dramatic incident in the West you could get a sort of test-tube sample, the local version of what had been standard treatment of the Indians and many free-thinking white men all the way west from the Pequod War. So I dumped the stuff I had written into the wastebasket and started over.

I had a sort of three-level analogy going. The people I had known in Reno, Virginia City, Carson, and on some of the ranches, where the children and grandchildren of the Old West people lived, and not very different really. And it wasn't hard to pick out counterparts of these people in the accounts we were getting out of Nazi Germany. If you'll run through the characters in *Ox-Bow* you'll see how this went.

Clark started ticking them off, telling what each character represented in a fascist society; some he equated with individuals, some with institutions. In *Ox-Bow*, Tetley is presented as a former officer in the Confederate Army; to Clark, he was a representative of the Prussian officer tradition. Clark even evidenced specific individuals, historical and otherwise, who had given him patterns to start from. The one I remember best—probably because I was amused by Clark's account—provided the original of Ma Grier, the powerful madam who becomes one of the leaders of the lynching party.

Clark said he had been coming home one broiling afternoon

from an excursion into the hills, riding a bicycle. He reached
a roadside joint, where a woman conventionally known as
"Ma" dispensed beer and hamburgers—whatever else she dispensed Clark had never asked, and probably the sheriff had
not. When entering, Clark noticed a partly filled, dilapidated
truck, backed up to the front door. He asked for a beer.

Ma said she was shut down. The highway department was
changing the road; it would run smack through her place and
she had to "git." Most of her stuff was packed a'ready. Sorry.

Several of Ma's men friends were lounging around; they had
been helping load the truck, and now were sizing up the huge
cookstove Ma had used to fry hamburgers. How could you get
enough hands on a thing like that to boost it into a truck?

Having finished with Clark, Ma went over to the stove and
wrapped her hamlike hands around the top of it. Alone she
hoisted it, and as Walter said, "gave it the knee," easing it
gently onto the truck bed. Years later, when Clark needed a
woman that all sorts of rough men would respect, and even accept as a leader, he resurrected the Ma of the beer-hamburger
joint and made her the Ma Grier whom Tetley named as a
lieutenant.

Thus we have record of at least two earlier versions of Ox-
Bow. Of the first, I now see no evidence. I must believe Clark
when he said he started by writing a satire on syrupy shoot-outs
in the manner of Riders of the Purple Sage, but if anything remains of that version it is now well obscured. Robert Clark,
however, suggests that the card game in Ox-Bow, which seems
needlessly long in its present context, may be a remnant of an
earlier version. Of the second version I had detected little until
I heard Clark speak, although some reviewers were alert
enough to suggest the analogy.

There must have been at least one later draft. In the class
discussion I have been recounting, Clark never got beyond his
anti-Nazi version, but the novel as we have it is not mainly an
analysis of fascism. It is more concerned with the problem of
evil, with the nature of goodness: Is the good man one who
means well, or must he also do well? What, in these days,
should men of good will do? These are much broader questions;

as Clark had gone from ribbing cheap westerns to using a basically western plot to warn against the dangers of fascism, he now went from what must have been a somewhat tractlike study of society to a true novel, to a story that is first of all a work of art, delineating the problem of human morality.

As we have seen, Robert Clark says his father dug the manuscript from wherever it was gathering dust and, after some revision, made mainly at the request of the publisher, it became *The Ox-Bow Incident*. We have no reason to doubt this statement, but the printed version is apparently the last of at least three drafts, or at least two extensive starts toward a draft, plus a third version that with some revision became the printed novel. The first version had started as a spoof of the sort that intrigued Clark; it was followed by two quite different versions, different from the original concept and different from each other, each stemming from a reconception that led to a whole new manuscript, from the first word on, not a revision of an old draft. Evidence from unpublished manuscripts suggests that this way of writing continued to be usual with Clark. Incidentally, Tim Hazard worked in a similar way when he tried to compose in *The City*, and a good sketch of the way Walter Clark worked as a writer can be inferred from the trials and failures—and the eventual success—of Tim as a composer.

Here we might notice that various reporters have recorded seemingly contradictory testimony concerning *Ox-Bow*. Robert Clark, for example, reports his father saying he wrote that story as a "finger exercise" to study the use of conversation to tell a story. I do not doubt that the elder Clark did say this, and that it is part of the explanation.

The fact is that Clark made several statements about the novel; and although they may seem at first blush to be inconsistent with one another, I suspect that they are all true. We need to consider the circumstances. For example, in the class I heard, Clark was responding to a specific question, and he never finished his answer. Clark loved detail, and he was suspicious of undocumented generalities. As a good teacher he encouraged students to think precisely, and he was himself scrupulous about answering a question that had been asked. We should notice the student's request. He had not asked what the theme of the novel was; he did not inquire what Clark had meant by the book. He asked how Clark came to choose the subject. If Clark had been a lover of peremptory answers, I can imagine him saying, "Young man, in the various versions of that story I chose the subject at least four times: (1) as a satire on 'westerns,' (2) as a warning against fascism, (3) as a case history of violence and bigotry in society, (4) as an inquiry into the nature of evil—and throughout as an exercise in composition." If he had been allowed to finish his lecture, he might have said something of this sort by way of summary, but the bell stopped him midway through the second segment of the explanation. At other times, asked similar but not identical questions, he had given appropriately dissimilar answers.

Notes

1. 527/1/16/3, in the Walter Clark Collection at UNR (University of Nevada, Reno). Of the introductions to the various reprints, that to the *Time* edition is noteworthy.

2. The Walter Clark Collection at UNR, 527/1/16/7 and 13.

3. The notes vary from a 3″ by 5″ card scribbled on one side to two pages, 8½ by 11″, covered with fine script, along with two copies of the Signet paperback edition, one with passages marked for reading, numbered to 42, and the other with slips inserted, with indication of the subject matter. These are so extensive that they imply several workings.

5

Clark's Western Incident: From Stereotype to Model

Robert B. Heilman

When the Christian Gauss prize for 1979 was awarded to The Ways of the World *(Seattle: University of Washington Press, 1978), the judges were recognizing what has become clear for some time, that Professor Robert B. Heilman is one of America's leading scholar-critics. For nearly half a century he has been publishing critiques distinguished by knowledge, wit, and insight—not to mention light verse. Among his other recent volumes are* The Ghost on the Ramparts *(Athens: University of Georgia Press, 1974) and* Tragedy and Melodrama: Versions of Experience *(Seattle: University of Washington Press, 1968). He has long been an ornament to the University of Washington Department of English, where he is now emeritus.*

Some years ago, when he was a boy of ten or eleven, my son occasionally, at the movies, would see some kind of action that he could not stand, and he would go out into the lobby for a brief respite. He was very tight-lipped about this; he did not explain what seemed unbearable. I was usually a little puzzled, for we did not take him to movies that might be expected to test his psychological stamina.

Yet his flight brought back memories—memories of my own responses to reading three decades earlier. In pretelevision days we read books over and over again. In certain books that I read more than once—boys' books that I can no longer identify, but

also novels by Dumas and Henty—there were some scenes that
I could hardly bear to live through again—scenes, I suppose,
of suffering or potential disaster. I dreaded those scenes even
when I knew that the key figures survived and things got better
later. Hence, when I came to the scenes, I would skip outright,
read very rapidly, or try to neutralize the painful episode by reminding myself, while agonizing through it, that life would
soon look brighter.

I am not, however, substituting family history for literary discussion. On the contrary, the memory of a childhood dread
leads right into my theme. When I was about to reread Walter
Clark's *The Ox-Bow Incident* last year, I found myself experiencing something very like that strange anticipatory dread
that I can hardly recall having known since the passionate
reading of more than fifty years ago. I do not think I am a hyper-
sensitive reader; I hope I am not an eccentric one; in general
I am not much moved by the "literature of the victim," in
which easy subject matter often stands in for hard mastery by
the artist. I should like to think, then, that my spontaneous
expectation of acute disquietude in the coming rerun was a tribute to Walter Clark's grasp of reality. I hope that, even though
they might use different words, other readers can join me in
finding an inner truth of the kind that evokes what I have
called dread. I will try to put my finger on that truth.

The word "dread" of course designates an emotional response. In casting about for a term to denote the objective quality of the events that cause such a response, I toy with the word
"inexorableness"—that is, fearful relentlessness. Yet as soon as
we think of some inexorable forces—violent storms, earth-
quakes, even terminal diseases—we realize that we do face up
to them as somehow in the nature of things. We may feel anger,
terror, or despair; but not, I think, dread. Dread implies the
presence, not only of danger, which can even be a stimulus,
but of a peculiar ominousness; it connotes, not so much a recognizable eruption within the norms of existence, as a threat
to the norms themselves. Furthermore, in *The Ox-Bow Incident*
we do not really have an inexorable course of injustice. There
is a powerful surge toward the murders, but there is also an ob-

servable resistance. It expresses itself in constant delays; one tension of the story lies in the possibility that the drift into delay may shape up as a decision to postpone. What causes dread is that the men may prefer the evil act. In the choice made, what is more, the voluntary is strangely compounded with the unwilling; the source of dread is the mysterious veto of a saving intuitive reluctance. But even this diagnosis is still on the surface, and we need to seek out the underlying reality.

A Residue of Millennialism

It is a critical truism that in *The Ox-Bow Incident* Clark showed what could be done with "the western"; he freed himself from a stereotype and came up instead with a model of fundamental human behavior. There is some obviousness in this approach, and it has been disparaged, but I choose it because I think it steers us to the heart of his achievement. What Clark did was to burrow more deeply into the stereotype and discover the secret bases of truth without which no stereotype could exist. A stereotype is not a falsification of reality but a sclerosis of reality: a pattern has become rigid instead of staying flexible and thus able to accommodate the inevitable varieties of unpredictable experience.

It is always interesting to try to define the kind of truth that is imprisoned in any stereotype. In approaching the western stereotype that concerns us here, I cannot help recalling the attitude of several British friends: they are devotees of the American western—not western literature as a reputable school, but actually the movie melodramas popular in England. There are varied motives for this fondness, which reflects a deeper passion old enough to deserve a name. I shall call it "hesperophilia," or the love of things western.[1] In Europe hesperophilia is related to a persistent habit of feeling that dates at least from the Renaissance: enchantment with the exotic, be it oriental or occidental. In America, the only thing left that can be imagined to be exotic is the special life attributed to the West, and Englishmen (or Americans) may want to believe that there is such a special life because they cannot bear to be without exotic relief from the too-well-known that is every man's fate.

We come now, however, to a deeper issue. Into the long-lived European fascination with the American exotic there entered very early another motive: the exotic, being by definition little-known and extraordinary, could readily connote a little known and extraordinary condition: perfectibility, in either an Eden that could be recovered or a utopia that could be founded. The lure of the utopian quest was exported from Europe to America. Deriving moral energy from the Puritan conviction of God's presence within, dreamers or idealists could seek to institute a heaven upon earth, moving west for the indispensable exotic scene as the East became known. The most familiar term for their spirit is millennialism, and it lies deep within hesperophilia and its literary offspring, the western stereotype. And it is what Clark found and obliquely utilized in a dramatic narrative in which the power of the surface is matched by the complexity of inner force.

We have been looking for the qualities in *The Ox-Bow Incident* that could evoke what I call dread. I propose that an underlying theme of this tale is the millennial impulse. The millennial impulse and the feeling of dread: surely these are incompatible terms, except perhaps to a diabolical being for whom the most ominous evil would be the appearance of a heaven upon earth. I hope, however, not to be the devil's voice, or, what is worse, to be attracting attention by a frantic paradox. So I will try to point out the quiet link between the apparently irreconcilable cause and result.

Millennialism can work in several ways. It may inspire a fierce total quest—that is, a campaign to root out or destroy evil in a grand way, literal or symbolic. This is a familiar American endeavor; it is what the governess does in *Turn of the Screw*, what Captain Ahab does in *Moby Dick*, what Curt Bridges does in Clark's *The Track of the Cat*—what all prohibitionists do. In ordinary fictional western millennialism we find a simple pursuit of a readier, more decisive justice than the actual world seems to offer. Misconduct is clear-cut and tangible and hence vulnerable, like a body to a bullet. Though evil may cause damage, it finally gets run out of the county. This is a seductive goal for good men, doubtless persuasive even to those ordinarily suspicious of stereotypes. Quick, pure justice charms many who may feel immune to societal mirages but are gladdened by the doctrinaire's mirage, the Platonic idea clamped like a mold upon everyday experience.

This justice triumphant has another charm: it offers a utopia without doctrine, a heaven without theology. The implicit slogan is "We all know what justice is; let's execute it." Winder, anxious to be off on the hunt, is driven "wild" by the question posed by Davies: "I mean, if you had to say what justice was, how would you put it?" (p. 46).[2] Winder, one of those more eager to execute justice, is like many for whom doctrine is always frustrating; it means laws, bylaws, rules, regulations—a maze where the noble ends that we all visualize seem hopelessly lost. Hamlet put the problem in a phrase we often quote, "the law's delay." The law's delay is rooted in procedure, and we tend to be of two minds about procedure, alternately valuing it as the safeguard of the innocent and disparaging it as the escape-hatch of the guilty. In the last decade we have often had doubts about procedure, and they have arisen on both left and right. For the left, the law undergirds the status quo and especially its inequities; for the right, the law protects criminals instead of victims. To both, procedure becomes what we might call undue process. The antidote is supposed to be direct action, and so from one side we get vigilantes, and from the other, revolutionary radicalism. Even in the middle there is much of that representative activity of the middle—grumbling.

I am trying to set up a perspective for *The Ox-Bow Incident*. Some things that since the 1950s we have often seen before our eyes are what Clark got hold of in 1940. He has one character after another harp on the law's uncertainty. "If we wait for [Judge] Tyler," Bartlett says, ". . . there won't be one head of anybody's cattle left before we get justice" (p. 34). The theme is pounded home in a dozen such remarks.[3] We can turn these complaints off as lynchers' rationalizations if we will, but we ought rather to recognize them as criticisms of courts such as we have made or might make ourselves, and certainly have heard made by angry people who are not extremists. The point, of course, is not that Clark is good because he anticipated a style often used in later decades; the point is rather that he speaks to us because he was accurate enough, when using a formula, to transcend it and catch a truth beyond history. That is, he dug deep enough into the stereotype to find there a perennial human reality that appears in the usual western, in his own special version of it, and in historical events at different times. He has authentically caught, in an actual antisocial outbreak, the tempting millennialism of "Come, we all know what the good and the true are, and let us establish them at once, for delay is unnecessary." Resentment against the law's delay is a quite literal thing, of course. But the law's delay is also a symbol of all the institutional habits that try our patience; we speak of bureaucracies, for instance, as if the word were a synonym of "law's delay."

Manliness and Membership

In the stereotype Clark not only found a residue of millennialism but also put a finger on something else of deep importance, and I turn to it now. It is a truism that the western excludes women or reduces them to marginal supporting figures: we all have seen the movie poster of the brave-faced blonde erectly outfacing danger from just behind the hero's shoulderblade on his trigger-side as he blasts away at the enemy. Clark squeezes profits out of the stereotype, but with great originality. He keeps women peripheral, but they help clue us into another phase of the ideal essence that is reduced to a mechanism in the stereotype. Only one woman goes along with the manhunters, Ma Grier—a great big woman, "strong as a wrestler, probably stronger than any man in the valley except Gabe" (p. 75): a man by another name and, "soiled and greasy," doubtless smelling unsweet enough to prevent confusion. The creature who spurs the men on to their hunt is a screaming harridan, Frena Hundel (the name means "frantic little bitch," which I suppose is not an accident), allegedly hating men because they found no female charms in her. The two appearances of Rose Mapen, the authentic female, and her new San Francisco husband seem like pointless intrusions from a softer, more convoluted world, in some way inferior because, in its less uncouth and more calculating style, out of harmony with the larger world of direct action in the name of justice.[4] The narrator's friend, Gil Carter, was in love with her, but this seems a mistake on his part, a deviation from the straight and narrow.

When we look beneath the stereotyped male world that Clark examines anew, we do not find, I am sure, anything so banal as sexlessness or homosexuality. On the contrary, we find another component of hesperophilia, a fantasy quite characteristic of heterosexual men: the fantasy of straightforward, uncomplicated action, aggressive, marked by physical rather than social ability, by blunt tactics rather than troublesome tact, by endurance rather than forbearance. It is uninhibited by the conflicting values of the whole world of men and women, but invigorated by an unmixed code that highlights the goal and the road toward it, and brings forth the heroic, in solitude or in comradeship—voyage, hunt, rescue, quest, crusade (the responses to the everlasting challenges of nature, beast, victim, grail, and pagan). Instance Walter Mitty, a Westerner without a West. This powerful motive buried beneath the detritus of the stereotype is what Clark gets hold of: virtually all his men feel the lure of the search, in the dark and in a blizzard, for rustlers and a killer.

Yet the terms of this search are ambiguous, and hence the imperative is less absolute than a man wants it to be. So the more committed instinctively translate the deficiency in the cause into a deficiency in the men not wholly persuaded by the cause. Farnley, as we have seen, is irate over the way in which a malefactor can be saved by sentimental pleas in a court. Such pleas are made, he says, by "Osgood or Davies, or some other whining women" (p. 87). The key phrase is "some other whining women." To men, that is, it seems effeminate to hesitate, inquire, or introduce conflicting evidence when the business at hand is the punishment of guilt. Gil Carter commands preacher Osgood, who argues against the expedition, "Shut up, gran'ma" (p. 32). When Davies calls extralegal punishment a "sin against society," Winder picks up the phrase sneeringly, "imitating a woman with a lisp" (p. 48). There is a steady flow

of such passages.[5] One significant word is used twice:
"stomach." Tetley ironically asks Gil Carter, ". . . is . . . your
stomach for justice cooling?" The Mex, superficially the tough-
est of the victims, alludes to Gerald Tetley with similar irony:
". . . without the stomach for the blood, eh?" (p. 176).
"Stomach," of course, is "guts," and guts, as we know, are a
male organ, the erectile tissue of the man who makes war instead of love.

Within the western stereotype, then, Clark has caught the
male lust for warlike adventure that is a human constant rather
than a historical accident peculiar to hesperophilia. At the
same time he has seen that adventure is not only an exercise
of male quality but a test of it: a man's nature volunteers him,
and then he finds out the quality of that nature. We have different terms for what is at stake: I shall use "manliness," because
it leads us to a certain duality in the concept.[6] Clark understands this ambiguity, and thus again he departs from the western convention. Whereas in the stereotype manliness is always
a two-fisted virility that makes no moral errors, Clark sees that
it may err grossly. Thus he implicitly moves toward the duality
already grasped by Shakespeare, who often has two counter-
definitions of manliness in competition—manliness as aggres-
siveness and revengefulness, and manliness as forbearance and
even forgiveness. Without overtly stressing the latter meaning,
Clark has put his finger on human uncertainty as to what is
manly, and thus he touches on an extremely interesting
theoretical issue: the problem of distinguishing what we may
call manly virtues, womanly virtues, and human virtues. He
does not deal with the issue explicitly. But he makes doubly
clear what Shakespeare brings out: the male fear of effeminacy,
the concept of manliness as a persuader to action, the immense
psychic force exerted by manliness as an ideal; above all, the
begging of the definition, and hence the tendency to enthrone
outrage as the only possible courage.

The impact of the ideal may cause anguish to men in solitude, but the immediate impact is greatest when the ideal is
voiced by society. Clark catches the subtle strength of the male
society that is forming about the nucleus of the quest; we can

imagine ourselves half subdued by it. There is the sharp vignette of the woman, beside her husband's mount, "holding
onto [his] leg with both hands" while he "wasn't answering, but
just shaking his head short" (p. 67). Despite his own doubts,
Gil feels pressed enough to say, "I'll see this thing out as far as
any man will" (p. 111), with "man" as the pivotal word. The
narrator makes a key remark: "Most men are more afraid of
being thought cowards than anything else" (p. 57). His words
are not "being cowards," but "being thought cowards"; the fear
is of condemnation by others, and I think the reader is taken
along by the narrator when the latter assumes, though he never
needs to say it outright, that withdrawal from the pursuit party
would seem cowardly rather than prudent and rational. In the
conduct and speech of man after man we feel the heavy, unde-
fined power of the group.[7] No man is an island, and we sense
the almost unbreakable tie of membership.

Clark has got hold, then, of three powerful impulses to action of a certain kind: millennial justice, manliness, and membership. Combined, they can sway men to pursue ends even
though their minds are troubled by doubts about those ends.
Clark is not doing anything nearly so simple as showing that
direct action, a staple of westerns, is unjust; rather he shows
the roots of unjust action in deep passions that may seek good
and may lead to it. The story makes us feel, as it should, the
almost irresistible pull, upon people not at all monstrous, of an
action that we eventually see will be monstrous. Indeed, given
the overwhelming trio of imperatives—millennial justice,
manliness, and membership—we may well wonder why the
hunt is so slow in pulling itself together, why it is impeded by
a hesitancy that no one ever acknowledges. Here we get to the
heart of the conflict: the men also feel, of course, the bonds
of the community that long antedated the immediate crisis.
The conflict is a great and potentially tragic one: it is between
the customs and values of their normal community, and the
pressures and values that seem to compel them to go outside
it. If Clark had been writing a quarter of a century later, he
might have made the men mouth a few clichés about "the system." But though momentarily disenchanted, they are not, as

we have learned to say, alienated; they have a substitute for alienation, and that is our next subject.

Rival Communities

From the time they receive reports of increased cattle-rustling and the murder of Kinkaid until the time they find and hang Martin and his two workmen, the men are sorely torn between two contrasting human styles. On the one hand there are the ways of the established community, which seems to have muddled along adequately if not gloriously; on the other hand there are certain basic drives, primitive and instinctual. On the one hand there are the received ways of dealing with errant behavior; on the other, a retaliatory and punitive spirit, a passion for quick death as the solvent of exceptional wrongdoing. On the one hand, there are the rational restraints to dam hot blood until a cool judgment can be made; on the other hand, hot blood, prejudgment, and cooling off only by cathartic violence. Within limits we can think of one side as classical, the other as romantic: the one committed to forms, balance, and measure; the other to compulsive inner voices that, divine or demonic, claim transcendence over form and balance.

Clark has presented in full the symbolic voices of the traditional community. We see virtually all its institutional forms. Osgood embodies the church, Tyler the law. Davies is the responsible citizen who has profound convictions about the value of the civilized order that society has slowly won. In the wife trying to restrain a departing husband we see the institution of the family. And finally, and I think more importantly than may be realized, there is Sparks, the black handyman and ex-parson. I suggest that he is essentially an old Shakespearian character, the special voice of human wisdom—the fool, the court jester. He says simply that the expedition means a "man takin' upon himself the Lohd's vengeance," and he adds, "Man . . . is full of error." The author makes a significant comment on this: "He said it jokingly, but he wasn't joking" (p. 118)—a good working description of the fool's style. As the sole black man in the community, Sparks is an outsider, as the fool was. He is liked but is the object of jokes, as was the fool.

Fools often spoke in verse; Sparks sings hymns. Above all, he
has the kind of impact that Renaissance fools had. Note the
words that Clark uses of him: ". . . Sparks had given a kind of
body . . . to an ideal which Davies' argument hadn't made
clear and Osgood's self-doubt had even clouded" (p. 75). He
had "given a kind of body"—that is, by images, by nonlogical
discourse, by a condensed statement of the heart of the matter:
the essential style of the fool.

So we have what ought to be the triumphant word of the
community delivered by all its voices—church, law, family, responsible citizenship, and the special corrector whom we might
call prophet or seer or, as I have done, fool. But they are defeated. And by what? How shall we think of the twenty-eight
men riding through night and cold and snow and dangerous ter-
rain to punish thieves and murderers? Judge Tyler calls them
"a lynching mob" (p. 65), and we must find the term "mob"
very tempting. Yet Art Croft objects to the term (p. 65), and
I believe we should shun it. When we are attempting to be critics, we should always avoid the quick clichés of condemnation.
The word "mob" is too easy; it begets self-approval in the user,
and it tends to conceal rather than reveal the inner life of the
pursuing group. The word that Gerald Tetley uses repeatedly
is "pack"; for Gerald it is a term of contempt, and yet it comes
close, I think, to the truth that we need to grasp. For "pack"
at least implies a group with a certain center and principles of
order, with a unity and instinctual bond. It implies a mode of
being to which I will apply a term that I now use for the first
time of the Tetley group—the term "community." It is a community, and we miss the underlying life of the story if we do
not think of it in terms of community.

The basic tension of Clark's novel is the conflict within man
between two different modes of community that have powerful
appeals to him. On the one hand there is the central, continuing community to which we have applied such terms as "normal" and "traditional." On the other hand there is the crisis-
born community that we ought not to underestimate by using
the facile terms of denigration that we are all rather fond of.
The Tetley group is a community that has its own cohesive and

hence magnetic quality. It does not make a random attack on existent order; it stands for a different conception of order. The seekers of millennial justice and the judges of manliness are other men, the group. The group constrains the individual; no doubter really challenges its force. No one can deny his membership—that is, they all belong to a community—a community whose commitment to the just and the manly shames any serious questioning of its authority.

The stature of the book is rooted in the author's sense of a profound conflict between two communities or modes of community. The new community resists efforts at definition. We can dig out the motives of millennialism and manliness and still feel somewhat dissatisfied, for these provide a rational form that does not encompass all the energizing irrationalities. Clark tries to identify these too—in such a phrase as Gerald Tetley's "pack instincts" (p. 101), but more strikingly in a description of Davies's dilemma. Davies, he says, is using "something remote and distrusted" in trying to combat "something that had immediacy and a strong animal grip." He is finding out that what "shaped men's actions" is "not the big misty 'we,' " but the "small but present 'we' " (p. 57). The word "we" implies community, and the two uses of it reflect two different senses of community: the inclusive, historical one, nonlocalized because reflected in all places, and the exclusive, local, present one mysteriously coercive in its "immediacy and strong animal grip." We might think of one of them as the large Western one, the occidental heritage, and of the other as the small western one, the limited blood brotherhood that shrinks into the western stereotype.

What Clark gets hold of is the authentic threat of this latter community to the other one in which we ordinarily live and find security. Let us risk a strained antithesis of terms and call them the community of the Holy Ghost and the community of the unholy guts. "Holy Ghost" can image the informing spirit of substantive human order; in Davies's terms, law is the "conscience of society." "Unholy guts" hardly needs definition, but we can use "id" as a loose synonym for it—the force that precedes conscience and ever seeks to supplant it. Its universal-

ity and primacy give it a bonding strength of exceptional tenac-
ity, the "animal grip" that makes the pack, or the pack-as-com-
munity—the inferior but dangerous rival community. There is
a nice symbolic representation of the two communities in that
Sheriff Risley speaks for one, and Deputy Sheriff Mapes automatically attaches himself to the other, thus giving it a quasi
legality.

It is this threat to the established community that is the
source of what I have called "dread." Others may prefer other
terms, but to do this book justice we need to have a sense, not
simply of an unpleasant danger of a familiar kind, but of an
ominous disruption and displacement of essential order. Clark
is not describing a standard kind of dis-order—a private, non-
communal violation of rules, such as theft, injury, or crime of
passion. Such events may create excitement, fear, or even anx-
iety, but they are mild affairs—small, curable wounds to some
part of the community—compared with the taking over of
power by a deviant, narrow community of faulty substance, and
hence more ruthless methods and more merciless bonds. The
situation, as Davies puts it, is "infinitely more deadly when the
law is disregarded by men pretending to act for justice than
when it's simply inefficient" (p. 47).

One physical source of dread, we might notice, is movement
from an open to a shut-in situation. Without ever using the
word, Clark has forced us into a kind of claustrophobia in the
key scene: we are shut in by the night, by the storm, by the
mountains. The specific scene is a tight little enclosure within
the larger enclosure of the mountains. It sets off exactly the
ironic enclosure by hard facts (Martin has no receipt, the Mex
is tricky), the moral enclosure of the prejudgment that shores
up circumstantial evidence, of the exclusion of counterevi-
dence, of simulated ritual that only seals a predetermined
doom, of emotional doors that cannot be opened to forces that
might revise these emotions—in sum, of "normal" men acting
"ab-normally."

Clark has found, it seems to me, an extraordinary narrative
image for the experience of being taken over by the deviant or
deformed community. He has said that he had in mind the Nazi

takeover in Germany, and his conviction that it could happen
here. But luckily he gave rein to his storyteller's imagination
instead of mechanically inventing parallels to the Nazi acquisi-
tion of power (many events of his story are not at all parallel
to the history of the 1930s), and he did far better than arbitrarily constructing a one-dimensional parable. Rather he discovered a paradigm of events of which the Nazi affair was only one
variant. For instance, many of us can still remember the ominousness of the 1930s, and the dread that it evoked. Those of
us who can do so could not help noticing remarkable
similarities between German goings-on of the 1930s and the
style of American violence from 1968 to 1971. Writing in 1940
Clark so interpreted a contemporary terror that he managed to
anticipate a near-terror of three decades later. The dread that
we felt ten to fifteen years ago was the dread of feeling a true
though imperfect community in danger of going under to a fake
community promising to enforce perfection. As many people
put it, the problem was whether the fringe destroyers with slogans would gain the ear of the middle. For a time they seemed
to be doing it, and the community hung in balance. We had
a new awareness of its frailty, and wondered whether the frailty
meant disastrous vulnerability. That theme is what Clark had
got hold of years before.

My phrase was "destroyers with slogans." The community of
the unholy guts is a pretty wily affair. For all its universality,
the id has limited organizing powers; hence it tricks itself out—
almost anagrammatically, one might add—in the idea. The instincts simulate an institution; the pack comes up with a program, the id with an idea. It is always the same one: perfect
justice. It is so simple that it can be proclaimed by rascals as
well as by honest idealists, by sick men as well as by the pure
id boys. In our day, the sick man often pretends to be, or actually mistakes himself for, the specialist in internal medicine.
He prescribes perfect health for all—that is, his own compul-
sory health insurance.

I am trying to describe some of the complex working
mechanics of the millennialism that Clark long ago detected
in the western stereotype. The rival community[8] becomes

menacingly effective because it looks simple and honest but mixes up two or three appeals that fuddle us. It is not easy for the unanalytical—the class to which all of us belong most of the time—to disentangle the mingled calls of the wild, of the sick, and of the ideal. It is hard to resist the fused and thus confused summons of the irrational force and the rational perfection, of the barbarous and the utopian, of the noble goal publicly proclaimed and the demonic leadership, of guts and dream, id and idea, of the simultaneous assault from below and above—the visceral fear that one may not be brutal enough to be manly, and the spiritual fear that one may lack the soul for a more nearly ideal justice. The final source of dread is the sinister marriage of the Platonic and the primitive, the ultimate coupling that begets the deviant community.

The Ultimate Obligation of Art

It takes a penetrating book to set us off on these meditations that can cross back and forth between literary and historical realities. The hardest problem is to clarify the combination of the insinuating and the tough in the rival community that we know is always on the periphery, waiting for some trouble in the circle of the going order that will mean vulnerability to destructive attack. I have spoken of the frailty of the established community; in this context it is a susceptibility to the blandishments that call simultaneously to its crude passions and its corrective instincts.

To pass now from the theoretical problem to the specific literary method: Clark makes us feel the force of these blandishments, but in a rather subtle way. It is not, of course, that our sympathies are drawn to the Tetley project. But we are compelled to know inwardly the power of the group, its strong magnetic field, its almost magical suasiveness. If we do not want to be in that community, we can nevertheless see how it tugs at people who are more like ourselves than they are like monsters, and we can sense the enormous difficulty of resisting its strenuous though unspoken membership drive. If the group were openly barbarous, we could simply flee; but these people are, in Art's words, "quiet, gentle men, and the most independent in the world too" (p. 55). They are hard to draw away from for an opposition that could seem censorious or priggish. Clark also sees them as striving for a certain decorum, always a mark of the legitimate institution; they are upset by loudmouths, unseemly jesters, arrogant predetermined hangmen. Thus by various narrative devices Clark so positions us that we can almost feel ourselves being drawn in, however reluctantly.

The use of a first-person narrator is important. We always tend to go along with him and share his feelings unless, by some device within the fiction, he is repudiated or, like Gulliver, made ambiguous. We are not seriously separated from Art Croft and his friend Gil Carter. Art's human decency is established by the fact that Davies sees him as a possible ally and gets some help from him, that Gerald Tetley feels quite able to talk intimately to him, and that he keeps wrestling with the problems of the crisis. Initially he and Gil fall in with the manhunt because they need to overcome the unspoken but communicated suspicion of themselves as outsiders and to be at one with the power group. In their desire not to be suspect outsiders, they are not special cases different from ourselves; in the long absence that makes others unsure of them we see projected our own weaknesses or skeletons that could be damaging to us if we directly challenged a community with a salvationary program. So Art and Gil never really act on their occasional impulses to feel apart from it all, to criticize the affair, and to assure themselves, as Gil puts it several times, that "this ain't our picnic" (pp. 54, 140). If they are bothered by the style of the quest, they tend to accept its premises and the circumstantial evidence that spurs the group.[9]

But though we instinctively go along with a first-person narrator who is not stupid or palpably self-deceiving or vicious, "go along with" does not mean "agree with"; obviously we do not share Art's conviction about the guilt of the prisoners. But we do understand why he feels it; we sense the deep pressures upon his belief and action. It is the paradoxical gift of Clark's novel to afford us two contradictory experiences. On the one hand it provides the esthetic distance that makes it possible for us to judge. On the other hand it gives us a felt proximity of crisis that enables us to know the frightening difficulty of maintaining, in the ultimately close quarters of actuality, the judicial separateness of art. We judge others while we know how painfully difficult it would be not to join them if we were there. In the art form of fantasy we entertain images of heroic individualism that we do not often transmute into an actual risking of public scorn and humiliation. We know the force of Art Croft's phrase, "each man afraid to disagree with the rest" (p. 48).

But now the next step: Suppose we do become bold and fight shy of the crime-hunters, where do we go? Here again Clark shows great skill, and I think more than may be apparent on the surface. He creates barriers, conspicuous or delicate, between us and almost everyone with whom we might ally ourselves. The minister's style puts us off; Osgood falls into homiletic truisms that gain no edge from his sincerity. We cannot join him. Judge Tyler's rhetoric spurts up and out in mechanical leaps, but it is more like Fourth of July fireworks than the D-day firepower that is needed. We might conclude that Clark is satirizing church and bench, but that, I think, is a too-easy reading. In my view, the stylistic shortcomings of both men symbolize the defective power of institutional order in this kind of crisis. What they say does not get hold of us, though we know it ought to. Then there is Sparks, but we could not hold hands with him, because an outcast cannot supply the alternative shelter that we need.

Why, however, not Davies, the good citizen, the passionate voice of the community conscience? All he says is right, but he remains impotent. What Clark catches hold of here is the insubstantialness of intellectual truth against the pseudo community of virility and instant justice. He presents the ineffectiveness of the right idea in various inconspicuous symbols that, in a real-life situation, would tend to push us away from Davies or at least make us diffident about allying ourselves with him. Davies *looks* ineffectual: "an old man, short and narrow and so round-shouldered he was nearly a hunchback" (p. 31); he "would have been a good figure of a miser" (p. 32); he is a shopkeeper, and he can be accused of the profit motive (pp. 37, 85). Art tries to duck him (p. 38); his Socratic questions seem, in this atmosphere, a little pedantic (pp. 46–47); at one time he looks "as if he were going to cry" (p. 48); after a while he "sounded defeated" (p. 78); Tetley's challenge makes him "confused" (p. 88); he is a target for jokes. Surely Clark's most difficult feat was to make Davies right but not quite convincing, almost persuasive yet lacking in what we now call charisma; wholly worthy of respect and yet weaker than the Tetley whom no one likes.

Finally, there is Gerald Tetley, who balances Davies nicely in the story: Davies articulates the theoretical principles of the true community, Gerald excoriates the working principles of the deviant community. Gerald is utterly right, too. But we shrink from him. For he is weak, hysterical, even neurotic; we doubtless remember that he is a "sullen, sick boy" who looks like his mother (p. 79); and he must remind us of another ailing son of a disciplinary Civil War officer, Orin Mannon in O'Neill's *Mourning Becomes Electra* of just a decade earlier. We fall away from him; he could never be a rallying point.

Clark has shown extraordinary ingenuity in leaving us, so to speak, nowhere to go—that is, as soon as the esthetic stimulus draws us away from esthetic distance and imaginatively into the interplay of actual society. In contemplation we can remain solitary; in participation we cannot be solitary unless we are saints or heroes. But when I say "we" I mean not saints and heroes but, in the familiar phrase, us average sensual men. Clark forces us to feel the pull of the deviant community, if not upon us as individuals, at least upon others like ourselves—the secret and unacknowledged attractiveness of the spirit of the new community, with its destructiveness clothed in a sense of mission and even of ironic decorousness.

But beyond our feeling the secret grip I think must lie another deep and unarticulated fear—namely, that under stress we might not be immune to the unwanted invitation. After all, we are the middle that may be drawn in by the devious, self-righteous, threatening, mesmeric fringe, which can always find an occasion and proclaim a virtue. The ultimate dread must be that of in some way being carried along by or consenting to the deformed society. If Clark has taken us to that point, then he has indeed met the ultimate obligation of art: to make us hold back the finger of accusation, and instead to look into a mirror—a clear mirror, neither flattering nor distorting, of ourselves. This is not the experience of satiric and melodramatic art and of their counterparts in societal art—politics and war—for in these we separate ourselves from the wrongdoers and condemn them. Rather it is the experience of comic art and of tragic art, for these must elicit from us the "there go I" of the no longer innocent.

From Stereotype to Model

Clark completes the story with another action of deep significance: the reordering of the community after its lapse into the ways of the fringe community of the unholy guts. This is in chapter 5, which I am inclined to think of as act 5 of the drama. It is, however, more detailed than drama could be, for it observes nearly all the possible ways of responding to disaster, of the conscience trying to recover ground lost to guts and dreams, id-cum-idea.

Judge Tyler applies the law literally: he declares everybody under arrest. Sheriff Risley countermands the judge's order. The sheriff's realism confirms the view that Tetley's posse is a community and you cannot hang a whole community. The sheriff's decision thus raises the complex question of penance and atonement for the guilt of a whole community. In the place of formal legal action the group tends to apply what we may call folk-law: purgation by scapegoat. Clark has prepared us for this quite early in the story by having Davies declare that the group needs a leader whom it can, if need be, turn into a scapegoat. Clark is very shrewd in seeing the inner tie between leader and scapegoat: leadership depends on a singleness of will made possible by a freedom from common scruple; the followers' absence of will frees them from guilt, and the leader's freedom from scruple is just what can be blamed if things go wrong. Again, Clark is wonderfully perceptive in handling the inchoate move to lynch Tetley; though a number of men might like this way out, we see only one man pushing it—Smith.

Early in the story Smith was defined as "the town bum, . . . balanced between begging and a conceited, nagging humor that made people afraid of him" (p. 7). Purification by scapegoat is the special cleansing style of a spiritually unclean man who needs an execution as a retaliatory consolation for his own maculate condition. Smith provides the unsavory alternative to the dry, unsentimental morality of Sheriff Risley, who says to Davies: ". . . there's nothing you or anybody else can do about it now" (p. 192).

But individuals can do something about it; they can respond in different ways that reveal different spiritual potentialities. Beset by different attacks upon his selfhood—guilt, public humiliation, the shame of a sensibility that seems unmasculine—Gerald Tetley commits suicide: the response of despair. For different reasons, rather unclear ones, his father too, in the old Roman style that befits a part of his personality, even if the act itself is, as I find it, a little too neat. In contrast with all the rest is Davies, whom Clark rightly makes the dominant figure of the final section. Davies's anguished, non-self-exonerating grasping for and grappling with self-knowledge is in the tragic mode, and to introduce the tragic is the final achievement of the book. Getting revenge, as Smith wants to do, or making a final exit, as the Tetleys do—these are in the style of melodrama, which is natural to the life of the western.[10] Yet Clark complicates the tone and actually gives us something of a tragic hero. Davies repeatedly makes an assertion that comes out of the tragic point of view: the others, especially Tetley, he says are not to "blame" (pp. 199, 202). Blaming is the spirit of satire and melodrama, modes of punishment and revenge; Davies blames only himself—the tragic style. Further, Clark makes the narrator say of Davies that "the flaw had been in him from the start" (p. 211). "Flaw" is the ancient term for the error of being or doing that the tragic hero, in the final phase, comes to know about.

Through the admirably paced revelation by which, step by step, we go deeper and deeper into his personality, we learn that Davies's flaw is unused knowledge. Davies knew that a gun, to threaten with or actually kill, was necessary to keep Tetley from going on with the triple murder, but he did not take a gun along, because he could not face this ultimate act of preventive force. Hence his tragic anguish, so sharply different from the irremediable despair of killing oneself, or the scapegoat method of killing someone else, or the ordinary man's living uneasily, without further killing, with the killing done.

The tragic climax is remarkable in several ways. Clark not only makes another break with the western stereotype; he also breaks sharply from a basic element in tragic form. In the stereotype the hero—ready with gun, firm of hand, certain of what has to be done—comes up fearlessly with the needed direct action. Clark, on the other hand, presents a virtuous man who does not and perhaps cannot have it in him to be the cool triggerman of justice in an all-or-nothing confrontation. As for the tragic form: Clark simply turns a central feature of it upside down. The traditional tragic flaw is hubris, the arrogance or insolence that bursts forth in violence; Davies's flaw—he calls it fear—was an unwillingness or inability to use a violence that would be only technically arrogant.

Furthermore, in breaking with both melodramatic and tragic patterns Clark not only closes doors, so to speak, but opens up a very large door upon a philosophical scene that is fused with the dramatic scene. The philosophical scene has to do with a disturbing issue, a possible vulnerability at the heart of civilization: the paradox that this ultimate secular achievement may have a built-in self-destructiveness. The mark of civilization is the civilized person who uses civility in all modes of intercourse. This is Davies: the civilized man who has a grasp of the culture, a feeling for its patterns of order, a passion for the rational discipline of passionate irrationality. But can all that knowledge and sensitivity coexist with the toughness apparently indispensable for crisis politics? Does not the civilized man, of his own nature, always act with civility? Can he of his nature achieve an incivility upon which the survival of civil men and of a civil order may depend? That he literally cannot do this is one premise of all deliberate destroyers of order: their initial rule of battle is to immobilize civilized man with a barrage of effrontery, insolence, and brutality that they think him by nature lacking

the resources to deal with. Tetley's lynchers do not want to destroy order, of course, but Winder's sneer at "law and order
crap" (p. 45) is remarkably like some battle cries of a later day.

Thus Clark's novel keeps expanding and reaching out; it
keeps revealing bonds of meaning with historical events and
with other works of literature. That is why we can say that
Clark has transmuted a stereotype into a model, an exemplary
shaping of reality whose presence we can see elsewhere in life
and in art. In presenting the recurrent problem of the civilized
man who shrinks, perhaps disastrously, from a critical confrontation, *The Ox-Bow Incident* inevitably takes us back two and
a half decades to Conrad's *Victory*, which has the same theme
(as does also Clark's *The Track of the Cat*, in a different way,
in the treatment of Arthur). Conrad and Clark both make us
wonder whether man must not deny something of his civilization to protect the rest of it. Beyond that, he may be subtly en-
trapped by a paradox of moral advancement: that the desirable
state achieved contains within itself the virus of a pathological
hypertrophy. That is to say, the process of becoming civilized
may trigger a mechanism that, unless we brake it by some extraordinary act of will, inflates the civilized into the over-
civilized which invites the undercivilized.

In *The City of Trembling Leaves* Clark can look at civilized
society hopefully, at least in the sense that the troubled artist
eventually finds himself—his way of living and of effectively
using his talent—not in solitude or in a commune but within
the ordered community. But Clark comes closer to achieving
a model when he treats the crisis within the community. *The
Track of the Cat*, recounting the family community in crisis, has
some striking resemblances to O'Neill's *Long Day's Journey into
Night*, which O'Neill was writing about the same time (1940;
published, 1955). It even has an affiliation with O'Neill's *Em-
peror Jones*—in the effect of severe unwonted pressure by nature
and solitude upon the personality accustomed to the ways of
societal living. But *The Ox-Bow Incident* is the model of greatest
usefulness. It provides, as we have seen, the essential pattern
of historical events of three decades later. What is more, it

anticipates by fifteen to twenty years a set of European plays
that brilliantly dramatize disorder within the community and
most of which, like the *Incident*, felt at least a partial impetus
in the Nazi revelation of what could take place in an apparently
sound community. Three of these are Friedrich Duerrenmatt's
The Visit (1955) and Max Frisch's *The Firebugs* (1958) and *Andorra* (1962).[11]

The tone of "it *can* happen here" may be frightening or saddening. It is ominous and appalling when we occupy the role,
not of defenseless victims, as in moments of grim light we know
that we may be at any time, but the role of contributing to our
own disaster, of having the tools and the talent for betraying
ourselves. The final dread is of what one's own humanity may
be capable of. Two brilliant plays use opposite technical ways
of exploring this dark possibility: in the one we see a representative individual, and in the other the whole community, losing
the right way and feeling the insidious pull of the deviant community. In Jean-Paul Sartre's *Altona* (1959) the central character, a young German officer, is driven virtually mad by the recognition that, in an episode in which Nazis tortured a Jew, he
had actually felt "some strange kind of approval." In Eugene
Ionesco's *Rhinoceros* (1960) we see a whole town throwing aside
its communal bonds and, with various rational justifications,
joining in a new, inferior, and indeed bestial community,
grotesquely symbolized in the rhinoceroses that the people become.

All this, Clark had already caught: the precariousness of
community because its members, people like us, choose the
wrong act, the wrong bonds. It is not that we approve the new
inadequate, shortcut, visceral order; it is simply that we recognize some part of ourselves in it. As we read, we experience a
deep-feeling knowledge of the intense difficulty of facing down
the deviant community, exerting an almost demonic pressure
in its millennial appeal to conscience, its code of manliness
that engages mysterious subconscious forces, its moral arrogance, and its call to membership that arouses our fear of solitude. Some part of ourselves has to fight another part. The new

crisis-born order makes an appeal that is hypnotic because it is directed simultaneously to the higher man, the lower man, and the social man.

What an immensely embracing model of reaction to a crisis Clark has constructed from the rubble of the old stereotype! When *The Ox-Bow* reached print, he was thirty-one years old. We wonder that a youth of so few years could know so much about humanity and could find so successful an artistic form for what he knew. In that knowing and that forming we see something of genius.

Notes

1. As it appears in a devotion to westerns, hesperophilia may reflect a number of motives. In an intellectual it may be only a form of play, of escape from the critical rigors of life; it must be much the same thing as the passion for detective stories often professed by writers and scholars. Sometimes there is an element of pure or playful perversity in this: you expect me to be above this kind of thing, so I will make a point of being, not above it, but with it. I am so secure in my professional exercise of critical or creative intelligence that I can flaunt my privilege of acclaiming that which will not stand rigorous criticism. I can display my exemption from ordinary critical canons, or even go to the opposite extreme of implying that there is a subtle superiority of taste in my addiction to the popular art.

2. Quotations are from Walter Van Tilburg Clark, *The Ox-Bow Incident*, A Signet Classic (New York: New American Library, 1960).

3. Bartlett uses a sneering phrase, "Wait for his eternal justice," and insists that it's Tyler's justice that has brought rustlers into the valley (p. 34). "Maybe if we do our job with our own hands, the law will get a move on" (p. 35). Suppose we do bring the guilty men in, Winder argues, "Then if your law lets him go?" (p. 48). Art Croft, the narrator, refers to the "times when [the judge] don't seem able to make up his mind" (p. 60). Farnley tells the judge, "The bastard that shot Larry Kinkaid ain't comin' in here for you to fuddle with your damned lawyer's tricks for six months and then let him off because Osgood or Davies, or some other whining women, claim he ain't bad at heart" (p. 87). Or, as Tetley tells the victims, "the law is almighty slow and careless around here" (p. 154), and "Law, as the books have it, is slow and full of holes" (p. 156).

4. After writing this I learned from Robert Clark that Rose's appearance was historically an "intrusion"—a response to the publisher's fears that the story was deficient in sex appeal. However, the

women's driving Rose out of town is structurally appropriate: it is an earlier, anticipatory instance of a special community's taking over an enforcement program to gratify its own needs, regardless of the well-being of the larger community.

5. Monty Smith calls the objectors "flower pickers" and adds, "in a thin little voice, 'Girls, shall we lay out the poor dear rustler wustler?' " (p. 52). A skinny old man fears that the hunt may collapse before it gets going, and he snarls in disgust, "What kinda stuff you boys made of these days?" (p. 68). Ma Grier jests at Davies for taking the line of the parson and the judge, and she blames this on his reading too many books—in this context clearly a way of calling him a sissy. The narrator's own incomplete assent to the operation is what is reflected in Winder's angry words to him, "You've been a lily since this started, Croft" (p. 121). Tetley rounds out this theme with an old simile and a sharp metaphor; he tells Martin, the leader of the victims, "you're taking it like a woman" (p. 158), and he applies the crusher to his son Gerald, "I'll have no female boys bearing my name" (p. 182).

6. D. H. Lawrence liked "maleness," but his emphasis was different from that of the western. More familiar are "masculinity" and "virility," terms that could apply to a permanent Hemingway problem. "Virtue" is interesting in its etymological sense: the qualities of vir or "man." The root meaning is perhaps best represented in "manliness," which I use.

7. Clark makes Gerald Tetley articulate, with equal fulness and bitterness, the influence of the group upon the individual. Men will "lie" or conceal the truth, he says, "to keep from looking queer to the pack" (p. 104). Nothing would make us reveal anything that would put "the pack at our throats" (p. 104). We would not admit "fear, or lust, or even anger" or anything "that would make the pack believe that we were either weak or dangerous" (p. 105). In sum, "we're afraid not to be in the pack" (p. 106).

8. Up to a point one might call it a community of the ill and injured, those who, having some psychic wound or moral trouble, or beset by a sense of injury, or lacking the normal person's ability to cope with actual injury, work off grievances in aggressive and retaliatory activities concealed under ennobling banners. Tetley's son is a severe disappointment to him, Winder is aggrieved by the decline of stagecoaching, Monty Smith is a spiritual defective, Farnley has lost heavily at cards. Tetley, as Robert Harvey has pointed out to me, may still be suffering from the Civil War defeat. The search for individual compensation and wholeness in a new order operating through punitive violence but proclaiming virtuous ends is of course a familiar event on the twentieth-century political scene.

9. Art "didn't want to look like [he] was anxious to quit; not any more than anybody else" (p. 86)—the hold of the magnetic field. Gil calls the supposed rustlers "dirty rats" (p. 90). Though Art at one point helps Davies, at another he acknowledges, "I, for one, wasn't with him" (p. 91). Though Gerald Tetley feels in Art a sympathetic confidant, Art finds Gerald "disgusting"; Art shifts to a more kindly note only after he has rebuked Gerald stingingly. Then Art is shot by the panicky stagecoach guard, and this "made me feel like I had a stake in the business" (p. 135). He believes that the party whom they are rounding up may be dangerous (pp. 142–43). Gil says "let's take them in to the Judge" (p. 157) but stoutly insists, "I'm not one of them"—those who may want to leave (p. 158). Then the Mex's gun turns out to be Kinkaid's, and Art sums up, "The gun was a clincher with us" (p. 178). He includes himself among the convinced, and neither he nor Gil joins the five who vote for postponement.

10. In spending all my time on interpretation I have ignored a subject that deserves considerable attention—the technical expertise of Clark as storyteller, especially in the melodramatic mode of authentic conflict. His skill appears in scene after scene—the card game, the visit to Judge Tyler's, the episodes that slow down and speed up the formation of the Tetley group, the incidents on the trail, the tension after the three innocent men are taken prisoner. The discovery that Kinkaid is not dead is handled with fine understatement, indeed masterfully "thrown away." The stagecoach episode, later addition though it is, functions as an excellent microcosmic symbolization of the larger community action: crisis, inadequate leadership (the driver and guard are at least partly drunk), panic, heroics, shooting in the dark, the wounding of an innocent bystander, and, above all, the near self-destruction of the community (the occupants of the coach) rushing headlong to save itself.

11. In The Firebugs a citizen helps destroy his community—symbolized in the burning of his house by professional arsonists who have moved into it—by his inability to take necessary action against the destroyers; like Davies, he can call upon force but is reluctant to do so. In Frisch's Andorra a community allows itself to fall into an unwanted but somehow irresistible campaign against its single Jewish resident; his innocence is identical with that of the hanged men in The Ox-Bow Incident. In Duerrenmatt's The Visit we see a community taking on a distorted form by accepting an enormous bribe to commit murder and then using the bribe as the cornerstone of a new era of progress and prosperity. In both The Visit and Andorra there is a Davies character who protests and fails; in each play the Davies character is a schoolteacher, both teachers take to drink, and both commit suicide—one literally, the other symbolically by acquiescing in the sweep of destructive public action.

6

To Escape the Tiger: The Short Stories

Max Westbrook

At the time the Hilliard series of lectures was being planned, the only book-length study of Clark was that by Professor Max Westbrook of the University of Texas at Austin, Walter Van Tilburg Clark *(New York: Twayne, 1969). The book was one of a series, with limitations on the length, and Westbrook's comments on the short stories were restricted to a few pages in a chapter that necessarily included other important topics. Hoping to give Westbrook an opportunity to comment more fully on the short stories, the editor of the present volume asked him to prepare a separate lecture, which he did. Finding the ideas in that lecture more appropriate for use elsewhere, Westbrook has written a new essay for this collection.*

Only the better known of Clark's shorter pieces are given individual attention here. With the exception of "The Watchful Gods" (see chapter 11), written at about the same time as The Track of the Cat, *most of the shorter pieces were composed before* The City of Trembling Leaves, *or were resurrected and revised when* The Ox-Bow Incident *and "Hook" had made Clark popular. Most of them have been reconceived at least once, and hence cannot be dated exactly, but in general they may be thought of as following Ox-Bow and preceding City.*

Many writers have treated Clark's shorter works individually. On "The Rapids" and "The Indian Well," see especially chapters 15 and 16, below; on "The Buck in the Hills," see chapter 11; on "Hook," see chapter 16.

W alter Van Tilburg Clark's "The Writer and the Professor: or, Where Is the Little Man Inside?" is a generic
paradox. Both essay and story, an allegorical comedy but also
a highly intellectual and independent instance of deconstruc-
tive criticism, it is a disturbingly honest and public confession
of personal problems and at the same time an objective and
helpful insight into the nature of literary art.

Portraying himself as the likeable but irrelevantly abstracted
professor of generalizations, Clark accepts with "acquiescent
imbecility"[1] an invitation to speak on "Communication and
the Arts," belatedly realizes that he has been asked to speak *as
the writer*, and promptly panics. For some time now, Clark explains, his writer-self has lived elsewhere; and *homunculus*, the
little man inside who fuels both, is seldom seen by either. In
desperation, Clark's professor-self hides a tape recorder at the
writer-self's favorite backyard table and reappears—openly this
time—lugging whiskey and beer. The plan is for the professor
to trick the writer into producing a paper, as artist, on "Communication and the Arts."

The relevance of "The Writer and the Professor" to my own
essay on Clark's short stories is that in sporting with his problems Clark describes also—mostly in long discussions centering
on Henry James—the splendid achievements of Walter Van
Tilburg Clark at his best. The following, from one of writer-
Clark's outbursts, is central:

> "James was great not because of his infinite refinements, eva-
> sions, tangential approaches, apparent ambiguities . . . , but
> because he never lost sight of [the] fact that most of the mo-
> tions of the mind are rationalizations, that language *is* a veil,
> that one must pierce through the veil to the feelings from
> which the thoughts and conversation arise, to the little man
> inside each of the people concerned, and in James the little
> man . . . is always the hairy ancestor, and the hairy ancestor
> is always hunting, mating, stashing away, or, like Strether, in
> *The Ambassadors* . . . , that man of infinite layers of self-de-
> ception, simply, at bottom, trying to escape the sabre-toothed
> tiger or the cave bear. In short, the old maestro never forgot
> the most important thing, that words are *not* the realities,

either as used by the writer or by his characters, or by any of
us in our daily intercourse, however honest we may try to
be."[2]

Self-deception through strategies available in civilization and
with the intent of avoiding confrontation with "the sabre-
toothed tiger" is, according to writer-Clark, a fundamental
theme in the art of Henry James. The implication, one borne
out by analysis, is that escaping the tiger is also a fundamental
theme in the art of Walter Van Tilburg Clark.

On the biographical level, Clark felt that he overexplained
himself even in his tightly dramatic *The Ox-Bow Incident*.[3] The
problem of trying to write stories against an intruding intellect
is a problem he faced from the start; and how the battle was
fought, how Clark managed to get the seven-eighths of the
iceberg below water after all, is basic to his accomplishments.
By the time of "The Writer and the Professor," victory had apparently turned to defeat; but he provides us there an opportunity to see three versions of the same story: professor-Clark's
intellectual generalizations, writer-Clark's cryptic and concrete statement, and—earlier, when the two were in harmony
with one another and with *homunculus*—the story itself, "The
Watchful Gods."

His intellectual generalizations about the words "communication" and "art," the professor explains,

> suggested that, as every infant in the mother's womb recapitu-
> lates the physical evolution of the race, so every child, in his
> spontaneous early endeavours at expression, recapitulates the
> artistic evolution of the race. And did not this recapitulation,
> since certainly all primitive art was essentially religious in
> source and intention, suggest in turn that even now the pri-
> mary impulse of the arts was religious, ritualistic—their cen-
> tral hope, however much diluted by time and civilized detach-
> ment and irrelevant rationalization, the same old one of prop-
> itiating or enlisting Nature, the Gods, God, or whatever name
> one wishes to give to the encompassing and still mysterious
> whole, and of acting, as it were, as the shaman, the witch doc-
> tor, the intermediary, between poor suffering man and the oc-
> cult powers which control him?[4]

When professor-Clark offers this to the writer as a précis of his original essay, the writer curses briefly, pointing out that it is not original, that he himself wrote all that years ago:

"Story of a twelve year old kid shoots his first rabbit without proper respect and fellow-feeling, and loses touch with nature. Stuck all by himself then, like idiot modern man."[5]

Unlike those who advocate dichotomies—reason only or the irrational only, practical action or religious faith, civilization or savagery—Clark believed in the total world. To confront the varieties of reality, especially when opposites appear in a single moment, both coming with ontological authority, is for most of us unbearable; and we rush back, if we can, to civilized rationalizations. For Buck, in "The Watchful Gods," returning seems just as impossible as not returning. He has seen "the words 'beautiful' and 'terrible' together" in actual experience. When he tries "to get it in words,"[6] the meanings seem to slip away, the experience being so much more profound than mere words about the experience. Clark's writer-self is right to say that Buck is lost. Having only bookish ceremonies from someone else's culture, Buck cannot propitiate nature, and he cannot go home without first making atonement. He cannot deny the god of death, the god of life, the simultaneous beauty and horror of a simple moment that swells into incapacitating profundities. The first solo hunting trip of a twelve-year-old boy has turned into a religious experience so powerful it melts the only ceremony he knows to offer. Though lost in the modern world, Buck is good-willed, and he has a chance to avoid the fate of Curt Bridges *(The Track of the Cat)*; but Curt and Buck have undergone a similar disorientation, witnessed the capacity of primal powers to collapse rationalizations whether in terms of macho ambitions or Kit Carson daydreams, and as Curt runs toward the last cliff, Buck walks toward the threatening ocean.

Without denying the variety of Clark's themes and techniques, while appreciating the range of his artistry, I believe nonetheless that his short stories (as well as his novels) are centrally concerned with the incapacity of words to capture the primal and religious immensities assigned to them, and with variations on civilized rationalizations of our confronting and failing to confront the primal "powers" that "control" us.

Peter Carr of "The Anonymous," for example, is a young Navajo who was born and raised on a New Mexico dude ranch that caters to rich and lonely women from eastern cities. Denying his own heritage—or what remains of it—he seeks a superficial education in white culture, just enough for the drawing room. Peter Carr will then marry the wealthy and much older white lady who sponsors his education, thus becoming a conversation piece who can join the social chatter he invokes.

Gates, the sensitive narrator, is a scholar with three college degrees who is teaching in a virtually meaningless high school on a reservation which is itself a cultural version of rationalization—for both races. Mrs. Varney, the grand lady who sponsors Peter Carr, is in the process of building and buying an Indian-doll husband. Cuyler has the personality of a big-shot executive, but he is in fact the principal of a remote and impoverished Indian reservation high school. Jenny is a warm, strong, and intelligent student who falls for Carr, is spurned, defeated—at least for the present—and who then becomes a runaway. Jim Blood, a young brave in love with Jenny, lurks in the dark, jealous of a phony Indian who is smugly indifferent to the lives he is disrupting.

The "anonymous," then, is the decultured Navajo who admires fancy automobiles and has the purchased (rather than earned) name of Peter Carr;[7] but "the" in the title may suggest the plural, for all of the characters in this story are "anonymous" in the sense that they are displaced, misdirected, cut off from meaningful development. A name, that is, should be earned by honest growth and achievement in a culture to which one—somehow—belongs; and that necessary culture must connect—somehow—our modern world with primal realities. Otherwise, one depends on props, tricks to avoid confrontation with the self and the place of the self in the world.

When making such critical comments, however, it is wise to remember Professor Charlton Laird's gentle but repeated and convincing insistence that Clark was a fundamentally kind human being. The chauffeur in "The Anonymous," who resents having to serve a "coffee-colored fake," comforts himself by saying, "Hell . . . , a fellow's gotta live!" (p. 92). Gates, with an ironic "sure," then goes back to grading papers, the teaching of white man's civilization to unreceptive students who do not want and probably could not use the culture of their conquerors; that is, Gates goes on with his own version of "a fellow's gotta live." Jenny persists against Peter Carr's rejections, barricades herself in his bedroom, and finally runs away . . . searches for a way to live. The pervasive sympathy, in short, is Clark's, the story's, and not just the narrator's. Peter Carr and all the rest, though engaged in roles and wearing costumes that are more or less false, are also human beings struggling to make a life.

Clark's sympathetic probing of civilized rationalizations is but one of many variations on a theme. In "Why Don't You Look Where You're Going?" Clark wrote a comic story of people protected from real confrontation by a giant ship, a state complete unto itself, a mechanical "leviathan" (p. 113). Their condescending and bemused brush with irrational power comes in a contemporaneous form: an outrageous pilot of a tiny craft who defies—in comic anger—the giant ocean liner and the ocean itself.

In other stories the contact with primal reality is direct and dangerous. This is especially true of Clark's hunting stories, "The Watchful Gods," *The Track of the Cat,* and "Trial at Arms," obviously, but also *The Ox-Bow Incident,* where the game is human, and buck fever (Arthur Davies and Gerald Tetley in public, and many others in secret) is shown to have a terrifying variety. Likewise, a journey toward confrontation may vary in that the touch is direct but the sport is internal merely. In "The Rapids," a city man plays with his own long-buried inclinations, plays with the total concentration and determination of a child, accomplishes glee, realizes the antic. Then word comes that his boss needs him back in town. His brief touch of another layer of reality has been voluntary, parenthetical, sportive; and the control of civilization—in the voice of his wife, who is like a mother scolding a naughty child—is total.

Clark's success in writing past his academic knowledge of such confrontations is due, in part, to his mastery of credibility. "The Wind and the Snow of Winter," for example, makes a strong appeal for the reader's empathy;[8] and it would seem to have, at first glance, no connection with the story of a twelve-year-old boy lost in the modern world or the story of an accomplished hunter pursuing a black painter. Mike Braneen, an old prospector, now senile, his day faded into history, comes to Gold Rock for the winter, his long-time custom, only to find that his favorite places are closed, his friends dead, and—one more turn of the screw—that he has suffered the same shock before, several times, and failed or refused to remember. At this level, we have a story about nostalgia that is not itself nostalgic. Mike Braneen's story is sad, but he endures the undertow of shock with dignity, and the reader is thereby asked to feel sympathy, not pity.

"The Wind and the Snow of Winter," however, is more than a well-crafted story. Several curious details suggest another layer. The first sentence describes an old road used in the Comstock days, but nearby now is a highway for automobiles. The contrast seems rather sharp, extreme. To be a decade or so past your time is more common than remarkable, but Mike Braneen—if not by the horrifyingly clear demarcation described in "The Portable Phonograph," then at least by hints—is traumatically severed from his own history. Similarly, Braneen's daydreaming is to be expected in one who has long followed a lonely occupation, but the specifics have an edge:

> Mike did not like to have his stories interrupted except by an idea of his own, something to do with his prospecting, or the arrival of his story at an actual memory which warmed him to close recollection or led into a new and more attractive story [p. 34].

Braneen is not merely an old prospector who has become senile. He is and has been since youth a maker of stories, one who prefers free imagination to actual events. One thinks of Tim Hazard in *The City of Trembling Leaves*, Buck in "The

Watchful Gods," Art Bridges in *The Track of the Cat*, or even Tad in "The Fish Who Could Close His Eyes." Brancen's frostbitten hand, further, may signal a connection with exposed hands in *The Track of the Cat*, and certainly his distinction between two kinds of "high-blue weather" (p. 37) ricochets all over Clark, from blue blankets in *The Track of the Cat* to recurrent distinctions between joyful and threatening vibrations in nature. Braneen, in short, seems to be one of the many Clark characters who have the sensitivity to sense and appreciate primal delights but who lack the toughness required to unify those delights with harsh realities.

Subtleties, of course, are hints toward possible interpretation. They could be misleading, but, again, "The Writer and the Professor" provides a striking encouragement. When professor-Clark plans to trick writer-Clark into producing an essay for him, he goes to Gold Rock, where the writer lives, spending much time in his favorite bar, the Lucky Boy. Mike Braneen is going to Gold Rock, and his favorite saloon is—or was—the Lucky Boy. Further, Tom Connover is mentioned as an old crony of both Mike Braneen and writer-Clark.[9]

The telling point—since details may recur simply because writers and other human beings repeat themselves—is that both "The Wind and the Snow of Winter" and "The Writer and the Professor" are about creativity and remembering. As the inept professor trying to make notes toward an essay on creativity, Clark refers to "three temporal functions of the mind which, though common to all men, are often exercised more promptly, fully, and intensely by the writer than by most. . . ." The first is "*Attention in the present,* which gathers the substance of his art. . . ." Second is "*Detailed recollection of the past,*" and third is "*An active imagination,*" which can, by processes unknown, unite discordant experiences and produce "a vision or recognition not previously present," that is, "the identifying characteristic of a work of art."[10]

The language of professor-Clark is self-mockingly ironic and turgid, but the mirror image of Clark's wit is a serious statement about his own problems and about the nature of art in modern times. The professor-self's intellectualized generalizations are nonetheless a fragmented and abstracted version of Clark's *actual* beliefs about literature. Subtle hints in the story of Mike Braneen can now be interpreted with more confidence. Braneen is and has been a decent human being, a good old boy whose qualities earned him many cronies and many good times in barroom fellowship; but he is also a dreamer, disenfranchised from within, and his long-discarded illusion of one day finding gold and—this time—investing it and thus escaping the chase, returns now to haunt him and tease him once again. The subject of "The Wind and the Snow of Winter" is, in the absurd generalizations of the intellect, "attention in the present," "detailed recollection of the past," and "an active imagination," the means of unity, if unity is to be achieved.

How to order a life is central to how to write a story. The quest, in either task, is for shape, connections between the stuff of whatever world in which you happen to live, both present and past, and that never-understood and never-analyzed faculty—call it the imagination or something else—which knows the "powers" below and thus can discover unity, something "not previously present." The experiences that force our reluctant recognition of successes and failures in self-organization will come in the forms in which they come, a black painter, the improper shooting of a rabbit, the aftermath—for a few—of holocaust, or—for some—the passage of time until friends and familiar places and other comforts no longer provide protection, and confrontation is forced.

Mike Braneen had only the Lucky Boy saloon and his drinking buddies, and outlived both, but others find a more secure place amidst the comforts of civilization. "White as a sainted leviathan, but too huge for even God to have imagined it," the giant ocean liner of "Why Don't You Look Where You're Going?" may well be Clark's allegory of the modern city-state. The passengers are comfortable in their "sense of well-being" (p. 113). They are secure in "the knowledge that their fate" is "somebody else's responsibility for the next three days." They know that there is "nothing an ordinary mortal could do about a ship like this; it was as far out of his realm as the mechanics of heaven." He could talk about it, as he might about one of the farther galaxies, in order to experience the *almost extinct pleasure of awe,* but he could not do anything about it, and what was even more comfortable, he could not be expected to do anything about it [p. 113, italics added].

The "un-Olympian calm" of this "self-sufficient creature" (p. 113) represents the modern human conquest of nature. It moves "independently" (p. 114). A machine that has appropriated godlike qualities, its very "joints" move with "perfect limberness" (p. 114). The liner usurps the role of God, parting the waters and securing its passengers from action and from contact with nature: more "like a white Utopian city than any the earth will ever bear, she parted the subservient waters and proceeded" (p. 114).

Using an ironic style much like that of Stephen Crane in stories exposing pomposities, Clark describes "the tall man," the "woman in white flannel" (p. 114), and others equally complacent, insulated. Suddenly they become aware of something dimly visible out in the vast and lonely ocean. Two qualities are emphasized: gamesmanship in jockeying for glories to be earned by being the first to identify the object and a vague stirring within of feelings long dormant. Safe, for this moment in their lives, these idlers will be observers merely. No black painter will leap from Cathedral Rock.

The passengers aboard this leviathan live, nonetheless, in the same world that Hook the hawk lives in. When protected, one's experience of another layer of reality may be comical. The little man shakes his fist at the giant that almost ran him down and shouts his protest: "Why don't you look where you're going?" (p. 120). The passengers are "charmed" (p. 120), with some vaguely nostalgic aftermath of deep feelings. It is funny, but somehow memorable. For Hook, there is no ship of state, and his confrontations are immediate and constant.

If it seems foolish to compare a hawk with a human being, the cause is not critical ineptitude but the excellence of Clark's writing. His skill seduces us into reading "Hook" as if it were what it seems to be, a pure animal story. The seduction is even more astonishing since Clark brazenly states in the first words of the story that his hawk has a name, Hook. Hawk parents do not name their children, or, if they do, the name would not be Hook or John or anything we would recognize. Hook's progress through life would also not include comments on "pride" and "shame," for these words carry too many associations with human consciousness and history. We readers do not know what goes on inside the consciousness of a hawk, and neither did Walter Van Tilburg Clark.

Appropriating a term from William Faulkner—"synonymity"[11]—and claiming that if Clark can deconstruct himself in "The Writer and the Professor" then readers may try it too, I would like to suggest something about Clark's "synonymity" in terms of the word "hawk" as it appears in another hunting story, "The Watchful Gods." After Buck has finally killed his rabbit, "a hawk rose out of the bench-land," rose "at that instant" and "seemed . . . to be ominously related to the rabbit, to have risen, indeed, directly out of it. . . ." To Buck's imagination, "it went up toward God with word of an unforgivable sin" (p. 259). Later, trying to pray, Buck thinks of his prayer as "being offered up for the undying, miniature-hawk part of the rabbit" (p. 271). Still later, his attempts in expiation having failed, Buck feels a "small motion . . . at the memory of the hawk-soul," but this faint stirring turns "out to be nothing but a weak imitation of the ascent and falling away of the real hawk. . . ." Buck forces himself to kneel for prayer, but it will not work: "Everything inside him was dead, or anxious to escape" (p. 298).

The version of the tiger Buck wants "to escape" is in Clark's "synonymity" confrontation with the hawk, that is, the realization that everything living—including a baby rabbit—is a part of the living world, a world that shines with beauty and threatens with death. The tugging at the reader's heart, below the story line, is a plea for sympathy with all life, much the same plea that is made at the end of "Hook," when the farmer's wife gives Hook the only last rites he will have: " 'Oh, the brave bird,' she said" (p. 30). We live, then, in a world that includes an incredible variety within the individual self, in nature and civilization, and in multiple gods. To confront that variety in a single moment is traumatic, and thus most of us, most of the time, develop strategies, seek to "escape the tiger."

Unfortunately, most of those who reject or want to reject the rationalizations of civilized trappings and who want to learn nature's secrets—Buck, of course, is included in this number—tend to identify with the joyful side only. These are Clark's heroes, in the sense that they are good people, but they have not yet learned what Clark knew. They are not allegorical representations of spiritual reality as understood by Walter Van Tilburg Clark. In fact, they have much to learn. The narrator in "The Buck in the Hills," for example, has achieved a Hemingwayesque union with nature: "God, I was happy. This was the way I liked it, alone, and clean cold, and a lot of time ahead" (p. 98). His friend Tom Williams, however, returns prematurely from deer hunting with a chilling tale. In an act of unspeakable cruelty, a third member of the party has purposely crippled a deer and made it stumble itself agonizingly down a mountain. Thus the deer bleedingly delivers itself and does not have to be dragged down the mountain.

The pilgrim who worships nature as ecstasy is booked to learn of brutality and death—animal as well as human, and there is even a god of death—and the resulting collapse within is often accompanied by threats from without. When Tom and the narrator head back home, there is "something listening behind each tree and rock" they pass, something that "didn't like" them (p. 109). In "The Fish Who Could Close His Eyes," another disillusioned lover of ecstasy stands watching "the bland, happy, heartless sea," and nothing moves "inside him to its dancing" (p. 175). In "The Portable Phonograph," after the holocaust, variation on confrontation is reduced to the stark essentials of a nocturne by Debussy and a piece of lead pipe.

The exception among Clark's collected stories of unity lost or spoiled or merely glimpsed is "The Indian Well." It is another hunting story—Jim Suttler waits a year to shoot a cougar that had killed his burro—but one with a difference that is essential to Clark's vision. In "The Writer and the Professor" the writer describes "The Watchful Gods" as the story "of a twelve year old kid" who "shoots his first rabbit without proper respect and fellow-feeling, and loses touch with nature." Suttler, it is true, kills his cougar for revenge; but he is angry on behalf of animal life—his murdered burro—and he undergoes ritual ceremonies before, during, and after the killing of the cougar. He acts *with* "proper respect and fellow-feeling." Jim Suttler does not need to escape or rationalize. He is not lost in the world. Instead, he repeats "his cleansing ritual" and moves on, "a starved but revived and volatile spirit" (p. 148).

From the antic moment of a businessman to the almost total destruction of civilization, reality for Walter Van Tilburg Clark includes the rabbit and the snake, the sophisticated intellect and "occult powers," the dancing sprites of joyful gods and the dark terrors of a god of death. For mere mortals, the desire to "escape the tiger" is an understandable weakness; for although confrontation may be comic or parenthetical, it may also be dangerous.[12] It is a weakness, however, that Clark treats with compassion, irony, humor, variety, and a brave honesty.

Notes

1. "The Writer and the Professor: or, Where Is the Little Man Inside?" *Chrysalis Review*, 2 (Spring 1962) 64.

2. Ibid., p. 88. It is significant that Clark displays (pp. 87–105) extensive knowledge of Henry James.

3. See Clark's introduction to *The Ox-Bow Incident* (New York: Time Inc., 1962), p. xiii.

4. "The Writer and the Professor," p. 72. I am quoting from a copy sent to me by Walter Clark in which he made a few emendations of the text.

5. Ibid., p. 78.

6. *The Watchful Gods and Other Stories* (New York: Random House, 1950), p. 304. Hereafter cited parenthetically.

7. In "The Writer and the Professor," writer-Clark teases Henry James for outrageous punning with characters' names, the purpose being, actually, to tease readers so in awe of the Jamesian style that they miss the obvious: Mille Theale in *The Wings of the Dove* is a "sitting duck"; *Fanny Assingham* is a triple pun (for these and other examples, see pp. 88–89).

The "sting" in this con game is that Clark does the same kind of thing. In *The Ox-Bow Incident*, for example, the Reverend Osgood oozes good, Greene is a green kid, Major Tetley is testy, Mrs. Larch is very arch, there is an ape in Mapes and a swan in Swanson, Ma Grier is an extremely masculine woman named Jenny, Bill Winder is full of hot air, and Art Davies and Art Croft are—like Art Bridges and unlike the curt Curt Bridges—associated in one way or another with art or the artistic.

8. See "The Writer and the Professor," pp. 72–73.

9. Ibid., p. 61. Note also (p. 78) that Clark's professor-self has "forgotten" "The Watchful Gods."

10. Ibid. In addition to the Knute Fenderson section of *The City of Trembling Leaves* (especially chap. 48), see "The Ascent of Ariel Goodbody," *The Yale Review*, 32 (Winter 1943)337–49; a merely personal form of perfectionism, for Clark, is another way "to escape the tiger," to avoid the challenge of Major Tetley, the challenge of the hunt, of creating art or literature or music.

11. "In my synonymity, 'living' equals 'motion' "; see Joseph Blotner, ed., *Selected Letters of William Faulkner* (New York: Random House, 1977), p. 429.

12. Although an unusually good person, Art Bridges of *The Track of the Cat* neglects the preparatory ritual of the icon for Joe Sam, fails to cleanse himself after delivering a coup de grace to a wounded steer, and thus gets himself killed.

7

On "The Wind and the Snow of Winter"

Walter Clark

First published in The Yale Review, *Clark's short story "The Wind and the Snow of Winter" won the O'Brien award for that year, 1944. Not surprisingly, the best comment upon it, printed for the first time below, comes from the author himself. It is the introduction to a reading of the story before the Friends of the Library, University of Nevada, October 19, 1967. For more on this short story, see chapter 16, below.*

Fiction, all fiction, I think we can say, has one basic purpose, no matter what kind it is or what particular realm or subject it is dealing with: to create the illusion of experience. We cannot, obviously, in words hope to create more than an illusion. With ink on pages you cannot actually present something worthwhile to the eye. Unless it is read aloud, you cannot present something to the ear, and, even when it is read aloud, you are presenting a representation, not the actuality. The senses are not really involved. The illusion of reality is the most we can hope for.

When I say "the illusion of reality," I mean essentially this: that the effort of the fiction writer, always, is to create the experience, to seek, in the first place, to put himself in the position of a major character or characters in a story and, by way of that, to coerce his reader into the same position—not to preach any sermon, not to state or expound any idea or theory—but whatever idea he may wish to present, to make it inherent in that experience. Implicit but not stated. In short, whatever reactions may come from a tale should come, as nearly as possible, as they might from your own experience—not something that anyone else is telling you, but something that, having gone through a given experience, you elicit for yourself in considering it.

Beneath this general intention of all fiction, it seems to me there are three possible approaches to story. One, which we might call the foreseen, begins with an idea, a moral, a purpose, a statement you wish to make, though you cannot make it directly or you destroy the illusion of experience. But you have the idea that you wish to expound, and you seek then the world in which you can embody that idea and take readers through the experience so that they may elicit the meaning themselves. The second approach, which one might call the exploratory, is that in which writers are suddenly moved by a memory, a personal experience, an intense feeling about something. They have no more, perhaps, than the ghost of a notion that there may be a story behind it, and when they begin to write they are not even sure that there is. And, perhaps many more times than not, there is not. They write the experience that does not turn out to be a story; it is not discovered. Finally, there is one that you might call the known story in which, to begin with, the writer is aware of both the idea, the moral, the theory—whatever it is he or she wishes the story to shadow forth without direct statement or preachment—and the world which will give body to that idea and shadow forth the idea. Historical fiction, for instance, is one, though not by any means the only, approach to this kind of fiction, wherein you take some actual scene and interpret it, present it in terms of a given meaning, a sense of it that you have that is not particularly implicit simply in the raw facts, though there are many other forms of fiction besides the historical. This is merely an example that works in that way.

For myself, I know, and I think for most writers of fiction, the happiest of all experiences is the exploratory story that really works out for itself. I doubt if it happens very often, but sometimes it does. You touch upon a memory that moves you. You are, for some reason or other, stirred by a recollection, or even by an imagination that has been touched off by a recollection, for an immediate emotional experience. And you have that happiest of all writing experiences: you start really presenting the little scene, the immediate thing that you wished to present, because it mattered to you emotionally, however slight it was, and you discover for yourself that there is a whole story lying there prepared behind it. A story that, once you have touched upon that first image and begun, to all intents tells itself.

"The Wind and the Snow of Winter" was that sort of a story for me. I was teaching in the East in upper New York State at the time that I wrote it. I was engaged in teaching seven English classes, a make-up class, directing twenty-four plays, coaching the basketball team, assisting the football team, running the yearbook, and a few extracurricular activities, and revising a novel, with which (revision has a habit of getting that way) I was profoundly fed up. At the same time there occurred one of the most beautiful blizzards of that winter, and upper New York State can do very well in the way of blizzards. And there came a clearing day, and this clearing day caught me. You will find a note in the story that is a description, in a measure, of it. It is still in the story. Though all I began with was that day. It was a very clear one, which is relatively rare in those regions; the sun was brilliant, there were two or three feet of new snow on the ground, and it was very cold. The house we were living in had behind it a little grove of spruce trees, beautiful spruce trees, heavily burdened, all their branches deeply in snow. In the bright sunlight they were casting very clear, blue shadows on the ground snow, distinct almost to the needle. The whole image was one that really did not belong to upper New York State; it belonged to Nevada. It was that kind of winter, that kind of sunlight.

And I do not know why—nobody ever does know why with this sort of thing—I got very restless (this will also be mentioned in the story, you can see it). What came to my mind was not so much the spruce trees in our backyard in New York as juniper trees and piñon trees in the hills of White Pine County. I do not know why White Pine; I have not the faintest idea. It just somehow became White Pine. I have looked at juniper trees and piñon trees in nearer parts of Nevada far more frequently, but somehow I was just drawn to White Pine. And I was drawn just to try to write something. I cannot remember distinctly now. I think probably what I was drawn to try to write was a sort of little bastard poem that would serve as a note or a relief or something that could relieve the restlessness and allow me to get back to the tedious duty of the revision.

But it did not quite work that way. Because the moment my feelings connected White Pine with the trees and the shadows, I remembered an experience that my wife still remembers with a shudder (I do not think she actually shudders any longer, but she did originally). We visited Hamilton and Treasure Hill in early spring with snow still on the ground and the temperatures very cold, a rather difficult visit because all the washes were washed out. There were no bridges and the road was precarious. Though the summer residents were fairly numerous, we discov-ered that the winter residents in Hamilton at that time num-bered two, one of whom was absent when we arrived. But he came over the hill very shortly after we arrived, a tall, a *very* tall—I do not know exactly, I did not measure him, but I would say he was six feet eight or nine, not exaggerating—very broad-shouldered, very thin, white-haired man, with a three-foot drill in one hand and a hefty hammer in the other. He had been out prospecting, but admitted to me later that it was just the spring that got him; he really was not looking for anything. He was just out. He was the last, you might say, permanent resi-dent of Hamilton, save for a lady he was living with who, from the moment of our arrival, darted from window to window to window in their little house, keeping track of us. I did not think we looked that dangerous.

The man had been the schoolteacher in Hamilton, the last schoolteacher in Hamilton, when it was still a working town. He was remaining there employed as simply a lookout, a kind of guard, for one of the big mining companies that was holding property though it had not operated there for more than twenty years.

The thing that gave my wife difficulty with this experience was that when the gentleman came down I asked him how the road was up to Treasure Hill. We could see it; it did not look very good. He said, well, the last time he was up, it had been pretty good.

"Well, how long ago was that?"

"Well, that was twenty-one years ago."

We asked him about several other things around and it was always, well, the last time he looked at that it was so and so, but that was twenty-one years ago. Apparently he had made a canvass of the region twenty-one years before and it finally boiled down to there was just one of the big main business buildings left in town, and it was now in ruins, just a shell, a quite impressive brick hotel that had, as its main feature, a lingering story to the effect that a notorious character had been hanged off a poker table in the back half of the bar. The old man had not been in that building for twenty-one years either.

So, he got curious, oddly enough. I thought he was beyond curiosity, that he had reached nirvana and perfect peace. But he was curious, so, by a very shaky flight of wooden steps that went up the whole three stories of the hotel in the back, we entered the hotel, and so far as my wife was concerned that was the last that was seen of us for three hours. She had seen my minuscule form disappearing through this door followed by Six Feet Nine, with a long iron spike in its hand. And we did not emerge again.

It was all very innocent. What happened was that we found part of the carpet torn up and we began to think maybe we could find some old bonanza-day papers because there were newspapers under the carpets all over. So we were just going around the hotel tearing up the carpets. The result was disappointing. We found nothing earlier than the Japanese-Russian war.

This man came back to my mind after I had had the first glimpses of blue shadow, the sense of cold, of clarity in the air, of the purity of sound that would come with that. I knew I had to have a prospector in the piece somehow. At that point it began to be a story rather than just a vignette of place, a scene that I was to remember. And I had found the prospector, though he had to be somewhat transformed. This man was just a little too much, so I shortened him, not remarkably, but by seven or eight inches, and I gave him a little more bulk and even more years than he had, though his numbers were respectable.

Some of you, I am sure, will remember the character who became—what should we say—the other half of this prospector. My friend Robert Caples had done a portrait of an old prospector whom I knew also. I am sure that many of you have known him because his face appeared for some years on every check from the First National Bank. He was stamped on it. A gray-bearded, rather stocky, elderly prospector.

From somewhere between these two my prospector emerged. I got him on the road. Again, I do not know why the seasons had to be switched. But yes, I do know why; I did not think about it, but you will know too when we get to the story, why I did not make it spring. It had to be on the other end of the season, the beginning of winter, not the end of it. And, once I was on the road with this man—again I have not the faintest idea whether I ever knew anybody by that name—he turned out to be Mike Braneen. The moment I was on the road with Mike, almost everything was settled; Mike just took over. It was his story. I followed. I had really only one problem: to be able to write fast enough to keep up with Mike, although Mike's gait was actually quite a slow one.

I wrote busily, happily, and furiously for something less than three hours and the story was complete. And, as I say, it was one of those things that is a pleasure, granting that perhaps now I should like to change some words. But why bother with it after all this time? I do not think I changed a half a dozen words after I had completed the story.

I had actually one, only one, conscious problem. I became aware of it quite early. As soon as I got on the hill into a fabulous town, nearly ghost town, called Gold Rock, which was

more or less—but only more or less—Austin, I was aware that
I did not want to make this a story just about Mike Braneen.
I wanted it to be a story about an old-time breed of prospector
that had, to all intents, disappeared, or certainly nearly vanished: the old walking prospector with his only companion, a
burro. Not a man with a blue light or a geiger counter or a jeep,
or any of those things; just a man who walked. And I wanted
to make my story a kind of *in memoriam* to this vanished, or
nearly vanished, breed of prospector.

This does furnish you a rather special problem in fiction, because nobody can believe in or be moved by something that is
purely a symbol. I had to make Mike Braneen individual
enough so that I could identify with him and feel for him, and
therefore, the reader following me must. But at the same time
I did not want to individualize him so highly that he could not
suggest at least this larger and more general meaning that I had.
So there are certain details that I used. You will notice some
of them—his far-back remembered evening with a little prosti-
tute in Eureka, a couple of specific memories among his many
burros, most of which have become now anonymous and all
one after all these years. And at the same time I tried to keep
him general enough so that he could suggest just old-time prospector, not a specific individual.

And, insofar as special devices used—it was not really a special device, it just developed and I was not aware of a conscious
use of it until the very end of the story. The snow that I used,
which is what impels Mike Braneen to make this last trip back
to his beloved town, is what we call in the gobbledygook of
creative writing an "objective correlative." Something happens outside that also represents a state of mind or spirit within
a person.

As I have already mentioned, language cannot really do the
job at all; the effort is to reach from the writer's imagination
to the reader's. The poverty of language is beyond belief. The
most one can do is try to suggest. You cannot possibly describe
the whole of even one small bare room. What one must do is
pick the selected details and trust the reader, the listener, to
do the other half, or more, perhaps two-thirds, of the job.

8

The Poetry of Walter Clark

Susan Baker

Susan Baker, who received her doctorate from the University of Texas, is an associate professor of English at the University of Nevada, Reno. She has published on Shakespeare and his contemporary, John Webster.

Walter Van Tilburg Clark's reputation rests securely on three novels and several short stories, but for the first decade of his writing career he was primarily a poet. He published numerous poems in the early 1930s: *Christmas Comes to Hjalsen* (a pamphlet); *Ten Women in Gale's House and Shorter Poems;* and several individual poems in anthologies and little magazines, including *Poetry.*[1] Although Clark ceased publishing poems after 1935 (except, significantly, those embedded in the prose), he continued writing poetry throughout his life. The University of Nevada, Reno, holds manuscripts of over two hundred and fifty poems, most of which have never been published. The majority date from 1931 through 1942; a very few may be earlier or later.[2] Clark's later ventures in poetry remain sealed until 1983; Robert Morse Clark describes them as "drafts of poems, often quick jottings, incomplete and never worked on, ranging from early 1950s to 1971."[3]

The poetry testifies, first of all, to a spirit of experimentation: it ranges from brief lyrics to extended narratives and verse dramas, its presentation from tight structures, traditional or invented, to those so loose only the lineation distinguishes them from prose. This diversity of form, however, counterpoints a

deep consistency in thought and image, and a perhaps more
surprising persistence of artistic strategies. Although one must
be cautious in ascribing influences to such a sustained individual imagination, Clark's work is much closer to that of E.
A. Robinson and Robinson Jeffers than to that of Pound, say,
or Eliot.[4] Like Robinson and Jeffers, Clark keeps his moral concerns close to the surface of his poetry and values statement
over image. Many of the earlier poems resemble Robinson's in
presenting portraits of eccentric or neurotic personalities
whose peculiarities illuminate us all. (Several of these are
labeled "for One Among Many," apparently a collection Clark
considered publishing.) And one hears echoes of Jeffers in
Clark's love for long lines, his compound modifiers, and a recurring exhortatory tone.[5] These elements are present
throughout Clark's poetry but become increasingly prominent,
as does the format of linked lyrics, which may well reflect Jeffers's influence.

   It remains true, however, that in reading Clark's poetry one
is less interested in looking backward to influences upon it than
in looking ahead to its role in his development as a writer of
fiction. Although the poetry lets us observe an artist at work
wresting a shape for his perceptions, poetry was not, finally, the
shape Clark needed. The particular demands of poetic forms
seem to have truncated his imagination rather than urging it
into unexpected insights. His handling of fixed meters is too
often labored, and where he uses rhyme it tends to be irritat-
ingly predictable (fire/desire began to clang in my ear). It is as
if the poetic line lacked room, fenced the open space Clark
needed to develop subtlety of description or fully to embody
abstraction in concrete particularity. Indeed, "the longer the
better" is a quick but surprisingly reliable index to the vast variations in quality among the poems. These longer poems derive
much of their interest from Clark's narrative gifts, especially his
eye for the telling situation and his ability to suggest the mysterious core of personality.

   Like the novels, the poetry ultimately addresses the question
of how a man is to live in this world. Clark's ethical focus encompasses explorations both of right behavior itself and of the

sort of knowledge in which right behavior is grounded. He well knows that these linked concerns resist easy resolution and final certainty; indeed, much of his poetry explicitly rejects public formulations that attempt to codify either knowledge or behavior. Wisdom and its ethical implications are difficult to evoke in words, and Clark's characteristic poetic strategy is to counterpoise such pairs as sanity and fear, beauty and pain, codified knowledge and intuitive apprehension, meaning and manifestation, obliviousness and alert attention, deadening religion and life-giving celebration of divine presence, isolation and engagement. These paired concerns sometimes enter the poetry as bald statement, but in the better poems are suggested within sharp delineations of particular personalities. These same themes pervade the novels, so that the student of Clark's imagination and thought is in the enviable position of being able to see similar materials rendered in three different modes: flatly stated in many poems, embodied through specific contrasts in the narrative poems, and developed into full complexity in the novels.

Here I shall focus on a group of narrative poems which animate the central tension between a solitary quest for wisdom and the need to participate in a world of human beings. These studies of loners invariably collocate the persistent themes listed above, giving them more life than in the short poems yet less subtlety than in the fiction. Before examining these poems directly, however, it will be useful to consider the double-edged quality of Clark's imagination as revealed in his poetic techniques. The habits of perception and thought indicated by these technical strategies suggest the roots both of Clark's central themes and of his characteristic strategies for presenting them. Inescapable in the poetry, and deserving of more attention in the fiction, is a persistent doubleness, manifested in many ways. In the poems Clark emerges as temperamentally a mystic and a romantic, as well as a crafter of language, but given his keen and educated intellect, he remains suspicious of mysticism, of romanticism, even of the power of words to communicate essential truths.[6] These tensions are reflected in his habit of seeing things, simultaneously, from at least two points of view, and this perceptual habit in turn is reflected in the very structures he frequently prefers.

Several of Clark's prosodic experiments employ the strategy of spatial juxtaposition. The early sequence, "The Temple: Colors in a Faith," for example, consists of several linked lyrics, each of which has typed beside it a key epitomizing image.[7] The poet's urge, clearly, is to set verbal exploration of a concept against a haiku-like embodiment of that concept—that is, to juxtapose two very different ways of understanding experience. Similarly, in "Cubist City Quatrains" Clark writes quatrains, rhymed *axxa* or *abba*, with one word printed sideways down the left side, another sideways up the right. Use of the word "cubist" in the title indicates Clark's conscious intent to render multiple perspective in verse, and he reuses this format in "Epitaphs" and "Undertones," where each quatrain presents a character type and the juxtaposed vertical words are often ironic:

> Macey trundles heavy things along the docks,
> And then goes home, takes off his shoes and socks,
> Puts his big feet close to the stove, and smokes,
> And tells his brown, stoop-shouldered, heedless wife old jokes.[8]

This use of juxtaposition is characteristic of Clark's writing. Max Westbrook observes that in *The City of Trembling Leaves* the chapter titles "are long, usually, and the characteristic tone is lofty, comic, pompous, constituting an ironic commentary on sacred escapades too many readers have taken literally."[9] This use of deflating titles can be seen as early as a poem (collected in *Ten Women in Gale's House*) that evokes at length a young man's desire for the perfect consummation of perfect love with a perfect woman. His motive for this ultimate consummation is revealed in the final stanza:

> I would that all of love and all desire
> Might purge my being in that one moon time
> And leave me for the seeking of the truth
> All nights as well as days until my end.[10]

This is hopelessly romantic in its idealistic self-absorption, but the poem is just barely rescued by its title—"Youth Seeks for

Truth"—where the blatantly awkward rhyme undercuts the speaker's romanticism, insisting that we join the poet in seeing it as slightly comic. Both the extreme romanticism and the amused skepticism toward it are, of course, Clark's.

Other techniques for providing multiple perspectives, often to present a mystic or romantic vision while establishing some intellectual distance from it, include the embedding of poems (within either prose or less lyrically extravagant poetry) and the use of multiple narrative frames; the pairing of these strategies can be seen in both the poem "Ten Women in Gale's House" and the novel *The City of Trembling Leaves*. Or we may be told the same story from two points of view—for example, Marnell's suicide from his own perspective in "Symphony for White Apes" and from that of his lover, Mona, in "The Path."[11] Or a new speaker may be introduced to provide unexpected, and ironic, information at a poem's end, as in "Carl Andread, Philosopher" or "Benedict Morales' Wife."[12] The point is that, again and again, Clark employs strategies that prevent our resting comfortably with a single point of view, with an exclusive way of seeing and interpreting experience.

This ambivalence in Clark's vision pervades his work thematically as well as technically. At once romantic, mystic, and skeptic, deeply concerned with questions both of moral action and of the sort of knowledge in which right behavior is grounded, Clark turns obsessively to central tensions in human existence. Crucial to both the poetry and the fiction is the conflict between a solitary quest for wisdom and the need for engagement in a human world.

Among Clark's most interesting and successful poems are several extended narratives, parables really, whose protagonists are best characterized as loners. These loners are closely related to the "primary realists" described in *The City of Trembling Leaves*, those who see beyond "manifestation" into "meaning."[13] This relationship is clearest in the poet's efforts to render the sort of knowledge and understanding available to the loner who rejects stultifying public formulations. It is possible to trace through these poems a group of related themes that invariably attend Clark's loners: sanity and fear, beauty and pain, codified knowledge and intuitive apprehension, a deadening religion and life-giving celebration. Yet—and here the double-edged nature of Clark's attitude is sharpest—for all his interest in and attraction to these loners, Clark repeatedly insists on the life-enhancing necessity of participation in a human community. So these poetic studies of loners, of what they gain and what they lose by their isolation, with all the themes that accompany their essentially one-dimensional portrayals, can best be appreciated as stages toward the creation of the multidimensional, "primary realist" protagonists of Clark's major fiction. It is not that Clark ever resolved the conflict between the will to isolation and the will to community, but his considered comprehension of that tension was surely honed in his repeated explorations of the loner's mentality. To examine these portraits, then, is to deepen our understanding of how this central tension reverberates in Clark's artistic imagination.

Consistently, the loners in Clark's poems are credited with an essential sanity. The speaker in "Hermit's Hill" describes the hermit Raphael as "sane and lucid."[14] "Mark Agnew's Cat" opens with a combative challenge to the reader:

> Mad, so you'd call Mark Agnew mad
> Because he had a house all to himself,
> And a black cat, and his own way of talking
> When there was no one to hear?
> Mark Agnew might as well have talked alone
> For all that you, or such as you'd have heard him say.[15]

Surely we cannot doubt whose side the speaker takes here. This question of sanity is paradoxically emphasized in "Carl Andread, Philosopher."[16] The poem's unnamed speaker seeks out the title character, now confined in an insane asylum, of which Carl says:

> "A nice name, Graylock, don't you think? I chose it.
> Perhaps, if taken altogether, this
> Is a somewhat eccentric gathering, but who's to say
> Who's not eccentric who is anywhere
> Alive in time, and these are never dull."

Carl's "insanity" has been doubly manifested. Its first symptom is his gift of making others smile and laugh; the speaker quotes Carl again:

"Well, here's the joke: that I have come into
This sizeable, if somewhat grim, estate
By holding true to what I felt quite certain
Was such a small and practical philosophy
As never to win such attention for me;
By shielding men from what they've always feared
Through never giving way to it myself,
Until they thought me knotted for this difference
And feared what was the shield against their fear."

Genuine laughter for Clark, as for most of us, is a sign of health. (See, for example, the characterization of Curly in "Ten Women in Gale's House."[17])

The second "symptom" is Carl's attitude toward fear. But attempts to hide from fear are always destructive in Clark's world. Particularly revealing is "The Great Comer" where such religious figures as Christ, Buddha, and Mohammed are portrayed as arising from men's "crazy fear" and "fear of fear."[18] The same poem emphasizes the carnage that results from evasions of fear:

Now I coming among them, will cleanse them of fear,
Wash the caverns of ribs to a coolness and stillness,
That they may cease this pouring of blood tides upon you;
The stone gods not so drenched and red dripping
          as you have been, Jesus;
The wooden idols squatted with blood bowls between their legs
Not so dark and so heavy with blood as you are, Mohammed;
Nor the gold sheeted, big-mouthed demons so thirsty of bleeding
As these, your shadows, peace men, Confucius and Buddha.

Pertinent too is *The Ox-Bow Incident*, where Gerald Tetley identifies deep fear as the source of the "cheap male virtues" that promote the lynching.[19]

The reader of "Carl Andread, Philosopher" has the inevitable feeling—encouraged in the poem by the speaker's attraction to Carl—that Andread in facing fear is more truly sane than those who label him insane. But Carl Andread exhibits a third apparent aberration. He describes his wife Enid to the speaker with Clark's recurrent images for female loveliness:

"Her ankles moved as silver fish in deep green waters;
Her hands were white birds in a blue and wind-curved sky."

And he adds,

"The only thing I ever feared in Enid
Was that such dreamy beauty someday would
Prove nothing but a dream indeed, and suddenly
Blow to a bright mist in the sea wind, and to nothing."

As in Clark's poem of the same name, "sea wind" is often associated in his poetry with the dream that is more real than ostensible reality, or with the idea Helga expresses in "Sea Wind" that "A dream is a reality."[20] (Too, the sea itself persistently signifies what matters—Gale in "Ten Women in Gale's House," for example, suspects that looking too long at his painting of Jacqueline, a figure of wanton and consuming vitality, would distract him from looking at the sea.[21]) Andread describes his relationship with Enid:

"   We were the sole reality
To one another in all creation, all the rest a dream
Such as it seems to anyone those afternoons
When sun and mist share the world without turbulence
Over the sea and shore, keeping a few white gulls above
And a few water shining seals below
To prove that we may have the dream again
And so not dispossess us of our laughter."

This private reality could not last, however, and Carl tells the speaker how Enid disappeared over a cliff by the sea. Further, Carl describes the sequel to Enid's disappearance:

"   —and then because I laughed,
And others found me laughing hours after,
They shook their heads and bundled me with kindness
Until my new estate here was prepared."

The poem ends ironically when a hospital guard informs the speaker, "Carl Andread never had a wife." So the poem raises but does not answer the key question of whether Carl's dream of Enid was madness or sanity, whether his surrendering that dream back to the sea betokened a new madness or a new sanity. Emotionally, however, the poem wholly endorses Carl Andread, suggesting that public definitions of sanity are irrelevant (rather than accurate or inaccurate) to a private reality attuned to a wisdom that transcends the merely factual.

This concern with a reality that transcends facts, with the meaning behind the manifestation, is sometimes associated in Clark's poetry with an artist (as it certainly is in *The City of Trembling Leaves*). In "Ten Women in Gale's House," Gale Winthrop is introduced as a portrait painter with eyes "which saw to cast the soul upon the screen."[22] Gale lives alone (except for an unobtrusive Chinese servant) in a house by the sea, and the speaker observes that "Gale Winthrop never had us there."[23] Gale does make an exception for the poem's speaker, because he paints the sea, and takes him on a tour of the house and its ten paintings of women, each of which represents either an absolute type (e.g., the self-possessed gracious lady, the temptress, the motherly aunt) or an abstraction (e.g., beauty, pain, death). Gale is obviously a precursor of Lawrence Black in *The City of Trembling Leaves*, and readers interested in Black should also look at "The Intimate Medusa," which offers a glimpse into reactions of the wife of a painter obsessed with portraying her soul (or his vision of it) on canvas.[24]

But Gale is also interesting as a type of loner. He appears to be utterly self-sufficient, content in his isolated house with his dream visions; his own mind and art are life enough. The poem's speaker is given privileged access to this life, but this exception seems to be motivated by poetic necessity (so that we can be told this story) rather than by any need of Gale's for companionship. In other of Clark's poems about loners, however, the central figure does seek an appropriate listener, and revelations frequently occur in communal situations—generally over glasses of wine or the smoking of pipes.

The one instance where the need to communicate is presented as desperate, "Benedict Morales' Wife," is, interestingly enough, closely related to "Ten Women in Gale's House" in its treatment of the interdependence of beauty and pain, particularly to one engaged in a search for perfection.[25] In Gale's sequence of paintings, *Cynthia*, his attempt to render perfect beauty, is followed immediately by *Kathleen*, who embodies pain.[26] Unlike Gale, a successful artist who moves from *Kathleen*/pain to *Dawn*, which he calls "the truth about love," Benedict Morales seems to be a poet manqué, a "strange and silent one who was alone," who has deliberately wed himself to pain. When the poem opens, Morales's wife has just died, and Morales insists the attending doctor listen to a bizarre account of how he came to choose that woman. Morales had loved another, Helga (namesake of the dreamer in "Sea Wind"), whom he describes as:

> "   the white one
> Whose voice is low and cool as the tide in the narrows
> When it is full and going under Raven's Head.
> She was a daughter of the sun and sea,
> A marble cup hissing with hot, white wine
> As sweet as burning in the throat,
> A strange white blossom from a mystery
> Awash in the green surge across the channel."

And he recounts his feelings for her:

> "I was alive with her, full of her always:
> Even the sea was only part of her.
> If I had taken her there would have been no wish
> For anything, ever again, in all my life,
> Except the blossom and the wine she was
> And the continual mystery
> In such a room as this, above the sea we hear."

But Morales deliberately rejected this beauty and contentment and married Marcia who had "An ugliness to dry a man's marrow in all his bones / And set his teeth like biting in a bitterness." Morales fiercely wants the doctor to understand why he chose this marriage:

> "Think what it meant to me to bed
> On that bare oaken couch each night of the long year,
> In fire-dust of stars or the tomb's breathing fog,
> With her; to stir desire only with a dream

Of someone else so hot against me there;
To kill the lamp seeing that death's head on the pillow,
And see it there again, with dawn crying upon the hills.
But I could sing!"

And he defends his choice: "It may have been wormwood I drank, / But man, the cup was silver and it rang!" Like "Carl Andread, Philosopher," this poem ends in irony. Although Morales says he now may marry Helga, the doctor later talks to a Mexican ranchhand:

"Morales? Yes—he marry two weeks past,
Andrew Handley's daughter from south ranch;
You know, the ugly one."

A larger irony is that Morales's self-imposed suffering and deprivation is apparently futile; we hear nothing of his "songs" from either the poem's speaker or the doctor except that "some said that he made rimes." Read in the context of the relevant sections of "Ten Women in Gale's House," "Benedict Morales's Wife" implies that although beauty creates pain, the reverse is not necessarily so. Moreover, when Morales rejects Helga, he essentially rejects his potential "conductor to / the infinite" (Gale Winthrop's phrase for Helen, his classical muse).[27] And certainly the poem indicates that isolation is not a sufficient cause of wisdom or beauty (things closely allied in Clark's world).

Given this suspicion of isolation by plan, it should not be surprising that some of Clark's loners are rather unattractive. Mark Agnew (of "Mark Agnew's Cat"), for example, is crabbed, even sullen, and somehow identified with his black, yellow-eyed cat, Charon, a deathly creature.[28] One clearly endorsed loner, however, is Raphael, the hermit of "Hermit's Hill."[29] Here, a man named Drake seeks out the isolated shanty of Raphael, of whom some men had said:

That he was more than different from the rest,
And had said it as much to say more
That difference was sometimes dangerous.

Drake, on the other hand,

had been certain that Raphael
Had seemed doubtful to some because he was
Too clearly sane and lucid.

(The paradox of madness and sanity again.) After many years of separation, Drake wants to discover what Raphael has learned in solitude. Raphael's hilltop cabin, however, is deserted, and Drake finds only a verse legacy to the world:

A little time I thought it great
To give the world
The key to beauty,
So to truth.
I wrote a thousand sheets
Beyond
The farthest thought before,
And then distilled them pure
Within a hundred lines.
When it was done
I knew it for myself
Preparing for
Beyond.
A thousand sheets,
And more within
A hundred lines,
Are ash.

Apparently, Raphael felt that the world would not be able to accept the distillation of his wisdom; Drake agrees, "For Raphael was wise beyond / The understanding of the rest how wise he was." It is also true that Raphael—by his own claim at least—had managed to express in words essentially inexpressible truth. This paradoxical will to express the inexpressible haunts Clark throughout his poetry.

One way to define this problem is to recognize that at least a major portion of "the inexpressible" represents the sort of knowledge that comes through the intuitive, alogical right hemisphere of the brain rather than through the logic-ridden and verbal left hemisphere. Gale Winthrop describes such apprehended knowledge:

The thought beyond thought that is feeling

More than feeling, thought which brings
Revelation without use of a laborious logic,
Revelation which the laws of logic at their best,
Cannot attain . . .
It either is or is not.[30]

One of Clark's short poems explicitly juxtaposes two orders of
thinking:

                         Go into the heart
                         I am near to the heart of this thing
                              in the luminous dark
                         I will be very still; I almost hear like
                              my blood symbol
                         of sunken rivers, like the ladder
                              of stars, like time
                         Like the heart of this thing forever
                         It will be very wonderful here, but oh,
Deny   I must open slowly
Savage Religions   Never whisper the fables
Break Prejudice   Unharden
Study Zoology   Know what the cricket thinks of the night
Botany   What the aspen leaf sees in the moon
Geology   The stone dreams in the dark
Physics, Astronomy   What is time to the stars and the terrible
                              time of men
History, Literature   in their dreaming more wild than of stone
Love   Hear their little rivers forever before
                         I hear my heart go through the edge of day.[31]

"Hermit's Hill" sidesteps the issue of finding means to express
the inexpressible, but it does suggest what mode of thought
Clark feels is required to experience it. The word "customary"
occurs three times in the poem: coming to Raphael's shanty
takes Drake "out of more customary life"; he expects to find
Raphael looking *not* at a landscape that has become "the customary unobserved"; as Drake leaves he sees a "magpie, higher
than his customary haunts." Consistently, "customary" and its
synonyms carry negative connotations in Clark's poetry: Carl
Andread likes his new home partly because it has "innumerable
chambers / Without a customary air in any," and Benedict

Morales knows he could have married Helga because of some "crazy, customary words" that implicitly had nothing to do with either's real feelings. The ground of Clark's objections to this word is clearest in the phrase from "Hermit's Hill": "the customary unobserved." To become accustomed to something is no longer to see it, to cease to pay it any attention. And there is a deep sense in which all of Clark's writing is an exhortation to pay attention to both the internal and external worlds. Only through continual alert attention can one perceive the realm of apprehended and intuitive knowledge or act appropriately. Thus, any mode of dealing with the world that becomes customary can harden into a system that precludes thoughtful attention to the things that matter. "Law," "fable," "habit," "custom," and related words are those with which Clark regularly attacks such systems, and they are frequently attached to organized religion, which, for Clark, is a major system to be rejected as a moral or ontological guide.

This view of religion as inadequate or destructive is embodied in the novels. Osgood, the Baptist minister in *The Ox-Bow Incident,* has "no heart in his effort" to dissuade the lynch mob—he can only orate, not move.[32] The mother in *The Track of the Cat* persists in a harsh and hell-fire religiosity, which is specifically contrasted with Arthur's gentle awareness of divine presence. In the poetry, this rejection of formal religion is explicit and encompasses more than Christianity: "You cannot sell Forever for a sign / of whatever cross or crescent" ("Even In Such A Night").[33] In his long poem "The Great Comer," Clark elaborates the failure of religion in the figures of Christ, Buddha, Confucius, Mohammed, and innumerable dark tribal gods.[34] He depicts these divinities as exhausted, wanting rest denied them by men who will not leave them in peace. Clark's indictments of humanity under these gods are grim: "The fear drooling soul of humanity"; "ingrown thinkers in patterns"; "axes biting necks for human blood"; and so on. The poem, however, announces the arrival of a new divinity, The Great Comer, which will put the old gods to rest and reawaken humankind to forgotten truths. The celebration of life that marks the new coming contrasts sharply with the deadened existence under the old gods:

On all the white roads of the earth men and women marching,
Arms about waists, singing with eyes in the flowering rain,
Thrusting glad feet in the fallen blossoms, tossing them spraying,
Petals caught in the wind of the moving, dancing the roadside;
Blossoms and birds and streaming and bursting of sunlight
Over and under and swirling within the mad going and circling,
Embracing, mouth upon mouth, hands tight within hands,
Arms about glad swaying bodies, nations mingling forgotten,
Dancers fringing, alone, and fast trooping;
Birds, blossoms, sunlight and beautiful bodies
In the wind of the triumphal moving.
In the swinging and ringing and turning of bells carolling,
Mad ringers riding, clapper hanging, swinging and shouting,
The blasting, continuous, high throated metal of trumpets,
The hailing and cannonading of drums, rattle and thunder,
And strident whistles, silver long in the uproar.

Clark's recognition of this need for an attentive participation in life, including the community, typifies his ambivalent attitude toward the loners he is so fond of creating. On the one hand, withdrawing from the world of men can enable—perhaps is the only action that can enable—one to perceive beyond the customs, fables, laws with which we persistently try to codify both knowledge and ways of knowing, both experience and ways of experiencing. Yet a full participation in life must include other human beings. Both the attraction and the fallacy of self-imposed isolation is expressed in the last two stanzas of "Now the Good Anchorite":

Often I envy the anchorite for what he has shed
    that is like the deadly gift of more than enough
But he as of old in the desert picking his lice and inviting the Lord
    To set the table for two
Is more evil, having a choice, than any of these.
The houris peopling his vision, and some as saints, however
        lovely,
    however delicate as lilies in shining cloth with their feet
    in the cool waters in the wilderness

Are the foul symbols his brain makes of self-love in his blankets.
Only lust and the crawling evil dwell in him and will not go
    for any whip of the mind.
Clearly the good anchorite bears desert with him now,
Seeking to behold each face alone, denying no eyes,
    Giving them for their own what splendid space he can
Knowing the only god dwells in their addition
    That heaven's in their children
        That the hand must touch love.[35]

Clark epitomizes this attitude in one line from a related poem
entitled "You Can't Alone": "Forever denies the hermit
mind."[36] But its finest poetic embodiment occurs in Clark's
long narrative "The Burial of Kitty Hemming: A Tale of the
Comstock," another parable of a loner, but one that resonates
its meanings through the fully realized telling of a good story.[37]

"The Burial of Kitty Hemming" opens by announcing that
a strange tale will follow and then introduces the loner at its
center, Black Bart:

He had come up when the great gold was struck,
From some dim pocket in the outer world,
And Bart was all the name he ever gave.

Bart clearly qualifies as a legendary hero: he appears out of
nowhere, and no one knows his name. He is, moreover, a creature of the gold rush—created by it, even perhaps its emblem.

Bart exists against the backdrop of boomtown Virginia City,
"built of gold and silver, and men's lives," and its wealthy
exuberance. In the midst of this fevered round of dance halls,
gambling parlors, and international celebrities at the opera
house, Black Bart "Walked easily, and never seemed a part /
Of the hot fever, save a watching part." And his smile seemed
to say, "I am the only sane one here."

In this quality of self-containment, of being a watcher and
a sane man, Bart suggests Clark's other self-possessed loners.
He moves in the world but is somehow detached from it:

He always drank, and he was never drunk;
He always gambled, and he never lost;
And women loved him, but he never loved.

After establishing Bart's detached character, Clark introduces Kitty Hemming. Much like Bart, she "came to gay Virginia from / Some hidden, quiet place." Unlike Bart, however, she plunges recklessly into boomtown life—and a wild life indeed is available to a beautiful girl in a town populated mostly by men. Kitty goes to Bart's cabin, but unlike other women before her, she takes up residence there. Clark contrasts Bart's and Kitty's responses to this unaccustomed stability:

> And she came down a few brief times and sang,
> And Bart came down alone, each day, each night,
> And played and won. He was the same,
> Silent and slim and smiling at the world as if to say,
> "I am the only sane one here." But she
> Came down from out another world, with eyes
> With happy stars sunk in their depths and lips
> That spoke Bart's name in every speech.

Bart and Kitty stay together for three years, during which "the Bonanza dropped as though the earth / Had tired of so sick a giving of her strength." One could still eke out profits, but the boomtown dreams and glamor have ended. And Kitty's dreams are dying too. Bart is restless, and Kitty finds his words "Fewer than ever." Her love cannot pierce his isolation, which is by now complete:

> He only sat and smoked and drank and stared
> Into the fire, while the thin
> White fingers drummed and drummed.

Finally, Kitty cannot bear *her* isolation from Bart, and she dies. Apparently unmoved by Kitty's death, Bart pays a few men to dig her a pauper's grave, but he provides no headstone and doesn't bother to attend the burial.

Bart seems prepared to continue in Virginia City life, but is moved into uncharacteristic activity by the news that Kitty had a mother. He presses for details: "Did someone send the word that Kitty died?" "Did they tell how Kitty has died, or how she lived?" "They wrote / Or telegraphed?" Finding that "they" had written, Bart rushes to the *Enterprise* and orders a new obituary: "Mrs. Mason died, Mrs. Bart Mason, of this town."

He then sends a telegram—"Your daughter and my wife died here last night"—and signs it "Bart Mason." It is in this act of compassion that Bart gives his surname for the first time. The symbolic meaning, of course, is that in acknowledging human responsibilities, Bart becomes more fully human.

Once his isolation is breached, Bart finds himself engaged further. He discovers that Mrs. Anna Hemming is coming to Virginia City, to see where and how her child had lived and to visit her grave. Bart responds to her need by commissioning a marble tombstone, buying a cemetery plot and a coffin, and hiring a stranger (who plans to leave town soon) to help him rebury Kitty.

In the poem's final section, Mrs. Hemming pays her visit. Bart takes her to Kitty's grave:

> **"She sleeps Here, Katherine Hemming Mason,**
> **Beloved wife of Bart;**
> **Who Sang in Life and Left Her Song**
> **In Heavy Hearts."**

He weaves stories of a happy marriage and an easy death, and he gives Mrs. Hemming $10,000, claiming he and Kitty had saved it for her. She leaves, saying "God Bless you, son." And Bart remains "With the thin smile that said, / 'I am the only sane one here.' " The next day Bart leaves Virginia City: "And no one knew when he went out, or by which road."

This long poem (49 composition-book pages in manuscript) is interesting in several ways. First, we see Clark using the materials of his well-loved Nevada history to create a setting for his parable, just as he so often did in the fiction. Indeed, it can be argued that "The Burial of Kitty Hemming: A Tale of the Comstock" is at least partly a parable of the Comstock. Bart and Kitty are both typical boomtown figures, as well as the stuff of which legends are made. When the boom is over, their lives are irrevocably changed. Kitty has always been more connected than Bart to the larger world—she at least has a surname—and she dreams of creating a "normal" life once the boom is over. She cannot do this without Bart, so she dies. And her death forces Bart into a situation where—apparently for the first time—he must accommodate the outside world, in the person of Mrs. Hemming. It is surely no accident that in dealing with her he finally acknowledges his full name. Bart, like a good legendary hero, leaves town, but those who remain will face the same challenge he did: that of creating an everyday existence in the boomtown setting, once its transient fever has passed.

Of course, the virtue of parables is that their meanings are not narrowly defined. Much as Clark's western novels have universal ramifications, so too "The Burial of Kitty Hemming" suggests something about the nature of a loner, whatever his specific milieu. Bart succeeds as well as any of Clark's loners in carving out an independent, self-sustained existence. But even he finally confronts circumstances which demand that he acknowledge his connectedness and his responsibilities to other human beings. Ironically enough, his lies to Mrs. Hemming suggest the truth about being a loner: it is neither possible nor, finally, desirable.

Obviously, the theme of "The Burial of Kitty Hemming" is very close to that of "Now the Good Anchorite" (quoted earlier). Yet even my paraphrase should convey the degree to which the narrative poem is superior to the briefer lyric. And "The Burial of Kitty Hemming" is a better poem primarily because by taking the form of a parable it suggests a richness and depth of meaning the shorter poem only asserts.

This observation about the relationship between "Now the Good Anchorite" and "The Burial of Kitty Hemming" applies as well to the relationship between Clark's poetry in general and his fiction. The same themes—those that cluster about the central question of perception and its ethical implications—persist throughout both genres. So too, throughout both poetry and fiction, one sees the double-edged quality of Clark's imagination, particularly the will toward romantic isolation and private mystic vision subjected to a skeptical demand that its perceptions be tested through attentive engagement in a human community. But Clark's characteristic techniques—juxtaposition, ironic undercutting, multiple perspectives—and his greatest talents—rendering significance through story and por-

traying believable individuals—are finally better suited to fiction than to poetry. Though the poetry is extremely valuable
in illuminating the artist's imagination, and although the narrative poems do have some inherent interest, it is as a writer
of prose fiction that Walter Clark best embodies his complex
ethical vision.

Notes

1. *Christmas Comes to Hjalsen* (Reno: Reno Publ. Co., 1930);
Ten Women in Gale's House and Shorter Poems (Boston: Christopher
Publ. House, 1932). For individual poems, see the bibliographies by
John R. Kuehl, "Walter Van Tilburg Clark: A Bibliography," *Bulletin
of Bibliography*, 22 (Sept.–Dec., 1956)18–20, and Richard Etulain,
"Walter Van Tilburg Clark: A Bibliography," *South Dakota Review*,
3 (Autumn 1965)73–77. Seven of Clark's poems ("The Sweet Prom-
ised Land of Nevada," "Kindred," "The New New Moon," "Over
Carson Valley," "Lake Tahoe," "Dawn—Washoe Valley," "Big
Dusk") are to appear in *The Nevada Poet*, Gary Short and Roger
Smith, eds., to be published by Frosty Morning Press.
2. The poems in Special Collections, Getchell Library, University of Nevada, Reno, are preserved in three formats. "The Temple:
Colors in a Faith" (10 pp., unbound), "Trilogy for Tired Lovers" (103
pp., bound), and "8 poems" (88 pp., bound) are in typescript, illustrated by Clark. A few other poems are in typescript; most are in
handwritten fair copies in 8 by 10½" hardbound notebooks. References in the present article will use the Special Collections call numbers.
3. *Walter Van Tilburg Clark: 1909–1971*; NC527. "Calendar of
his papers in The Special Collections Department, University of
Nevada, Reno, Library. Compiled, 1972, by Robert M. Clark; revised, 1979, by Kenneth J. Carpenter," p. 10.
4. Four poems written in the early forties (527/1/21/7) exhibit a
style markedly different from that of Clark's other poetry. These
four—"Boardwalk Parade," "Madonna and Child," "Carolyn Plays
Chopin," and "Modern Exhibition"—are characterized by convoluted or abandoned syntax and language that is highly associational,
with the associations sometimes triggered by rhyme. This radical shift
in style in nearly the last of the carefully finished and preserved poetry
suggests Clark's dissatisfaction with poetry as a vehicle for his imagination. [Some of the verse may have had its origin and its use as what
Clark elsewhere called "a small bastard poem." See his comment on
"The Wind and the Snow of Winter," above. —Ed.]

5. Henry J. Nuwer, "Jeffers' Influence upon Walter Van Tilburg Clark," *Robinson Jeffers Newsletter*, 44 (March 1976)11–17.

6. Max Westbrook examines Clark's "sacral" view—which locates intuitive thought in the unconscious and believes in the unity of being—in *Walter Van Tilburg Clark* (New York: Twayne, 1969), *passim*. I find Westbrook's analysis quite persuasive, except that he finds "sacrality" the theme of Clark's fiction, whereas I see it as the backdrop for exploration of ethical concerns.

7. 527/1/21/3; n.d. (1931–33).

8. 527/1/21/4; probably 1929–31.

9. *Walter Clark*, p. 75.

10. *Ten Women*, pp. 24–26.

11. "Symphony," 527/1/21/6; 1933–39. "Path," 527/1/21/5; 527/1/21/12; no later than 1933.

12. "Andread" and "Morales," 527/1/21/5; 527/1/21/12; no later than 1933.

13. *The City of Trembling Leaves* (New York: Popular Library Edition, 1962) p. 14.

14. 527/1/21/4; probably 1929–31.

15. 527/1/21/4; probably 1931–33.

16. 527/1/21/5; 527/1/21/12; no later than 1933.

17. *Ten Women*, pp. 51–52.

18. 527/1/21/10; 527/1/21/12; probably 1932–33.

19. *The Ox-Bow Incident* (New York: New American Library, 1960), p. 104.

20. 527/1/21/4; probably 1931–33.

21. *Ten Women*, p. 44.

22. Ibid., p. 34.

23. Ibid.

24. 527/1/21/6; 1933–39.

25. 527/1/21/5; 527/1/21/12; no later than 1933.

26. *Ten Women*, pp. 59–62; see also "My Lady," 527/1/21/4.

27. *Ten Women*, p. 42.

28. 527/1/21/4; probably 1931–33.

29. 527/1/21/4; probably 1929–31.

30. *Ten Women*, p. 42.

31. 527/1/21/7; dated "Indian Springs, Nov. 26, '41."

32. *The Ox-Bow Incident*, p. 33.

33. 527/1/21/7; 1941–42.

34. 527/1/21/10; 527/1/21/12; probably 1932–33.

35. 527/1/21/7; 1941–42.

36. 527/1/21/7; 1941–42.

37. 527/1/21/9; 1931–32.

9

The Gospel According to the Trembling Leaves

Charlton Laird

Three sorts of trees with trembling leaves shadowed the land of Timothy Hazard, the home also of stripling Walter Van Tilburg Clark, who dreadfully needed to say something, and labored learning how to say it. The mature Clark, speaking with the voice of an imaginary narrator, tells us that "the trees of Reno have regional meanings within their one meaning, like the themes and transitions of a one-movement symphony. It would be impossible to understand Tim Hazard without hearing these motifs played separately before you heard them in the whole."

This "whole" is presumably something more than the meaning that fictional Tim Hazard is said to have attributed to all trees, that "any city containing a region in which you can look all around and not see a tree" is "moribund," for it "is drawing out of its alliance with the eternal, with the Jurassic swamps and the Green Mansions." Such a place will "choke out the trees in the magic wilderness of the spirit." Presumably the trembling leaves have messages for us, separately and about this whole, messages in the sense that the Gospels were messages. They are esoteric and fugitive, and they must constitute, or be associated with, what Timothy in other surroundings calls "the nuclear," a concept to which we must return.

The City of Trembling Leaves opens with a Prelude, which I have been quoting, in which somebody, presumably a fictional

Walt Clark, endeavors to suggest these motifs. He starts with
cottonwoods, which even in their short lives may grow to be
huge and assume a craggy, dilapidating majesty. In the novel
they are associated with Wingfield Park, a shadowed place
suggestive of Corot's wood nymphs and an "ever-lasting late afternoon somnolence of a Watteau painting." They line Court
Street, where pillared mansions have "high-ceilinged rooms
with the shades drawn in late afternoon in summer." The cottonwoods are said to stand for "the Court Street theme," as we
might remind ourselves that *The City of Trembling Leaves* is the
title both of a novel by Walter Van Tilburg Clark and a supposed symphony composed by Timothy Hazard, who along
with "Walt Clark" must be some sort of alter ego of the novelist.
These trees "dispense an air of antique melancholy," so much
so that as you walk under them you grow "sad and old." They
must have something to do with vested pride, with moneyed
elegance, with somewhat smug self-satisfaction, with something other than "the magic wilderness of the spirit."

Cottonwoods are exotics, as the culture they towered over
was exotic, imported from farther east, and they canopy the
older parts of residential Reno. Young Tim Hazard seldom approached the exalted seats of the Court Street quarter, though
his dearest friends lived there, Lawrence Black whom he found
kindred and Rachel Wells whom he worshiped. He ventured
into the domain of the cottonwoods, but could not move naturally to such a theme. In his world "the grown trees are marching
files of poplars, in love with wind and heavens . . . always
trembling so they nearly dance." There were three of these poplars near the house where Tim lived, in a homely area near the
race track.

Two sorts of trees called poplars are common in western
Nevada: the Lombardies, brought by Mormon settlers, and the
native poplar that grew along the streams and guided pioneers
to water. In *The City*, trees called poplars seem all to be Lombardies. Timmy Hazard can hear them rustle when he is lying
in bed at night, and they are sufficiently prophetic to warrant
Timmy's happiest experience in Book 1 to be labeled "The History of Mankind According to the Poplars of Bower's Man-

sion." The fictionalized "Walt Clark" tells us that Tim's world is a "city of dissonant themes," that the pattern of the Lombardies is a "thin, hasty brightness," that it is "almost strident, and saved from being as intolerable as persistent whistles only by the yellow hills, like cats asleep in the north." The theme of the Lombardies somehow stands for life as Tim is living it.

The other sort of tree with trembling leaves is the aspen, of smaller growth, fragile, but capable of thriving on the gales and the inundating snow of mountain winters. It can be resplendent with its birchlike bark and its sprightly leaves, gold in the autumn sun. All the aspens I recall in *The City* are young, most of them brought down from the mountains by people who loved them. One such aspen became a talisman for Tim, when at a teenage party he finds out about kissing girls and about the softness of their bodies. Aspens characterize what Clark calls "the Peavine Quarter," the section of Reno nearest to Mount Peavine, where both the youthful Tim and his friend Lawrence agonized about their art, and where, with Lawrence's wife, Helen, they constituted a "triumvirate against destiny"; we are told that Mount Peavine itself "begets love." Here Tim and his friends talk for hours, and "all their thoughts and words were touched by the twinkle of sun on the aspen and by the whispering and rushing of its leaves." Aspens recur repeatedly in the novel, usually in association with some spiritual crisis, and when we last see Tim, now a father, he is watching his children playing with a young aspen that Tim had replanted from a mountain canyon. Tim's little daughter quiets one of the dancing leaves, only to find that, when released, "it began to dance again, by itself." As with the poplars, we are not told what aspens symbolize, but a young aspen must have something to do with youth, tremblingly expectant, but fearful, too, in a strange but meaningful world not much given to loving and dancing, to creating and living in harmony with the universe.

Reno in Tim Hazard's day had also another section, the downtown commercial and gambling area, treeless and busy, which the fictional Walt Clark calls "the ersatz jungle," where "the human animals, uneasy in the light, dart from cave to cave under steel and neon branches." But the jungle was small, and

almost obscured by the trembling leaves on all sides of it. Tim
and his friends have little to do with it. Whatever *The City of
Trembling Leaves* is trying to tell us, the message is not much
concerned with the ersatz jungle, except by implied contrast.
In fact, one may plausibly surmise that the first chapter of *The
City* is a remnant of an earlier version, so beautiful that Clark
had trouble wastebasketing it.

Sequence of Events

Formally, the novel is broken into two sections, designated
as "books," but not otherwise titled. To draw the contrast between them we might concoct titles for them: Book 1, "A Sensitive Boy Grows Up in an Insensitive Town"; Book 2, "A Tortured Artist Finds Himself."

The City can be read in a number of ways, notably in at least
three. To the casual reader, perhaps especially to the casual
Nevada reader, it is a leisurely, comfortable, rambling sort of
yarn, about young people growing up among homey surroundings, about human needs and their fulfillments, about the good
life in a young land, the mountainous, semidesert West. There
are no murders, no rapes, no nationally newsworthy events,
only the daily doings of people known mostly to their friends
and their communities. The author tells us about them as
though he were a favorite uncle, at once tolerantly amused by
them and absorbed in them. Their lives are sharply etched in
unobtrusive detail, but the lives are not very unusual in themselves, except that Tim and Lawrence Black are presumably
young geniuses who have not as yet found themselves. Even
Tim's "dark period," at the beginning of Book 2, is little more
than the essential agony that many serious artists experience
while they are learning technique and finding their voices. The
reader is never in much doubt that something will come of
Tim's genius, and that the action, however the book wanders,
will lead to some sort of "happy ending."

We might add that the novel contains some of the most brilliant writing thus far done in American English. There has
been little critical dissent on this point, however much the
critics may have differed about almost everything else in the
book.

Tim is an intelligent, sensitive boy, but neither adventurous nor worldly-wise. Told that two girls are going to "give out" during the noon hour, he asks, "Give out what?" For a father he has "a kind of yard boss" of a lumber company. For a mother he has a mildly prudish, devoted woman who tends to her family, her flowers, and her vegetable garden. For a sister he has a pretty, pleasant girl who marries a boy she knew in high school, who thereupon gets a job running a filling station in California. For a brother he has a shrewd little dropout, who becomes involved in petty crime and goes off somewhere to become a jockey. Tim finds a few promising youngsters among his peers, but most of his playmates are as dull and mundane as one would expect. Superficially, the tale suggests home movies more than a powerful epic of the West.

When we first see Tim he is about eleven, discovering exciting mysteries, especially about girls and the natural world around him, along with—a bad third—art. Classmates of both sexes help with the girl-mystery; he learns about "it" from the talk of braggart boys and from Lucy in the basement of the school auditorium. He learns about women as the ideal of purity and spiritual humility from a demure child named Mary Turner, whom he sees at family picnics and who does little more than simply be there. We do not know much about her except that she is beginning to jiggle when she runs and has red pubic hair, these details not from Tim, but from his peeping-Tom brother Willis.

As for the natural world around him, Tim needs little help. It seeps into him gradually: "Outside, the end of the year was beginning, and the poplars along the front walk were quietly letting go yellow leaves which came down whirling, or dipping like heavy feathers, making a sound, when you listened to enough of them along the walk, like the scattered beginning of rain." Religion is involved in both the girls and the natural wonders. Formal religion comes through Bible-reading encouraged by Mrs. Hazard. Tim loves the stories, but is troubled by all those harmless creatures that could not get into the Ark, the tired birds he could imagine falling into the waters, and the dead butterflies carpeting the lifeless

informal religion, presided over by the unseen presence of Mary
Turner. For Tim, prayers and kisses, not necessarily physical
kisses, get all mixed up.

As for the art, two boys help: Lawrence Black, the son of
aristocrats in the Court Street area, and Jacob Briaski, son of
a Russian-Jewish pawnbroker, who has a shop on Reno's skid
row. Lawrence is a princelike boy, already something of a
sculptor. Tim tries to imitate him, creating things. Jacob is
learning to play the violin, practicing devotedly, but he has no
ear, and his desperation will eventually drive him to suicide,
but meanwhile the friendship leads to Tim's acquiring a good
violin and learning elementary music, both from the elder
Briaski. The early parts of the novel include incidents with
these children, notably at Pyramid Lake, a magical body of
water in the desert, which becomes for Tim a sort of sanctuary
and temple, although dedicated to a panoply of gods more
sensed than conceived.

With high school, both Tim and his surroundings change.
He elongates into a gangling, stringy creature, too odd to be
popular, but with unexpected powers, as inexplicable to him
as to his peers. He becomes the hero of the class fight, not because he and his classmates win—the freshmen are badly
beaten—but because he fights with such furious ineptitude.
Later, as a blackboard cartoonist he so entrances his fellows
that the faculty has to stop him—after all, life in school must
go on despite the vagaries of genius. He discovers the most en-
chanting creature in the world, a rather prim, sensible, capable
girl named Rachel Wells. Mary, and the memory of her, are
now only an embarrassment to him. He develops into something of an athlete, winning races as a distance runner; he practices tennis and plays in tournaments with Rachel. He becomes
enough of a musician to tootle a horn in a jazz band, and even
to arrange music for the combo.

Meanwhile, he becomes aware that surreptitious education
goes on among his classmates, and he is somewhat mauled at
a party, but he is mainly protected by his perdurable innocence.
His relationships with Rachel are sporadic; she rather likes
him, but he does gauche things such as talking compulsively

about nothing when he knows he should not, and trying to give her a moss agate, unaware that the days have gone in which a fashionable girl could wear Victorian gewgaws. For a time Tim is ravished, body and mind, by an unstable girl named Marjorie Hale, who eventually drops him for an older man. Toward the end of this period Tim and Rachel seem to be approaching some kind of accommodation. Red, a rival, has been disposed of, partly because Tim becomes a better runner. Tim and Rachel have one idyllic evening under the Lombardies at Bower's Mansion, but shortly thereafter Mrs. Hazard dies of cancer, the Hazard family breaks up, and Rachel goes away to college. End Book 1.

Book 1 often mentions the various sorts of trembling leaves, especially those of young aspens, which are linked to "the nuclear," which has something to do, also, with sustaining "the magic wilderness of the spirit." It appears in both persons and things. Later, when Tim has become more retrospective, we learn that it moves in sensitive recipients and can be felt better than described. Burns's songs are nuclear, but Milton's *Paradise Lost,* although a mighty work, is not. Neither is Bach, although the *Pathétique* is. During this time Tim experiences the nuclear mainly through its effects; if he can get himself into harmony and in tune with his surroundings, he can run unbeatably—"running with the stallion," he calls it. (He had been entranced by a wild stallion at Pyramid Lake, probably the same stallion that is the protagonist in the short story "The Rise and the Passing of Bar.") Touched by the nuclear, Tim even finds he can compose a bit.

Starting Book 2, Tim goes into his "dark period." He is bored by the trivial jazz he is expected to write, and tries to compose more serious music, sleeping and eating precariously. We find out more about the nuclear, mostly in flashbacks. Tim encounters Rachel; she has become a social worker, and is now mature enough to recognize that Tim, not she, is the profound character, a dedicated and perceptive artist. They climb the neighboring Mount Rose, play at believing she is being initiated into the sanctuaries of the local gods, and take a ritual swim in a sacred lake. She goes back to her job, and Tim never sends the letter he writes her. Meanwhile Lawrence Black has become a recognized artist, a highly innovative and creative one, who wants to paint what he feels, but is thwarted. He has married a wealthy woman named Helen, who wants him to do fashionable portraits that will sell. Tim and Lawrence have developed great community of feeling; they eat steaks and drink beer together, the latter in moderate quantities, especially at Pyramid Lake and at the Blacks' cabin in the Peavine quarter, but if they talk much about art, we do not hear them.

Eventually both Tim's spirits and his finances improve. He reencounters Mary Turner, who still loves him. She works for an eccentric in a music store, and she gets her boyfriend a job there. Tim plays occasionally with bands, sometimes doing his own compositions, and during one such session he encounters a maverick musician from Carmel, one Knute Fenderson. Tim has been writing at various abortive pieces, including a major work about the city of trembling leaves, of which he has burned his various starts. Knute encourages him, and he follows Knute to Carmel. There he meets more musicians, plays in a quartet, and eventually graduates into highly professional bands, both jazz and semiclassical. Knute proves to be an eloquent teacher of musical composition, but also a great troll of a man. There is also a conductor-composer, Teddy Quest, and a journalist, Stephen Granger, who concocts droll, satiric tales, some of which are introduced into the narrative. Meanwhile, Tim goes on burning his musical compositions. He has an affair with an intriguing but troubled girl named Eileen Connor, but little comes of it, except more incinerated music, including a piece called "The Stone Woman."[1] Having corresponded again with Mary Turner, he decides to go back to Reno and marry her. She passionately agrees.

Tim learns from Helen that his friend Lawrence has gone off somewhere, and she is worried about him. Tim goes to the Blacks' plush home in Beverly Hills, where he finds Helen and her friends intolerable and learns that Lawrence has been seeking something, apparently artistic truth and new techniques, and finding some of both, especially in remote parts of Nevada such as Austin and Virginia City. Tim traces Lawrence and overtakes him in Death Valley in time to save him from death by desiccation and heat. The two of them live an idyllic sort of life in a desert hangout while Lawrence recovers enough to travel. Before Tim and Lawrence go separate ways we learn more about Lawrence's search for art in remote places. Mary and Tim are married and indulge in a deeply satisfying honeymoon at Lake Tahoe, almost marooned in snow. Tim now has the peace of mind to write his symphony, *The City of Trembling Leaves*, along with other music imbued with a primitive sense of religion. We last see him, now several years a contented husband and father, watching his children become aware of a little aspen.

Genesis

That is the novel read as a sequence of events, an approach that Clark himself would probably have approved: he believed that all readers should make their own assessment of a work of art. Furthermore, some of the people whom Clark liked to drink beer with, common folk generally free of cant and hypocrisy, would be likely to read the novel as a good yarn, if they would at all read a book so long and speculative. But that is not the way most critics read the book; they tended to apply the commonly recognized canons of criticism. The more academic of them pointed out that *The City* is an "apprenticeship novel,"[2] one in which a person, usually a young man who has gotten himself into some sort of trouble, journeys for a time, has various adventures, matures in the process, and goes home to marry "the girl" and become a success of some sort. Obviously, the category fits *The City*, which not only exhibits the broad classification by plot, but adopts some of the minor characteristics. Chapter titles such as "In Which Tim Becomes a Pack of Hounds in the Enchanted Wilderness" reflect the elaborate titles of the older novels, except that Clark's titles tend to be ironic and whimsical. Likewise, as in many eighteenth-century tales, characters in the story introduce lesser narratives—witness the satirical tales of Stephen Granger. Obviously, Clark was imitating the older genre. He was well read in literary history, and knew what he was doing, but the parody of a by-gone day does little for all but a few modern readers. Even for them it may not offer much except a precedent for casual plotting. The whimsical titles grow sparser as the story advances, and were omitted from the paperback edition.

A few of the more artistic critics praised the book, most of them with reservations. Sterling North, in the *New York Post*, predicted that "Clark will shortly become a cult," but many commentators found the novel variously flawed. Perhaps typical is the review by Edward A. Laycock in the *Boston Globe:* "It is an imperfect but vital piece of work, tremendously moving, long-winded, but never dull. It is not tight and compact, but formless and sprawling, as is America." Orville Prescott, in *The New York Times*, thought it had too much of almost everything, including too many characters and "too much youthful sex." The *New Republic* called it a "hugely uninteresting success." Paul Engle liked it, saying there is "a great deal of earth in the book," but added, "sometimes too much." Wallace Stegner called it "exciting," but added: "it is in part overwritten." Jennings Rice, in the *Herald-Tribune*, said *The City* "possesses a magic charm of its own," but found it uneven and generally too long, as did several critics. One called it "disappointing yet distinguished. . . . Clark begins by being intriguing; he ends by being interminable." Most frequently derogated were the monologues, although only a few reviewers found them dull. Ray West, writing in the *New Mexico Quarterly*, characterizes *The City* as an attempt "to express the emotional relationship of a man to a particular natural scene," and says it might be called "Portrait of the Artist as a Westerner." Writing some six months after the book was published, he concluded, "It is pretty much agreed by now" that *The City* is "an advance over . . . *The Ox-Bow Incident*," but if so, a good many commentators must have changed their minds without announcing the fact.

Some of the more journalistic critics offered what seemed like the obvious explanation for the supposed faults of the novel. Like many young writers, they conjectured, Clark had written an autobiographical novel. Jejune, it was rejected. With time, Clark learned how to write a novel and *The Ox-Bow* became a best seller. To cash in on his success, Clark resurrected the older manuscript, but he or the publisher or both rushed The City into print with inadequate revision. This explanation looked plausible, except that five years had elapsed between The Ox-Bow and The City, which should have provided time enough for revision, if only time was needed.

Most charges of weaknesses in The City are not easily disposed of, but this one can now be put to rest. Clark made a practice of ignoring adverse criticisms, but he did firmly reject this description of The City when anybody raised the subject, most quotably in answer to a question put him by Max Westbrook:

> No—The City of Trembling Leaves was not written before Ox-Bow and published later. That assumption, I think—and the question has been put to me often—arises from another equally incorrect assumption—that the book is intensely autobiographical—and was just one of those things every young writer has to get out of his system. Another reaction—common to nearly all the reviewers—whether they liked the book or not—arose from those assumptions, I believe—that City was a loose, picaresque novel, a mere loose, sequential accumulation of remembered experiences. . . . I did make several bad passes at something like The City before I wrote Ox-Bow—but the book as printed was a complete reconception, and no part of it was written before Ox-Bow. Nor is it anything like as autobiographical as has been generally assumed.[3]

I believe we must accept this statement as essentially true. Clark was a meticulously and conscientiously honest man. He would not knowingly have lied about himself, and although any of us can be mistaken, this is not a detail that Clark might readily have forgotten about. Furthermore, there are reasons to believe that Clark's statement provides a judicious and essentially accurate description of both the inception and the content of The City.

We have few Clark manuscripts prior to 1938; he must have burned a great deal of paper before returning to the West, but his statement accords with the evidence from later manuscripts. He says he made "several bad passes at something like

The City" before *Ox-Bow*, but that the book as it was printed "was a complete reconception, and no part of it was written before *Ox-Bow*." As we have seen, Clark tended to incinerate anything that savored of a "bad pass"—he must have been a true Savonarola for consigning his own brain children to the pyre. With him a rewriting, particularly after a lapse of years, tended to start with a reconception, to include a fresh start from the first word, and to continue as a newly inspired piece of writing, not chunks of an older structure stuck together with fresh mortar. Even a revision is likely to suggest an earlier draft at least partly from the fact that themes and symbols recur in Clark, not necessarily because he has lifted a paragraph out of its old context and has given it a new direction.

As might be expected, much of Clark's early work had autobiographical leanings. As its Christmas greeting for 1930 the family used a narrative poem, "verse and cover design copyrighted by Walter Van Tilburg Clark," in which a disturbed writer from San Francisco builds a cabin on a lake beneath a peak, spends a winter snowbound, and finds peace and understanding after talking with a Christlike visitor.[4] One need have little doubt as to who this disturbed writer is; Clark had recently spent some time in the Bay area, and the snowbound winter suggests Tim and Mary's honeymoon at Lake Tahoe. The peak and the lake parallel Mount Rose and the lake beneath it, both of which occur as spiritual settings in autobiographical scenes in several of Clark's works. Likewise, "Ten Women in Gale's House" recalls Clark's having visited Thor House, and reminds one of the Carmel sections of *The City* and Clark's summer with his family in Carmel, where he met an eccentric musician who is probably the ancestor of Knute Fenderson and other Carmel oddities. And one would expect Clark's juvenilia to include various sorts of Arthurian tomfoolery that antedated the Tristram daydreams in both *The City* and *The Watchful Gods*. But such earlier bits that appear also in *The City* can be no more than "bad passes." All the evidence suggests that Clark had not learned to write mature prose until after he left Vermont; anything he did before about 1934 could not have been incorporated into his mature work without being conspicuous.

The legend persists among the Clark family—I have heard it from several of its members, including Walter's mother— that Walter wrote a version of *The City*, then wrote *Ox-Bow*, then rewrote *The City*, which was then published. This account must have foundation, although what Euphemia Clark would have considered a novel might have been what her son would have deprecated as a "bad pass." Robert Clark has found evidence that his father did an autobiographical piece about 1935, and he is known to have burned a manuscript, presumably autobiographical, in the summer of 1937. Some earlier version seems to have been a long philosophical discussion, including talk of "multiplicity" and "idealism," between the fictional "Walt Clark" and Tim Hazard. Some of this survived, much reconceived, in the Prelude to *The City* and in the talk about "the nuclear." It probably represents an important stage in Clark's thinking, but it must have been reconceived and much more than revised before it could have become *The City* or any large part of it.

An earlier draft of *The City* has now come to light, started presumably at Indian Springs in 1941—*Ox-Bow* was published in 1940—and continued when Clark had returned to Cazenovia. He was very firm, however, that this was not Walter Van Tilburg Clark's autobiography. He writes:

> I am not Tim Hazard, nor did I ever behold, nor did ever exist, the people and deeds which will probably encumber and shine upon his slow circular progress. And what's more, I shall even do my best to make the love and life of Tim Hazard himself a befogging vision of absolute unreality, not a voice to be heard, not a place in it, in spite of their names, to be actually found. I shall even do my best to mix up time, to so indissolubly entangle past, present, future, and never was, that finally even the most ancient and alert citizen of Reno will give up, and understand the eternal nature of his city.

This draft, dashed off at Clark's usual furious pace, led to rewrites, at least some of which have survived. A version went to the publisher, who wanted it cut to about half—the rumor is that some two hundred thousand words were expunged. Clark obliged, but also rebuilt the manuscript, working on it almost to the date of publication. In short, no extensive juvenilia have survived that Clark could have dug out of a desk drawer to provide a quickie refurbishing to quiet an impetuous publisher. Considering what we know of Clark's writing and publishing history, no such work could have existed, nothing that could conceivably have been reglued to embody the maturity of thought and the sophistication of prose technique that characterize *The City.* And we know so much of what Clark was doing after 1934 that the postulate that he was, during that time, generating another sequence of autobiographical accounts that were scrubbed up to become *The City* is equally unbelievable.

Autobiographical?

Most of the other charges against the book reflect individual taste, but one other matter is subject to somewhat objective examination: the autobiographical element in *The City.* Of course the book is autobiographical, if not "intensely" so. Every creative book is autobiographical; no one can create what he has not experienced, at least intellectually and emotionally. Clark need not have undergone such events physically; he was not himself hanged, nor did he hang anybody else, but he must have lived through something like death by rope when in the *Ox-Bow* he recounted Martin's writing the letter to his wife and young Tetley's refusing to become a hangman. But *The City* is more autobiographical than is *Ox-Bow,* and nobody who has read the two books and knew the author can doubt it.

Clark had special reason for insisting that the book was not "intensely autobiographical." When it was published various local people were shocked; some were horrified at what their offspring had learned, and might still be learning, at Orvis Ring School: anatomy that was not included in the school curriculum. They were troubled also because the book was widely accepted as a roman à clef; girlfriends of Tim Hazard and Lawrence Black were linked with various matrons, now happily married or unhappily divorced. All this must have pained Clark; as I have indicated before, he was a gentle, kindly man. That he now found he had not been sufficiently discreet in the words he had written—words that once published could never be withdrawn—and that he had encouraged gossip about friends whom he had loved and who had loved him, must have disturbed him very deeply.

Without any question, Walter Van Tilburg Clark and Timothy Hazard are intimately linked. Even the minutiae attest this; the cartoons that Tim scrawled on the school blackboards must be the same as those "colored chalk cartoons that Clark drew on the blackboards all over the school." Little girls like Mary of *The City* must have been among those "twenty or twenty-five deathless loves, only a couple of whom ever knew about it." In fact, the whole account of Clark at Orvis Ring School so much parallels the adventures of Timothy Hazard at Orvis Ring School that one would expect there was an original for the Lucy who tried to seduce Tim in the school basement, except that such a tale is probably not one that Clark would have included in an autobiography intended for the schoolchildren who wrote to him. These parallels go on; Tim's teacher, Mrs. Lydia Boone, is obviously Mrs. Lybbie C. Booth, Clark's teacher at Orvis Ring. Clark, as a young athlete, teamed with a high-school friend in tournament doubles. There is no doubt that Tim's best friend, the artist Lawrence Black, is Walter Clark's best friend, the artist Robert Caples, to whom, significantly, *The City* is dedicated. Robert Clark has pointed out that sequences in the latter part of the book reflect Clark's meetings with Caples in Reno in 1937— Clark had made a brief trip west in hope of getting a job—and later at Indian Springs, and on explorations from there. Lawrence's desiccation in Death Valley was a Caples exploit, "right down to the can of tomatoes." Robert Clark recalls an argument between Caples and the elder Clark about the scene in Luigi's bar: Caples felt Clark had romanticized the affair; Clark insisted that he had recorded it accurately, just as it happened. Both Tim and Clark delighted in the *Pathétique*; both loved beer and steaks—on and on. The details, and the corresponding broad outlines, are too numerous to be misleading.

Some of *The City* is obviously not autobiographical, no doubt deliberately not so. Young Walter did not grow up on the

wrong side of the tracks with a sort of lumberyard foreman for
a father, addicted to playing horseshoes. He lived in the presi-
dential mansion (though there were trembling leaves outside
the window, as there were outside the fictional house by the
racetrack) and his father had been an economist with an international reputation, professor at a reputable college before he
became president of a small university. His mother was an artistic, well-read, witty woman who had studied to be a concert
musician. Neither of his sisters resembled Tim Hazard's sister,
and Walter's brother is a distinguished physician and surgeon,
not the crafty, opportunistic dropout who is Tim's brother Willis. Walter's wife Barbara was not his childhood idol, the
onetime virgin of Pyramid Lake; he met her at the University
of Nevada.[5]

But the number and extent of these links between young
Walter Clark and Tim Hazard are not much to the point. That
Clark, with the Ox-Bow printed, or at least gone to press, decided to write a novel making extensive use of his own childhood and youth would seem to be obvious. That Clark used his
own experiences and those of his close friend Caples are matters of no small interest for the novelist's sources and his
methods of working, but they are of only secondary concern
when we consider what the author was trying to do in the book,
and why he elected to put it together as he did. Accordingly,
we have to ask ourselves whether there may not be a third way
in which The City can be read, not that of the reader mainly
interested in a sequence of events, nor that of the critic who
expects a serious novel to be closely knit and neatly polished,
a linear journal in time that leads to something approaching
a conclusion.

We must assume so. If Clark's second published novel was
in some ways inferior to his first he was not alone in this, but
to accept the charge that the author of The Ox-Bow and such
masterpieces as "Hook" and "The Wind and the Snow of
Winter"—all written prior to The City—did not understand
conventional plotting is to tolerate nonsense. Obviously,
Clark knew how to build a tight plot if he wanted to. If he did
not shape a plot neatly before 1932, we may attribute the blun-

der to youthful incompetence; but if Clark declined to plot a story in a conventional manner after 1940, he did so because he preferred something else. We might note also that Clark on several occasions said that he liked *The City* best of his novels, though he may have thought "The Watchful Gods" his best writing. He sometimes qualified the statement by saying that he had personal reasons for the choice, and no doubt the auto-biographical matter in the novel influenced his preference, but we should recall that Clark was a stubborn self-critic, and that he knew good writing when he saw it.

Symphonic Structure

Robert Clark has told me that his father said that of all the reviewers of *The City*, Professor Charles Denecke of the University of Scranton had come the closest to understanding the intent of the novel. The elder Clark did not elaborate, but the passage he must have had in mind—the review is mostly sum-mary—is as follows:

> **The City of Trembling Leaves is a story of extraordinary beauty and charm. Its effect is like that of a symphony which, beginning softly, gradually works up to a series of crescendos. What seems at first to be a jungle of unimportant incident and irrelevant detail shapes itself gradually into unified meaning.**

This hint at the structure of the novel finds confirmation in Clark's notes for the book and in the final version itself.[6] In his plans for the novel, cited above, he assumes that the plot will be circular, not linear; he refers to "the people and deeds which will probably encumber and shine upon [Tim's] slow circular progress." The final chapter is entitled, "In which the Circle Closes," and we should recall that the title, *The City of Trembling Leaves*, serves as the name of both the book by Walter Clark and the symphony by Tim Hazard. Referring to that, Clark provides a long list of persons, places, and events in the novel and explains, "The music arose from these, but it led it-self onward, and told no stories. It was whole, circular, com-plete, and in the last rustling notes the question was there as much as in the first. There was no answer, but the question didn't die." This perpetual question appears on the first page, "the trees of Reno have regional meanings within their one meaning, like themes and transitions of a one-movement symphony." And the last words of the novel, as we have observed above, tell of an aspen leaf released from a child's grasp, which immediately "began to dance again, by itself." That is, life is a circle, endless, or it should be, and a work of art that expresses this life will be circular if it embodies the unity of humankind and the universe. Tim ends the book a happy man because he has found a unity for himself in his love of Mary and the creation of music; Tim's friend Lawrence goes off to Salt Lake City because he has not. Tim has found peace in the assurance that "the sacred Truckee Meadows would never check the trembling leaves." Lawrence goes to Salt Lake City because there, at least, he found a man devoted to "the unhappiness of beauty, for which there are no words."

Before endeavoring to apply such theories we should note that *The City* is not a monolith; much that can be said about parts of it would not apply to all of it. Notably, it breaks into two, a division emphasized by the author when he divided it into Books 1 and 2. The two differ in style, content, and much else. Book 1 takes Tim through high school; it is rather consistently chronological, and probably represents Clark's youth in its essentials, even to personalities and incidents, altered only superficially. It concludes with the "fall of the House of Hazard," the exposition of "the nuclear" and its application to Tim's ideas and ideals. Book 2 takes Tim from his "dark period" of doubt and uncertainty, his sexual and artistic inhibitions, to his marriage and the writing of his symphony. It is set only partly in Reno, contains many events devised for the purpose along with incidents reordered—the Death Valley sequence took place during Clark's stay at Indian Springs, the Pyramid Lake episode during a trip west in 1937, though the order is reversed in *The City*. The style of Book 1 might be called avuncular, with the fictional "Walt Clark" observing the antics of teenagers with amused curiosity; Book 2 is at once more tense and more objective. We hear little of "the nuclear," but much about the search of thwarted artists.

This variety no doubt reflects in part the various stages in the growth of the manuscript. How early Clark started writing his "bad passes" at an autobiographical novel we do not know, but presumably he destroyed a draft of this sort in the late summer of 1937, or soon thereafter, one that he perhaps started the previous year, or was prompted by a trip west, when he saw his old friend Robert Caples and laid the foundation for the Pyramid Lake and Peavine Quarter episodes in *The City*.

The earliest draft that survives is incomplete, but is long enough to fill seven notebooks of very fine script, begun at Indian Springs, late 1941 or early 1942, worked on at Cazenovia and Essex, New York, and laid aside in 1943 or 1944. It relies on long discussions between the adult Tim Hazard and "Walt Clark," the narrator. Some of its character can be inferred from its title: *Autobiography: Or the Biography of Flesh Become One With the Intellect With the World*. It contains much of what became Book 1, along with parts of what was to become Book 2, with notes for other chapters. The printed version is clearly founded on it, although whole sections were removed, inserted, or extensively revised, often by the increase, sentence by sentence, of objective detail.

The draft has the philosophy if not the charm of the printed version. In line after line, in scene after scene, Clark is making real the art he had laboriously learned, but the theme of the novel is made even more clear in passages expunged from the printed version. There Tim explains:

> [He had been] a dweller in two worlds, unconsciously intent upon uniting them, upon bringing into his actual life the glory and movement of his dreams. . . . Through the love of Rachel this love of life began to be the test of his acts. This direction could not have been possible for him without the trembling leaves, and that abundance of being beyond the human which is part of what they represent to Reno. These themes are not separable. They *are* aspects of one theme.

Later he puts the same attitude this way:

> If Rachel gave me the world, on the mountain, Louise [the Eileen Connor of the printed version] taught me that I still wasn't living in it.

That is, Book 2 differs from Book 1 partly because it reflects
more of the Walter Clark of 1945, less of what survived from
the 1941–43(?) version, and possibly from the 1937 attempt
and other "bad passes."

Thus, if the structure is circular, if there are wheels within
wheels, if it is symphonic, and if it is built upon recurring
themes—as I believe it is—we need not be surprised if these
evidences do not appear equally in all parts of the book. The
most frequent theme is that of the trembling leaves, which is
associated with expectancy and creativity. Clark explains that
it is identical with the Mary Turner plus the Rachel plus the
Marjorie Hale plus the Eileen Connor plus the Mary theme.
It is various enough to encompass the book, from the first two
sentences to the last two, and in various circles between.

A contrasting theme is the internal conflict, expressed in the
oft-repeated phrases *Rachel vs. Rachel, Lawrence vs. Lawrence,
Timothy vs. Timothy,* and the like. These are many, and some
of them, such as the incident involving Doris, an alcoholic
poet, are treated lightly. With Doris it scarcely becomes a
theme at all; Tim chats with her a few times, and she disappears, but she enters enough into the pattern of Tim's being
that she is mentioned months later, during the scene at Luigi's
Bar. Many of the themes are recognized as such: the turtle
theme, the Court Street theme, the moss agate, sacramental
bathing, Mt. Rose, and on and on.

Construction by themes seems to me more characteristic of
Book 1 than of Book 2. If there are movements of the sort that
build up to Denecke's crescendos, they are more readily traced
in Book 2, which can be broken rather readily into three parts:
(1) set in Reno, ending with the coming of Fenderson and
Tim's tearing down the primitive prayer he had hung on the
wall; (2) set mainly in Carmel, and ending with *The Stone
Woman,* Tim's "vilest act," and his proposal to Mary; (3) set
in various places from the Black mansion in Beverly Hills to
the Reno area, and closing with the idyllic winter at Lake
Tahoe and the writing of Tim's symphony. These movements
could be broken into submovements, and they account in part
for the great number of characters who appear and then vanish

for good; they are parts of only one movement in the sym-phony.[7]

The most extensive attempt to provide a fresh view of *The City*—along with almost everything else that Clark pub-lished—is that of Max Westbrook, cited above. He reads the novel in light of Jungian archetypes and oriental concepts of sacrality:

> *The City of Trembling Leaves* is a study of a sacred youth who lives in a profane age. . . . As a novel of adventures into the sacred world, [it] is structured in terms appropriate to cyclical time [p. 73]. . . . It is a story primarily of spiritual growth in a moribund city [p. 74]. . . . Clark is seeking some image beyond words, a sense of unity which is nonverbal and yet American . . . a consciously realistic and therefore ironic ver-sion. . . . The analogy between music and the life of Tim Haz-ard is that music, like life, must be apprehended in parts, in linear time, yet is real only as a complete whole. Man lives in pieces, lives in the minutiae of the given day a life which is real only insofar as he attains to unity. It is for this reason that Clark describes in such detail Tim's schooldays [p. 76]. . . . The primary cause of irony is that sacrality tempts the be-liever to dreams of perfection, and this temptation—which represents the chief psychological danger of the sacred man—is the subject of [the novel] [p. 77]. . . . [which] is a story of a primal nature in twentieth-century America. . . . a story of the ancient quest for the golden answer [p. 80]. . . . Book I . . . is a lyrical and ironic record of Tim's wavering progress toward a realistic sense of the sacred, from abstract images of himself and the world through a more concrete image of him-self as an ironically comic yet holy member of a realistic world [p. 85]. . . . The nuclear . . . is Clark's version of the ar-chetypal, the sacred. . . . the central principle of art, religion, and life [p. 86]. . . . In Book II the trembling leaves have not been explained, and there is no guarantee for tomorrow, no suggestion that Tim became a great composer and lived hap-pily ever after, but some shape, at least for this time, has been given to primal reality, a shape which is realistic to life in the moribund city, beneath the shadow of the indifferent Moun-tain [p. 90].

No sequence of excerpts like this can do justice to Westbrook's thesis. The entire chapter is required reading, and it should be viewed in the context of at least Westbrook's first two chapters, in which he endeavors to establish the existence of something he calls "western sacrality." This western growth is rooted, he believes, in the human need for myth, which is expressed in unconscious archetypal ideas. For western writers these are at once an inspiration and a plague, because they inhabit land so new to white men that there is virtually no history in which to seek their own roots. Westbrook believes he finds evidence of this "western sacrality" in all serious western writers—Vardis Fisher, Wallace Stegner, John Steinbeck—and perhaps especially in Clark, because he was an unusually sensitive, conscientious, dedicated person.[8]

One should point out—because Westbrook has frequently been misread—that he is not suggesting that Clark encountered Jungian archetypes and then fashioned his fiction to dramatize such ideas, nor is he suggesting any approach to such a thesis. He insists that Clark's beliefs are his own and strictly American, even strictly western, but that they parallel oriental and some Jungian thought, and that Clark's work can be illuminated by noticing these similarities. He particularly likes archetypal philosophy as embodied in Mircea Eliade.[9]

Westbrook's beliefs must have some validity. *The City*, with its shifting pattern of characters and action, its protracted, undirectable seeking, its sudden and nonlogical solutions, does not make sense—to say nothing of the highly adult sense that would content a keen intellect such as Clark's—without some sort of deep-seated philosophical conviction. This "western sacrality," as Westbrook fully recognizes, is similar to what Clark called "the nuclear," and is suggestive of what Tim called "primary realism." Clark divides Tim's human world into "dreamers," the primary realists, and "factualists, or secondary realists," who must have included almost everybody else; they were "in their usual numerical superiority." And we can scarcely avoid noticing that, although Tim Hazard was a generally rational, sensible person, anything creative that went sing-ingly with him, whether it was running a race or developing a musical theme, responded to something in him that he could encourage but could not firmly control, some sort of harmony, a balance between him and something he could sense, mostly without understanding it.

One corollary of Westbrook's thesis, of course, is that creative work at its best must be rooted in the unconscious. Probably most generators of serious modern fiction believe something of this sort. Even a writer as hard-fisted and hard-working as Hemingway believed it, but Westbrook notices that Clark trusted something nonconscious to an unusual degree. When Tim Hazard, now happily married and surrounded by the purity of white snow, found that he could at last write his symphony, Clark said it "came," and he said similar things about himself. He seemed to feel that when his writing was good enough, it came fast; or if it was so bad that he had to throw it away, it had not "come." In an interview on *The Track of the Cat*, Clark was quoted:

> When I started work in transforming the poem to a novel, the story bogged down. The male characters wouldn't come alive. I was trying to follow the same story line as the poem, and I couldn't find that discovery, or anxiety, I needed in order to write. I just couldn't get the male characters away from the breakfast table. Then, one morning, after many nights of thinking about the problem, I put the mother in the story, and the story came alive for me. She was a new character and highly motivating for the men in the story. Then came the daughter and the girl friend, and the story really took off.[10]

Clark is using conventional terminology here, but the words can probably be thought of as strongly descriptive. He "started work." The characters "wouldn't come alive." He spent many nights of "thinking about the problem." When he got things right, with two sexes instead of one, "the story came alive for me." Then he provided some younger women and "the story really took off."

In part, Clark confirmed Westbrook's analysis. He mentioned to me that he had seen the book in manuscript, and praised it cordially. Being the kindly person he was, he would not have wanted to appear carping, particularly concerning a book about himself, but he was also honest enough that he would not have said much in praise unless he meant it. I had the distinct feeling he was surprised at how much Westbrook had divined, as though Westbrook had told him things about himself that he himself had not observed before. Robert Clark reports that his father praised the book, and he tells me he had much the same impression I did, that his father believed that Westbrook had found implications in *The City* that were genuinely in the book, although Clark the author had not consciously put them there.

This much I remember for certain, that Clark said Westbrook had understood more than had most of the critics. And in this connection one should add that Westbrook's basic ideas so permeate his volume that Clark could scarcely have approved any of it without subscribing to much of it. One might notice also that in answer to one of Westbrook's written questions, Clark declared his preference for "oriental faiths and philosophies," which he preferred generally to European thinkers whom he considered "divisive," and added to the list of his favorite reading "all primitive faiths, philosophies, folklores, especially those of the American Indians," which he characterized as "unifying and inclusive."

On the other hand, I should add that Westbrook's Clark does not sound to me like the Walter Clark I knew. I never heard him expound anything so systematic, so philosophically ordered, so intellectually distant, so burdened with archetypal terminology as is Westbrook's study. I have heard him counseling students by the hour. He always approached the student's paper as composition, talking about scenes, characters, and style, never about providing philosophical significance for the story. He believed that writing had to come out of the writer, and I never heard him suggest that students whose work was inadequate should build themselves up by reading books about ideas. Various students have made similar observations, that Clark talked about writing as expression and art, not as a veil to be cast over philosophy.

Meanwhile, we should recognize that nobody—Walter Clark or anybody else—is one thing, always and ever. Writers expand and shrink, and they undergo changes that cannot be described either way. In the years after Ox-Bow Clark was inevitably more concerned with criticism—criticism of his own books and the reviewing of other books. He was more caught up in the juggling of ideas that is much of the terminology-in-trade of critics, especially of academic critics.

On the other hand, idea permeates Clark's work, all of it. Some kind of moral, or principle, or admonition, or something thematic and symbolic can be found in all his writings, even the briefest, such as "The Rapids" and "Why Don't You Look Where You're Going?" He was, himself, aware of this quality, and apparently wanted it that way; we have seen above that his later manuscripts are sprinkled with admonitions to himself to realize his underlying purposes in overt character and action. He wrote with people and place, with talk and action, but he wrote for the theme, and this fact surfaces, as such underlying convictions are inclined to surface, in both expected and unexpected places. We might recall that Walter's final sentence to his young admirers (see chapter 17, below) concludes as follows: "I have several . . . [stories] in mind, all dealing . . . with various happenings, ideas, and beliefs about which I still have strong feelings." He does not say he has various characters in mind; he says he has "happenings, ideas, and beliefs."

Cyclical Movement

We are entitled to assume, then, that The City is essentially different from Clark's other major published works—although perhaps not essentially different from some of the later works he attempted without ever getting them to the point where they would "come"—and probably different from most of his shorter pieces. As we have observed above, waverings have not gone unnoticed, and on the whole they have been attributed to haste and juvenile incompetence. That explication, I take it, is no longer tenable. We must ask ourselves whether we can find any better explanations of why Clark planned and wrote as he did.

In some ways *The City* does not differ notably from Clark's other works. His tone is different; he is here more relaxed—at least in Book 1—more tolerantly amused by his characters, but this tone is dictated by the reminiscent position of the narrator, not by any fundamental philosophy. Basically, the writing does not differ much; Clark has not lost his craftsmanship, his amazing recall of sharply etched detail, his sense of the wonder and variety of the world around us.

But factually precise reporting probably does not account for the fact that *The City* was Clark's favorite among his own books, as he repeatedly said it was. Almost everyone, apparently, likes to relive his own life and recreate it. Clark seemed to take unusual satisfaction in such yarning, probably in part because he could reconstruct with a sharp-edged accuracy that is denied most of us, who have fuzzy memories when compared with Clark's. But such an explanation must be inadequate; without doubt *The City* lacks qualities triumphantly present in *Ox-Bow* and *The Cat*, virtues that have been identified and applauded by Heilman, Wilner, Stegner, and others. Clark must have known that most of these virtues were there—he put them there—and he must have valued the work for containing them. But he also prized *The City* for somewhat contrasting virtues.

Here we might notice some contrasts within Clark's works, including a tripartite division. It is my own invention, and I am by no means sure Clark would have accepted it, but at least three sorts of writing can be distinguished: the whimsical-satiric, the realistic-symbolic, and the somewhat messianic-symphonic. The first group contains nothing that is now well known; it might be characterized by the novella about a chess-playing poodle. The second is well represented in the *Ox-Bow*, many short stories, and somewhat less clearly in *The Cat*. The third category is best represented among the printed works by *The City*; these last have their realistic qualities, of course, even though the purpose seems not mainly to offer a slice of life. Of the published works, obviously those in the second group are at once the most extensive and the most admired, particularly by the formal critics. An interesting detail, however, is this: Robert Clark, who knows and understands his father's work better than anyone else now living, estimates that if we include the unpublished manuscripts in our survey, then the third sort seems to have been the main stream of Walter Clark's thinking and writing.

I doubt that anybody knows, or is likely to know with any precision, what Clark was trying to do in *The City*, but in a broad way, the answer seems to me obvious. He had something he wanted to tell others. He believed that this underlying truth is dreadfully important, important for him to get said in appropriate form, important for others to hear. He believed he had said more of this, and said it more profoundly in *The City* than in any other of his published works—perhaps not more or better than he hoped to say it in works he expected to live to finish, for which we have even less basis for speculation than we have for the affection he bestowed on *The City*.

What was this idea? I doubt that Westbrook has told us, but he may have come closer than did anyone else, and for that reason especially Clark liked Westbrook's study. Whether or not Clark knew about oriental "sacrality" we have no evidence. He had read widely in oriental philosophy, but I doubt that he elected himself as a "sacred youth." He was too modest for that, but he certainly did nominate both Timothy Hazard/Walter Clark and Lawrence Black/Robert Caples as "idealists," as "primary realists" who had within limits found their way to "the nuclear." Without doubt he felt that an increasingly polluted world—polluted both ecologically and socially—needed to find a better way of life. He probably believed that primary realists such as Lawrence Black and Tim Hazard could help their fellow idealists. He may even have hoped that some of the "secondary realists" might learn how to cultivate the nuclear. Or perhaps his devotion to primitive American Indian thinking had imbued him with the messianic potential of the Two Brothers, a folkloristic belief common among Amerindians.

The City, then, is not a naively conceived attempt to spin a good yarn. It is not mainly a looking glass calculated to reflect the life and times of the artist as a young Westerner. It is not merely a venture toward writing a modern Ox-Bow Incident, although somewhat surprisingly that may be a better epitome than either of the other two. It is a different sort of thing, with different purposes and different techniques—the latter perhaps not well developed, because the author had not previously tried this genre much and he had few models, as the highly experimental Caples had few models for some of his paintings. Of these techniques, the one most widely noted—and deprecated—is the plot. Westbrook has praised it, without saying very exactly how it is good, but he is the only critic I know who has given it more than tacit approval. In general he relates it to primordial rather than sequential time, to circular rather than linear movement.

The contrast will appear if we set a western and an oriental epic side by side. In the Christian Chanson de Roland there are protagonists (Charlemagne, the Douze Peers, the Francs, and the noble Roland) and antagonists (various perfidious pagans). The action mounts to a climax in the treacherous attack at Ronceval, where Roland sounds his horn too late, and reinforcements sent by Charlemagne arrive to find only the corpse-strewn battlefield. The whole is built on the familiar pyramidal plot, each action leading to the next, and the whole resolved after the climax.

An epic such as the Mahabharata, on the other hand, has no antagonists but human nature, no protagonists in the western sense, no sequence of events that leads from a problem through a climax to a solution. The Mahabharata are not fighting for anything, and no one is fighting against them; they have indiscreetly but honorably lost money gambling, and they go into voluntary exile for seven years. These years provide no interrelated sequence of events; they provide stories leading to implied misconduct such as that in the war with the monkey-men, and to triumphant virtue, as in Sita, who exemplifies wifeliness. But there is no climax, and the Mahabharata do not reform as in a Bildungsroman. They come home because they are now grown up. They come home because the seven years have ended; they are still the princes they have always been.

A similar pattern appears in a comparison of The City with

much of Clark's other published work. In *Ox-Bow* the antagonists are the forces of uncivilized brutishness, giving rein to prejudice, violence, hate, fear, and greed, variously embodied in Tetley, Farnley, Monty, Ma Grier, and others. None of them is totally bad, but they combine to support totally bad action. The protagonists are the forces of law and justice, embodied especially in Davies, but also in Gerald, Osgood, Sparks, Art, Gil, and the sense of decency in the community. The plot is a sequence of incidents, each leading to a subsequent event and to the climax when the innocent men are hanged and the posse learns that there is neither a stolen herd nor a murdered man. The action slows as the community adjusts to its sense of guilt. What is almost a minor secondary plot grows out of Davies's propensity for self-guilt, but we can ignore that.

Whatever the plot of *The City* may be, it is not like this. There are no antagonists; nobody wishes Tim or Lawrence harm, and nobody tries to keep them from writing music or painting pictures, albeit Helen wants a different kind of picture and Reno—even Tim's friends—would settle for less than a symphony. Tim and Lawrence are protagonists in the sense that they elicit the reader's sense of involvement, and they do grow into something, survive their frustrations, and Tim, at least, enjoys a well-earned peace of mind. There is something of a train of events; as Tim and Lawrence grow older, different sorts of experiences become natural to them. And some events pursue logical sequences. Tim does arrangements because he had learned some music. Fenster is attracted to Tim because the arrangements show originality. Tim goes to Carmel because of Fenster, and has an affair with a girl, partly because of the glamor that now surrounds a brilliant young musician, but such scattered sequences add up to nothing like an ordered plot. People wander into this book and out of it. Tim's brother leaves home, and it does not matter much, nor does anybody find out what kind of juvenile delinquent he had been. Sunday Wind, an erratic racehorse, does something to bring Rachel and Tim together, but the horse provides an isolated incident and Rachel herself drifts off somewhere and has only a prelimiinary part in Tim's salvation. There is no clear climax leading to a resolution; Tim marries Mary, but she does not do much in the first half of the book but jiggle some, and little in the second half but get Tim a job and not marry anybody else, although during the snowbound honeymoon she picks up the St. Francis theme associated earlier with Tim.

The plot of *The City* is not a tidy sequence in the classic Aristotelian manner; it involves circles aplenty—broad circles and tight circles, circles within one another. There are the intertwining circles of Tim and Lawrence, brilliant and sacralic children who have trouble, each in his own way, finding himself in a world run by and for secondary realists. Likewise, in his own way, each can work toward peace through his art and a new life that gives him something he needs. There is the distinctly separate circle of Mary, who so far as we know longed for little, except possibly Tim and a family, who changes from being The Blessed Virgin of Pyramid Lake, to Saint Mary of the Mountains, and finally to the mother of a little girl sensitive to a trembling aspen. She proceeds through this three-part cycle mostly without knowledge of what roles she is playing, and doing little but say yes with convenient expedition. She has the potential to remain herself and be a good wife.

We have already observed the recurrence of the trembling aspens at key points. In Carmel, Tim flounders while he learns to swim in a life intriguing but for him distractive. Meanwhile, Lawrence flounders in the Sargasso Sea of wealthy dilettantes. Both flee and are reunited in Death Valley. They later consider going back to Pyramid Lake to look at the turtles they made as little boys, but decide not to—they are in a hurry—but the inference is there. The circle is in effect completed, except that both Tim and Lawrence recognize that they are now moving in circles beyond turtles shaped out of mud.

The cyclical movement relies on repetitions, and at the same time promotes them. The doings in which Tim learns how cushiony girls can be are repeated in party after party, from each of which Tim goes on to another plane of his learning. These probably include the week at Pyramid Lake when Tim and Lawrence drink beer and eat steaks and Helen very much does not fit into the community they share. Tim's love for Rachel comes to a sort of fruition in the ritual swim in the lake below Mount Rose. One cycle, which I assume must have been deliberate, and is so extensive that it underlies the broad structure of Book 2, concerns Clark's beliefs about artistic creativity. Notice the following sequences: (1) Tim escapes the humdrum life of Reno; (2) he learns more music in Carmel; (3) he has an affair that is trivial, not to say tawdry; (4) he writes a piece of music called "The Stone Woman," which he destroys. Tim's needs, neither artistic nor sexual, can be satisfied by a stone woman. Later (1) Tim escapes the Sargasso Sea of artistic triviality; (2) he discusses art and life with his fellow-creator, Black; (3) he marries his childhood sweetheart and lives among the heaped-up purity of deep snow; (4) he writes his symphony. There are dozens of such echoes, big and little, brief and attenuated, isolated or interlocking. Which of these are accident and which follow from planned structure I am not usually sure, nor do I believe Clark was, at least not always consciously.

Thus much of the meandering quality of *The City* grows from a plotting that is not the traditional sequence associated with the five-act drama. Consequently, many scenes and characters that may seem irrelevant, and would be if *The City* had been built along a straight line, or a pyramidal line, may not be if the book is built on a pattern of circles. The long account of how Tim lost and then won a race with Red is not well plotted if it is about one boy losing the first race and winning the second, and another losing both a race and his girlfriend; if it tells only how Tim grew a little closer to a girl whom he was eventually going to forget about anyhow. But the scene is not about winning or losing high-school track meets; it is about the nuclear, human nature, the futility of triumph, and probably some other things. It has its place in the "slow circular progress" of the novel, not in a line that passes through it in going from beginning to end. Probably no one who moves within the western literary tradition knows how to do circular plotting, and how consciously Clark was flirting with the technique neither he nor we know very well.

In spite of such waivers and apologetics, however, I doubt

that Clark can be entirely exonerated from having published what is at times a prolix book. Much of *The City* is excellent, and I do not see how anyone can fail to recognize what is for me a fact, not an opinion. But I cannot justify all parts of the book, and I do not know anyone who has. I personally enjoy the Quests and their cats, although I do not see how they help the progression of the book much. I am glad Walter included "The Sweet Promised Land"; that way it was spared the flames that consumed other pieces. As for the Luigi interlude, it may be "just the way it happened in Tonopah," but I doubt that it should have happened that way in *The City*. And why are we exposed, at such length, to the poseur and impostor to whom Helen most gullibly becomes a gull? Did it really need to take that many pages for Lawrence to recover from his burning in Death Valley?[11] The list could become a long one.

How consciously Clark shifted from one type of plotting to another is not clear. Without doubt he deliberately set out to write an experimental novel, and he would have known instinctively that an Aristotelian plot leading to catharsis by pity and terror, well suited to the progress of an emotive tale, is not well suited to philosophic revelation. And he would have known he was writing a moral work, the sort of thing that in the West has often taken the form of allegory, but allegory was foreign to Clark's ways of feeling and thinking. Faced with the plotting of a philosophical tale, did he consciously turn to oriental storytelling for models? Or did he, knowing well the value of recurrence of theme, work himself into something approaching cyclical plotting? Either answer would seem plausible, and the correct one may appear only when Clark's correspondence is examined more carefully than it has been, or other letters become available.

One might reconstruct the growth of *The City* somewhat as follows: Clark set out to write a novel embodying his major philosophic, social, and psychological ideas, a sort of theology as such structures were conceived in the Middle Ages, the summation of all major truth. He would use the material he knew best; in that way he could write best. Inevitably, this material would be autobiographical, but he would avoid the pitfalls of autobiographical writing, both for the progress of the book and for its local impact, by scrambling the details beyond recognition. Now Clark the spinner of yarns and Clark the maker of myths—Robert Clark points out that his father tended to romanticize all people and places he came to love—took over more than Clark the artist had ever intended they should. With his almost total recall, he was inundated in material, and as Tim grew older and had the wider experiences of young Walter Clark to pillage, the confusion grew. The book ballooned out of all proportion, and the publisher counseled drastic cutting. Clark obliged, but being Clark, he also enlarged. Tim Hazard sometimes found that he could not say anything without saying too much, and Walter Clark found that at times he could not write anything without writing too much; the evidence is scattered all through the unpublished manuscripts. This process went on, cutting by excising, expanding by rewriting, until the publisher or Clark or both decided that five years was long enough, and the book came out without ever being quite finished or sufficiently pruned and honed.

Thus *The City* is a rich and varied book that offers many things to many readers. Clark recognized it as his most ambitious book, and he apparently felt that if it was not entirely successful—and he was troubled that others thought it was not—he believed he had spoken more seriously here than he had in any other finished and published volume. Some readers have been bothered by it because they have tried to make it into the second step after *Ox-Bow*, something that would lead to *The Track of the Cat*. Inevitably they are thwarted and not infrequently irked. Some Clark fans delight in it; they find here a picture of the period after the Old West—what from our perspective we might call the intermediate West—and they welcome it for what they experience by means of it, quite sensibly ignoring whether it does or does not read like other novels. To some readers it is a genial, happy-ending book that one can live with. Robert Clark tells me that for him it is a sad book torn by the wrenching between Walter Clark the man and Walter Clark the writer. And we are reminded of the oft-repeated observation that all comedy leads ultimately to tears. Some of us treasure it because we like good writing, connected or disconnected, and are attracted more by an unsolved puzzle than we could ever be by a solution.

Notes

1. It seems to share little but the title with a manuscript poem left by Clark.

2. Often called a *Bildungsroman;* the genre is a subclass of what is known as a picaresque novel, the adventures of a *pícaro* (Spanish for "rogue").

3. Max Westbrook, *Walter Van Tilburg Clark* (New York: Twayne, 1969), pp. 65–69. Actually, the first draft of *The City,* worked on from 1941 to 1944, but of course not known to reviewers, adequately refutes any pre-*Ox-Bow* thesis.

4. *Christmas Comes to Hjalsen* (Reno Publ. Co., 1930).

5. In private correspondence Robert Clark has pointed out that in some ways *The City* may be anti-autobiographical, with Tim and others in the book acting as Walter and his acquaintances had not, but the author wished they had.

6. Stegner noted the analogy with musical structure, as did a few others, but reacted adversely: "I am dubious of the confusion of the arts implied in a symphonic novel," he explains, and adds: "we are expected to feel themes coming into the tight texture of the symphonic web."

7. A somewhat similar thesis is mentioned, but not developed, by J. F. Powers, writing in *Accent.* He calls the novel a masterpiece, and says that "it is in motive, concept, structure, and progress, cubic." He does not define "cubic," but quotes several passages on "the nuclear," apparently to that end.

8. One might add that some other writers have found more evidence of Freud than of Jung in Clark's writings.

9. Especially as in *The Sacred and Profane* (New York: Harcourt, 1959).

10. Anthony Amaral, "Walter Van Tilburg Clark: The Writer as Teacher," *Sage,* vol. 2, no. 3, p. 10.

11. This may be an evidence of patching, not quite smoothed over. In the unpublished version the stay at Stovepipe Wells is the occasion for much philosophic talk.

10

On *The Track of the Cat*

Walter Clark

Perhaps the best brief statement about The Track of the Cat *survives in a letter that Clark wrote but never sent. Now in the collection at the University of Nevada, Reno, it was written in Iowa City, Iowa, probably in 1952. Clark wrote four pages in his close, beautiful script, nearly two thousand words. Sometime later he scribbled at the top of the first page: "Never sent—told too much." The letter to which Clark responded had come from a woman whose book club was about to discuss the novel and who, like many another uncertain student, sought clarification of the novel's "meaning" from the author himself. The letter is especially interesting for its indication of Clark's reaction to the comparisons several reviewers had made between his black cat and Melville's white whale, and it certainly re-veals some of his intentions for both the themes and the structure of the novel. Doubtless he then held it back for fear the book club would take it as the final word, something he would not have wanted. As he wrote in an autobiographical statement (see chapter 17): "Something must be left to the reader to find for himself, or there won't be any experience." With that, and the never-ending debate amongst critics concerning authorial intention in relation to actual achievement as a caution, it is here printed, with the text lightly cut, and edited in punctuation. A number of contributors to this volume have discussed* The Cat *(see chapters 3, 4, 15, and 16).*

Along with several other rather basic questions, the woman had asked: Was the black cat real?

I n the first place, yes, there was a real black cat, the one that Curt took his first shot at, the one that Harold and Joe Sam finally killed in the box canyon. But, as Joe Sam says, unless they find this one (and there really are such "black" mountain lions—the color of these cats varies greatly with the country they normally inhabit, and the season of the year. I have seen them all the way from an ashen grey—brush country in winter—through rufus—California red-earth foothill country—to very dark—"black"—Sierra evergreen country—like that in the story—remember this is an unusually early storm) dead in the willows, "it's not the black painter"—not him . . . him being a mythical cat, an avenger, whom he sees at first as the instrument of the gods to bring about the end of the Indian, but sees in the story, after years on the ranch, as now active against the white man too—especially Curt's kind—since the white man has succeeded the Indian as the chief offender against the gods. (As, say, a "civilized" man's offense against nature [rising and by his mistaken notion that he can "conquer" nature, as if it were a separate and hostile entity, which, of course, he cannot, since he is himself only a part of nature, and his own very existence depends not upon "conquering" nature but upon fitting himself into its patterns] [Clark's square brackets] is much greater than that of any primitive.) It is this cat, working in his own long-denying mind because of fears and Joe Sam's stories and rituals, which destroys Curt—the materialist, the "conqueror" of nature—and Joe Sam, of course, knows this. He knows how such visions work . . . (note the parallel activities of Joe Sam at the ranch—Book 2—and Curt in the mountains—Book 3—Joe Sam's little rituals of vengeance in the bunk-house coinciding with the critical points of Curt's hunt [i.e., the primitive beginning to work in the materialistic skeptic as soon as he is sufficiently alone and in trouble], his little circling of the ranch, during which he kills the quail, foreshadowing the big circle that brings Curt, without any realization of where he is, back to his death, at his starting point—and Joe Sam's attack on Curt's horse, coinciding with the attack of the vision cat as Curt lies by the fire.) Arthur, of course, would wholly have understood this, but Harold, who has only begun to think as Arthur does, only vaguely senses it, cannot yet get clear of the feeling, not altogether of mere accident. But he is beginning to see, and he realizes that there is a valuable kind of "understanding" in the primitive Joe Sam, which he, like Arthur, must learn to understand, or else act as blindly, and finally fatally as Curt. So the Moby Dick parallel is dangerously misleading—despite the mistaken insistence on it of a number of reviewers who are more at home in cities than in mountains, more believers in the codes of "civilization" than in the laws of nature. Moby Dick, of course, is not "evil" either—in this sense, as a careful reading of the chapter on the whiteness of the whale is enough to demonstrate—he is black and white—unsettled—and either is the color of either good or evil. But he acts merely as a depicter of the god. (Note the sun had images, and then the chapter on the lights in the rigging—which is really in all its form a black mass—in which sun worship is also proven false [the Parsee turning away] and this inscrutable actual force is openly defied.) The god, however, from man's point of view, is evil. Ahab is mistaken in challenging him, because he cannot be challenged, but he is nonetheless, humanly speaking, the hero, the one who dares the ultimate.

The two cats in *The Track* are quite separate—the one—not like Moby Dick—quite real and killable—the other an invention of the primitive mind—and everlasting. (There is no connection between the also real cat which killed Joe Sam's family forty years before, and the real one Harold kills. Mountain lions are relatively short-lived animals. The only link is the legendary cat which Joe Sam has created out of the one which killed his family.) The elements are separated, and neither of them is evil, save in the limited sense that a man might call them evil because they oppose his particular interest. Actually in the larger patterns of nature, the evil is his, not the cat's, for evil comes into being only with the conscious and inventing mind. There is, however, a relationship between the real and the legendary cat to this extent that both are avengers against man's evil—i.e., forces of nature worship against man who has sought to override the laws of nature. In the largest sense, then, if we put it morally, the cats come near to being good, since they act against the one conscious and disproportionately destructive force in nature—man. And by the same token, all the evil would be in man. And to put it in the truer way, there is no good and evil, save as man creates it. There is only, as the basic truth, the "that" which does exist: the balance of nature, in which any action begets reaction, any misuse of power bears the seeds of its own destruction. This works, then, upon both hands, the physical or actual, and the mental or spiritual—the visionary. The real cat destroys Curt's treasured steers, because Curt has willingly cleaned the hills of its natural game. (Man—and America—has been a particularly horrible example of this haste—has persisted in creating these imbalances by destroying beyond need—the primitive least, modern man most.) The visionary cat destroys Curt—i.e., Curt destroys himself—because Curt, the materialist, the "conqueror" of nature, will not believe in its reality as Joe Sam does, and cannot understand the nature of reality as Arthur does—because, in short, he is in the evil middle ground of most of us, who no longer understand our place in nature instinctively, like Joe Sam, and will not attempt to understand it consciously, like Arthur—thinking man, idealist, whatever you wish—artist, perhaps—in the largest sense—and least urban.

Well, too much about that. But you can see now why Arthur must die. He is the ineffective idealist (unfortunately that is simply a fact)—akin, let us say (for there is a historical pattern in the book), to the New England Transcendentalists—which cannot stem the mad destructiveness of the "materialist" who overrules him in all matters of action. He takes upon himself the guilt of his destructive brother, because he knows that destruction is wrong, but has been unable to curb it. (In terms of the action of the story, it is he who performs the mercy killing of the bull, the bearer of the seed of the ranch's future sustenance, although it is Curt's fault that the cat has injured the bull, and the feeling of guilt for this act renders him impotent—he forgets to reload the gun, and he cannot move fast enough, because he is lost in thought, in self-judgment—when he is himself attacked by the cat which Curt, ahead of him, in the box canyon, has driven from its feeding.) In other words the idealist, the dreamer, because he cannot act, is killed by reality, and the realist, the materialist, the "conqueror," the man of action, is killed by the dream cat, the vision—i.e., he goes mad, and acts madly, because he won't think.

Nevertheless, I have tried, insofar as the truth of man's history will let me, not to despair. Note—Curt, when dead, *is* dead. The consequences of his acts remain, but of himself, nothing that will work; and with him gone, feelings and consequences of his acts may be mended, at least modified. Arthur, on the other hand, is not dead.

[*About here in the margin is inserted:* Note the bearing of the dreams upon all this. Even Curt, in the part of himself he denied, is visited by Arthur and by Joe Sam.]

Even the dogmatic mother, who has believed Curt her favorite, begins to see things differently while she sits with Arthur's body. Grace remembers him, perhaps falsely, but she will preserve his signs. Gwen remembers him, Joe Sam, who *is* what Arthur *thought* in large part, is still alive, and Harold, during the preparations for the funeral—in part because of Joe Sam— begins to understand the truth in Arthur, that he has always in part felt. And during the funeral he dedicates himself to seeking a fuller understanding, and to acting upon what Arthur knew but, because of the rest of the family, could not act upon. In short, Arthur lying dead in the cold north bedroom is still more alive in the larger sense than Curt has ever been. Joe Sam, the primitive, under the present pressure of events, is the very central character of the action, though he is inarticulate, but Arthur, who recognizes the truth of the primitive, but the necessity of *consciously* getting back to acting upon it, is the force of the future. The big question—and how would I make it more than a question—is what will Harold, having enough of Curt's power of action, and beginning to understand as Arthur understood, but without the forces around him which nullified Arthur's thought—what will Harold be able to *do*? He sees the ranch house only fitfully and distantly through the after-scud of the all-enveloping storm, and he is dragging—and dragged by—the dead body of Curt, and he has Arthur's

teacher, old Joe Sam, still with him, and quite himself now—
and he is on good terms with him, though he has much to learn.
He has to cope with Grace's near-madness, but, as Joe Sam
said, he can take the panther hide to Gwen now—the future
lies with them. Will they have children? Or will they succumb
to the burden of inertia in the father and mother, whose favorite child was Curt?

[The next paragraph, partly a warning against trusting the
first Signet edition of *The Cat*, which was abridged, is crossed
out.]

11

On "The Watchful Gods"

Walter Clark

No entirely adequate introduction to "The Watchful Gods" is in print, partly no doubt because it has been somewhat obscured by being first published in a volume that received but little attention when it appeared, and where it was obscured by the first book publication of some very attractive short stories, including "Hook" and "The Wind and the Snow of Winter." It is a major work, and Clark always treated it that way.

The following text is from a letter Clark sent to his editor at Random House, Saxe Commins. Most of the contributors to the present volume mention "The Watchful Gods"; see especially chapters 3 and 6.

Virginia City
Nevada
January 31 [1950]

Dear Saxe—

Hereafter—*The Little Gods, the Watchful Gods.* The first version of it—much shorter, about 10,000 [words]—I wrote two years ago—and used, because I felt it to be in a preliminary stage, as the basis for a lecture and discussion of technique of fiction for the writer's group at Stanford two summers ago. It struck me then as little more than an outline of the tale it should be, and I think this version comes pretty close to what I wanted. The incidents of the rattlesnake and the rabbit were part of my own childhood—though not so closely related—and for some reason, minor as they were, have always haunted me as something I had to use someday. The theme I finally used has also interested me for a long time—made me watchful of many pertinent manifestations in youngsters while I was teaching, and since, and an explorer, insofar as memory can be trusted—and mine is pretty good—of the same things in my own childhood and adolescence. You will recollect hints of it—the running and the kind of prayer Tim Hazard used, for instance, in *The City*. Very roughly speaking, the idea is that religious development is a continuously repeated experience of the race—each individual in his childhood and early adolescence (barring such ideological straightjacketing as that of the Catholic Church—and often even then) recapitulates in capsule form, as it were, the religious history of the race, from primitive anthropomorphism, through the more regular and limited classical pantheon (or some counterpart thereof—it wouldn't be the same of course) into the simple two-force (good and evil) conception basic to Christianity, and finally, given a sufficiently strong urge to unity and honesty in appraising the events of life, into the complete unity of mysticism—a spiritual evolution comparable, that is, to the recapitulation by the foetus and infant in the womb of the biological history—though coming, of course, with the development of mind and strongly with sexual maturing, and complicated by many social factors.

[The remainder of the letter mainly concerns personal matters. Apparently the publisher was responsible for the shortening of the title.]

12

Problems in
"The Watchful Gods"
and Clark's Revisions

Robert M. Gorrell

*Dr. Robert M. Gorrell, onetime vice-president of the University of
Nevada, Reno, was chairman of the Department of English and later
dean when Clark taught there. The two became fast friends, the
more because they liked, as a doubles team, to beat the graduate students at tennis. Gorrell has been involved in the writing or editing
of several books, of which the best known is* Modern English Handbook, *now in its sixth edition.*

A basic paradox for the writer of fiction is that the enunci-
ation of abstract truth is at once the most frequent
mark of the beginner's failure and of the master's success. Flan-
nery O'Connor comments on the tendency of the beginning
writer to fall into the trap of abstraction:

> It is a good deal easier for most people to state an abstract
> idea than to describe and thus re-create some object that they
> actually see. But the world of the fiction writer is full of mat-
> ter, and this is what the beginning fiction writers are very
> loath to create. They are concerned primarily with unfleshed
> ideas and emotions. They are apt to be reformers and to want
> to write because they are possessed not by a story but by the
> bare bones of some abstract notion. They are conscious of

problems, not of people, of questions and issues, not of the texture of existence, of case histories and of everything that has a sociological smack, instead of with all those concrete details of life that make actual the mystery of our position on earth.[1]

Preoccupation with the search for the great truths stimulates in the writer the temptation to expound rather than reveal, and expounding is not the business of fiction.

Some kind of philosophical insight, a vision of truth, distinguishes literary greatness, but a shift of focus from concrete details to abstraction is usually disastrous for the writer of fiction. If we are forced to make critical judgments, we are likely to try to evaluate the work's insights or wisdom—but not as philosophical pronouncements, rather as revelations from the interpretation of events: the flight of a skylark, the blowing of the west wind, the mental wanderings of an idiot, or Napoleon's retreat from Russia. Serious writers of fiction almost always struggle with this paradox, with their knowledge that their medium is a story and their desire to say something significant.

Walter Clark was a serious writer, and he was occupied with both narrative details and literary devices that suggest abstractions—symbolism and allegory and myth-making. But Clark usually uses such devices only to reinforce the narrative, deriving meaning primarily from the ordering and interpreting of events, the analysis of character, and the descriptions of nature. Criticism that focuses on Clark's symbolism is likely to be misleading.

Like most serious fiction, however, Clark's stories are susceptible of interpretation on more than one level, and I want to consider abstraction and reality in two of them, "The Buck in the Hills," a relatively early story, and "The Watchful Gods," the last story Clark published. I want to look particularly at Clark's revisions of the latter story because I think they reveal some of his struggle with the paradox I have been playing with.

As in so many of Clark's stories, nature—in "The Buck in the Hills"—has central importance. The story is a frame story, with the shooting of the deer and Chet McKenny's grimly ingenious laborsaving method inserted between the scenes of the narrator's exalted happiness in the company of the mountains and the cold water. The scene is described sharply and accurately: "the big rock barrier, which a million winters had cracked into terraces," or the valley that could be seen from the mountain, "squared with fields and pencilled by the straight roads." Nature appears vividly and realistically, but almost always through the story it is introduced for its effect on the characters. Nature revives memories: the "dry, shriveled clumps of leaves" make the narrator remember the place in the summer. Another place revives an earlier feeling:

> [the little valley where he] had stayed for two hours to watch a hawk using the wind over the hollow to the west of me, feeling myself lift magnificently when he swooped up toward me on the current up the col, and then balanced and turned above. . . . [At his campsite] the place gave me the hawk lift again.

The purpose of the frame of course is to emphasize the contrast between the effects of nature unexploited and friendly, and the effects of nature violated. The narrator is uplifted in the cold water—"God, I was happy"—but Chet, by driving the wounded buck, reveals a callous inhumanity that makes him unworthy of the mountains and the lakes. Thus, in a way, nature becomes almost a character in the story. But it does so in "The Buck in the Hills," except for the ending, as in most of the short stories, without contrived devices. Nature is not personified, not presented symbolically. A particular quality of most of Clark's stories is that nature acquires abstract, universal significance without ever being presented as anything but real rocks and trees and water.

The functions of nature vary in the stories. In "The Wind and the Snow of Winter," for instance, nature again serves as a frame, but less as an acting force in the drama than as background. The winter of Mike Braneen's life is partly a reflection of the change of the seasons, a relationship long standard in metaphor and myth—archetypal, if you like, as Northrop Frye points out. But the treatment of nature in the story is not essentially symbolic; the snowflakes at the beginning and end are wet and cold. Even in "Hook," where the views of nature are multiple and complex, the story is primarily about a real hawk. The hawk embodies both the beauty and cruelty of nature, the triumph and defeat that are part of the world. And Hook, like almost all animals in literature, from the white rabbit to the white whale, is anthropomorphic; we constantly identify the struggles and courage of the bird with human problems and characteristics. But the brave bird of the woman's final comment in the story is the brave *bird*. Nature, in the hawk and in his surroundings, is not treated symbolically.

In "The Buck in the Hills" various incidents and things assume symbolic importance. The execution of the deer by slitting its throat and the blood that drenches Tom's arms and hands clearly function as natural symbols, and as such they are plausible. That is, they represent what can be expected to result from the characters and situation; they are not introduced for their own sake, to point to some broader significance of the event. The method of the killing works symbolically to suggest something about Chet's character and also to characterize the act as alien to the world of Tom and the narrator and the mountain. It does not function, it seems to me, as a conventional symbol linking the event to ritual sacrifice or to the Old Testament—although in other circumstances such an event might—and I doubt that the story gains by reading into it this kind of significance. Similarly the blood and Tom's elaborate and unaccustomed care in washing his hands later are primarily natural symbols, only incidentally associated with such conventional symbolic functions as the spilt blood of ritual sacrifice, or the complications of being washed in the blood of the lamb, or washing as an act of purification. In "The Indian Well" the cougar figures symbolically as Jim Suttler's obsession, as the object of his combined revenge and atonement, but it is not Blake's or Eliot's tiger, nor is it the black panther of *The Track of the Cat*.

The final paragraph of "The Buck in the Hills," however, takes a somewhat different approach, one that is not characteristic of the early stories. As Tom and the narrator start down the mountain in the snow:

> There was something listening behind each tree and rock we
> passed, and something waiting among the taller trees down
> slope, blue through the falling snow. They wouldn't stop us,
> but they didn't like us either. The snow was their ally.

Here, it seems to me, Clark is consciously working to make
explicit the abstract statement of the story, to emphasize that
the indignity on the deer has violated a code, angered nature
or nature's gods; and in spite of their innocence Tom and the
narrator share some of humanity's guilt for the outrage. The
passage moves the story directly toward myth, toward presentation of the stories as explanations of the universe, of the relationships of humankind and nature, of good and evil. I cite
the passage mainly because this kind of direct move toward the
mystic, the personification of nature and the emphasis on the
abstract, is not characteristic of the early stories.

It is, however, very much like numerous passages in the later
story, "The Watchful Gods"—for example:

> Several times, when he felt himself most closely watched, as
> if for an immediate purpose, he looked up quickly, thinking,
> "There's really somebody in here watching me."

"The Watchful Gods" is different from the early stories. It
makes use of a great variety of literary devices. In many ways
it is the most complex of Clark's works. At one level it is a story
of the initiation of the boy Buck into adulthood, probing the
problems and thoughts of youth meeting an inconsistent world.
It is told from the point of view of the boy, to reveal the conflicts in the boy's mind, through passages recording the boy's
thoughts and through such devices as dialogues between Buck
and the "counsel for the world," or between Buck and the
watchful gods, the fog god and the sprites who are the little
"gods of life." At times Buck's mind is primarily occupied with
his dreams of Janet Haley, who has some kinship with Rachel
in *The City of Trembling Leaves*. At other times, it is concerned
with his efforts to outwit the fog god. The story becomes more
than Buck's introduction to life, as the watchful gods become
identified in various ways with nature and as the book employs

complex symbolism—allegory at times—and myth to develop insights into nature and life.

Clark arrived at this complexity, however, only after the kind of painstaking revision and rewriting that was characteristic of all his work, and a comparison of surviving manuscripts of the story reveals a good deal of what Clark was trying to achieve in "The Watchful Gods." The comparison also, I think, confirms that both the fascination and the partial failure of "The Watchful Gods" result from the writer's concern to say something significant and the difficulties of doing this directly or doing it too frequently through artificial devices. The successive revisions suggest that Clark was quite aware of the paradox I have been exploiting and that he was working in various ways toward reconciliation.

At least three handwritten manuscript versions earlier than the final text of the novella exist, all in the University of Nevada Library:

A. A pencil draft, 65 pages, undated, entitled "The Little Gods, the Watchful Gods." It was probably written in late 1946 or 1947.

B. An ink draft, 72 pages, inscribed "Washoe Valley, 1947," entitled "The Little Gods, the Watchful Gods." A note inside the front board of the cover reads "First Draft," but the manuscript is a fair copy of A, with only slight revisions, apparently used as an example for a creative writing talk at Stanford in the summer of 1948.

C. A notebook draft of more than thirty-three thousand words, in ink, with many ink revisions and inserts, inscribed "Little Gods—second draft." This version is almost identical with the published story and reflects Clark's nearly final reworking of the prose. It is undated, but apparently was worked on in the fall of 1949, perhaps into early 1950.

Although there are some differences in all the manuscripts, the interesting comparison is between the earliest version, A, and the printed text, which is substantially C. It is impossible here to catalogue all the revisions, but I want to mention some of those that seem to me to record Clark's concern to reconcile

narrative and statement and to reveal Clark's skill in dealing
with the problems of the story.

Many of the revisions simply reveal the experienced
craftsman taking a second look. The following type of comparison could be repeated dozens of times. The 1947 draft (A):

> Still carrying the rifle and the rabbit, he worked down the
> steep side of the ravine. Toward the bottom he could smell the
> sea more distinctly. When he reached the little trail just above
> the rough bottom with rocks in it, where the water boiled
> through in the spring rains, he turned down toward the beach
> and began to run. He was very eager to abandon the rabbit and
> the gun and plunge into the cold, clean ocean.

The printed text:

> Still carrying the rabbit by its ears in one hand, and the
> twenty-two in the other, so that he had to go very slowly,
> balancing himself, and testing each foothold, he descended the
> steep side of the ravine. When he reached the trail, he turned
> down toward the beach. The smell of the sea was strong in
> the ravine, and the quiet seemed thickened and closed in, only
> the more complete for the pulsing whisper of the surf, which
> sent small, communicative ghosts of itself up along the brushy
> slopes above, and among the shelves and caves of bare
> sandstone in the chasm below. When he had gone a short way
> along the trail, Buck lifted the small rabbit against his sweat-
> shirt and worked his hand around under it, until he could
> carry it safely upon his forearm. This relieved him greatly, re-
> moving a painful strain from his own ears.

As Clark imagines the episode more precisely, he adds details.
As he revises, he becomes more intimately aware of the boy's
problem in carrying the rabbit and the possibilities for using the
wounded ears.

Revisions of this sort would be likely in any second draft.
Many of the revisions, however, which extended the first version of about ten thousand words to the final thirty-three
thousand, show a shift or perhaps a focusing of the intent of
the story. One major accomplishment of the revisions is the
strengthening of the narrative structure. To oversimplify, the

first draft is a summary of a myth, an extended outline; the revision is a story about Buck, with the myth in the background.
The change in the beginning of the story illustrates this difference. The draft (A) opens with an analysis of the little gods:

> The gods were indefinite to young Buck, but they were real
> and they were everywhere. They were gods, not a God. They
> were too different in different places to be a God.

With material that appears in the second section of the printed
text, the draft goes on to relate Buck's gods to the Bible, observing that "they were primitive gods . . . in most ways more
primitive than the Old Testament gods," and then moves to
discuss the god that watches Buck from the cliffs along the sea.
The revision shifts the emphasis at once by opening the story
with the narrative:

> Buck woke when the first gray light stole in at the window
> over his bed.

This version continues as a sequential account, with Buck's
movements on his twelfth birthday providing the pattern. It
drops summary statements such as the following from the draft:

> Buck's father gave him the twenty-two for his own on his
> twelfth birthday. It was the custom, in Buck's family, to cele-
> brate the young birthdays at breakfast.

It replaces them with detailed narrative, consistently expanding dialogue.

The change in the story of Janet Haley—Braley in the
draft—is another example of the shift to narrative structure.
The draft briefly summarizes Buck's visions of Janet, with a sentence each for Robin Hood and Tristram, and an outline of his
tennis triumph:

> And as himself, although with the physical attributes of a fine
> athlete of perhaps seventeen or eighteen, he saved her from
> the same malicious and decadent being in the form of a much
> more experienced tennis player with national ranking, defeat-
> ing him in a terrible and exhausting five set final match, for
> which Janet, somehow, had become the real trophy.

The revision changes the scene from summary to narrative:

> [Buck saves Janet] from the decadent intentions of a tennis player of national ranking and of thirty or even more sinister years, who was almost exclusively given, aside from tennis and seduction, to alcohol, cheating at poker, and miscalling his opponent's winning shots.

Buck loses two sets and is down 4–1 in the third, but:

> [he] pulled himself together and lifted his game to new heights by virtue of his cleaner living and more suitable youth.

The scene has developed as a separate daydream, recounted in detail and with understanding humor—which is usually absent from the story, even in the accounts of Buck's imagined romances.

As an almost inevitable accompaniment to the shift toward narrative structure, the revision centralizes the story on Buck, retaining the third-person approach but working consistently from the point of view of the boy. The revision, more clearly than the draft, is essentially an initiation story, Buck's story. And the gods and sprites, as well as the dreams of Tristram or Kit Carson, gain plausibility because they come to the reader through the mind of Buck. They also come nearer to fitting together into a kind of complex myth as the imagination and fantasies of Buck develop in a counterpoint relationship to the Old Testament myths or the hero stories that are expanded in the revision. In the revision the events of the story become a broad religious experience for Buck, combining with the myths of Buck's daydreaming early in the story to become a comment on all human religious experience. The most significant changes in the revision seem to me directed toward expanding and clarifying this comment, but doing so mainly by expanding, and sometimes complicating, the interpretation of Buck's experience.

The expansions of the central episodes are typical—of the shooting of the rabbit, the encounter with the snake, and the ending.

In the revision Clark prepares for the shooting by adding ex-

tensive details of Buck's attitudes and fantasies as he climbs
through the fog:

> Here he became Kit Carson, acting as scout for a cumbersome
> military expedition . . . he felt much more convincing as Car-
> son than he had ever felt before, yet he felt himself drawn out
> of the part too often to follow it consistently.

As he moves higher, Buck feels "himself the hunter and himself
the hunted," feels the "confusion made by the quality of legend
in reality." Then, as he walks across the plateau, Buck's
thoughts turn to the forces around him in a passage Clark reworked. In the first draft (A):

> The tiny sprites of multitude and life had given warning and
> withdrawn themselves. It seemed to Buck at moments that
> the malicious spirit was in the dark birds which fled briefly
> about him and chittered from hidden nooks, giving warning,
> not of concern for the possible victims of the twenty-two, but
> merely in order to prevent his ever firing it.

A few revisions appear in the fair copy (B). Then comes the
final version:

> Life on the plateau was not deceived about which power he
> was representing now. It knew he had gone over to the enemy.
> Gradually, because of these bird warnings, he began to realize
> that the multitudes that watched him were no longer sprites
> or the hunter parts of himself, but traitorous outposts of his
> new party, hostile, perhaps, to the brightness he had deserted,
> but also suspicious and envious of any new power among
> themselves.

As Buck approaches the discovery of the rabbit, the revision
looks more minutely at his state of mind, but also elaborates
the details of his imaginings, making the gods and sprites more
consistently a part of Buck's thoughts but at the same time
moving them outside Buck and regularizing them into allegory.

The description of the kill, including the puncturing of the
rabbit's ears, underwent relatively little change in the revision;
Clark's original imagining of the scene held for the final version. The one or two significant alterations, however, are in-

teresting in that they illustrate again Clark's concern with developing myth and also expanding the account of Buck's thoughts. One illustration is the passage describing Buck's preparation for the first shot. In A:

> Considerations pertinent to the shooting floated loose in his mind, as if they had been learned by rote and had arisen of themselves. "The gully is wider than it looks," he thought.

One of the relatively infrequent revisions in B renders it:

> Considerations pertinent to firing floated loose in his mind, as if they spoke with voices of their own, or perhaps with his father's voice. "The gully is wider than it looks," he thought.

The final version carries the revision considerably further toward myth, developing the report of Buck's memory in the draft to a dialogue of several speeches involving the father's voice of B and another "voice of the moment":

> Old warnings and instructions came up, but as if into airy spaces in his mind, floating free, like the fog clouds in the ravine, and with a voice of their own, or a voice like his father's, save for the unwonted urgency. Among them entered observations drawn from the particular moment, and much longer and more emotional than the instructions.

The comment on the width of the gully is transferred to the voice of the moment:

> "It must be an awful big rabbit to show that clearly across such a big gully," the voice of the moment put in, and added, getting clear down into his belly, "which is practically a crack in the globe, which is twenty-five thousand miles around. . . ."

And the voice continues with a long comment on the globe as a "speck in the dark abyss of eternity."

The flight of the hawk just after the death of the rabbit provides a further instance of revision to emphasize the significance of natural phenomena. In the draft (A):

> . . . a big hawk, floating on rigid wings, . . . rose out of the ravine below. . . . For a moment the stillness of the rabbit and

the phantom, unexpected rising of the hawk, seemed to Buck
related and ominous. Two aspects of the same being, a being
against which he had committed a crime.

The fair copy (B) revised the final sentence to make it more
explicit:

> Two aspects of the same being, the flesh and the spirit of one
> against whom he had committed a crime.

And the final version comments still further on the significance
of the hawk's flight:

> ... it seemed, so tiny, quick-rising and unexpected, to be
> ominously related to the rabbit, to have risen, indeed, directly
> out of it, and so to be the other, the enduring, portion of the
> creature against whom the crime of murder, in a peculiarly
> lengthy, deliberate and despicable form, had been committed.
> It went up toward God with word of an unforgivable sin.

In each rewriting Clark attempts to draw more from the flight,
to make it contribute more to the religious statement of the
story.

When the boy finally gets to the dead rabbit, the draft (A)
describes the act briefly and then has Buck make a direct judgment on it.

> Only its downy fur stirred a little when the sea-wind touched
> it. Buck's act, although he did not think this, but only felt it,
> became clearly an act of evil as he bent there looking down
> at the very small soft rabbit.

In the revision Clark deletes the direct judgment of the act, but
expands the use of nature in the scene, investing natural
phenomena directly with human qualities:

> Only its downy fur stirred a little when the sea-wind lightly,
> tenderly caressed it. At each touch of the sea-wind, also, the
> nearby grasses bowed a little in suppressed agony, and the top-
> most leaves and twigs of the bush close above trembled stiffly
> in unison.

Clark echoes the image half a dozen paragraphs later, speaking
of the "silently lamenting bushes and grasses of the ravine."

The pathetic fallacy escapes sentimentality because it registers Buck's interpretation, does not literally give the grasses capacity for agony, but the suggestion is there. And it is fortified as nature manifests itself more extensively through the story in more than rocks and waves, in a variety of abstract forces represented by all the little gods.

The encounter with the rattlesnake also illustrates Clark's use of nature to make abstract observations and provides another example of the direction of his revisions. In the draft (A) the rattlesnake appears in the path as Buck is making his final descent to the seashore, and the episode becomes the climax for the story, motivating both Buck's decision about the dead rabbit and the disposition of the watchful gods:

> It was a supernatural snake. It was the appointed guardian of the gate of his end. . . . It was clear without reasoning that the death of the rabbit and the sudden, frightening presence of the snake were related. . . . He had been let off. The god of the place, for it seemed now one god, curiously and unpredictably compounded of all the little ones, both hostile and friendly, had seen fit to let him escape with a warning.

Clark amplified the comment about the significance of the snake in the fair copy (B):

> It was, with such size and silence and fixity, more than a snake. It was the appointed conductor in the gate of Buck's end, an end deserved because of the rabbit. It was the avenging antithesis of the rabbit in creation.

The final version keeps much of the language of the central part of the episode but shifts it to become a flashback, an encounter Buck recalls as he comes upon the spot in the trail where he had met the snake. The version expands considerably the discussions of Buck's thoughts as he approaches the spot, fantasizing that he is a college sprinter and tailback, and it shortens the comment but shifts its point:

> It was the coiled spring of evil, the agent of the dark meaning, the very perfect, appointed conductor in the gateway to the other side.

The snake takes on a broader symbolic significance, and the revision moves toward a different sort of ending.

More than any other part of the story, the ending shows Clark at work as a reviser. All three of the manuscripts have significant differences, and the published version differs from C. The draft (A) provides a simple, direct ending that has some attraction. Buck solves his dilemma about the dead rabbit by contemplating a burial ceremony—much like the one that provides an ending in the revision—but he abandons the notion as he thinks of the practical problems of his return home.

> When his father . . . looked up from the writing board on his knees and asked the question, it would be necessary simply to hold up the rabbit for him to see.

Buck takes the rabbit down to the beach with him and looks at the water, approaching "in slow, depressed, black rollers":

> There was an indefinable presence, but there were no presences.
> Buck no longer felt the ardent desire to plunge into the sea. The swim had become something near a duty. He leaned the twenty-two against a whale rock, and laid the rabbit carefully near it on the top. Then he took off his shorts, dropped them on the sand, and walked slowly down to where the last reach of the foam could cover his feet.

Clark was apparently concerned about the ending of the story at an early stage, and the only very extensive change from the first draft in the 1947 fair copy B is a six-page extension of the ending, much of it adopted in the final revision. The additional material does not alter the events of the ending; it finds Buck standing with the foam at his feet and discusses his thoughts as he contemplates the rabbit and his return home. The passage introduces more of Buck's fantasy, especially of Janet, suggests that Buck's scratches from his encounter with the bush remind him of Christ's wounds, and then moves to a second ending much like that of the published version:

> He closed his hands into tight fists, and cried out, "Oh, God, God," in a voice he did not recognize. He was shamed by the

vehemence and spontaneity of this exclamation. He looked away from the shafts of light, and assuming the expressionless countenance of the boxer advancing from his corner, he began to wade out slowly into the dark water, which was now faintly colored upon its ripples by the distant splendor.

Manuscript C and the published version change that ending mainly by expanding the material leading up to it. In the most notable change Buck ceremoniously buries the rabbit rather than keeping it to take home as explanation, as the first two versions have it. A second change is expansion of Buck's adaptation of myths of Janet and Tristram and Kit Carson, along with his creation of a new sort of fantasy as he listens to dialogues involving voices of the gods and then more elaborate discussions between the counsel for the world and the defender of the rabbit as they speculate about what Buck will say when he returns home. From these additions the final revisions move to an ending not greatly altered from the fair copy of the first draft. Manuscript C starts the ending with a passage altered from the fair copy and labeled "key" in the margin of the manuscript:

> He was about, thus stirred, as by a great and distant music, to venture into the Tristram legend, when he noticed that everything was turning brighter around him, because of a faint but permeating glow, seeming to come from nowhere in particular. He looked north along the coastline and saw that great shafts of sunlight were reaching out to sea from the clefts of four canyons. He was searched by this surprising magnificence in a new and not altogether pleasant manner, which made him wish to sing and weep at the same time. It was the mood of the Tristram legend at its best, suddenly brought to painful yet exhilarating reality in his body, so that the dark unanimity of the secret beach was all at once more vital and more provocative and more bewildering than in the very brightest day of its benignity.

The published version alters this paragraph again, cutting the references to Tristram and interestingly making it closer to the paragraph in B. And then both C and the published version go on to the cry "Oh, God" and the walk on into the sea.

Although these major revisions make the story less a discussion of the gods, less a direct exposition of myth, they do not curtail the mythmaking. Rather, in the shift to narrative and to the point of view of Buck, the revision allows expansion of the mythical material and makes it more plausible. Although they are made more clearly subordinate to the story of Buck, the references to traditional myths—Tristram, Robin Hood, Gareth, or Old Testament heroes—can be expanded and treated naturally as parallels to Buck's other fantasies, like those involving Janet, or to his flashback memories like that of the snake. And the sprites and gods, even though their appearances are multiplied in the revision, function more plausibly as they are linked to Buck's view of nature. It is possible at times even to broaden the significance of symbols and to make them more explicit. In the first draft the snake that becomes the "coiled spring of evil" is only the "appointed guardian of the gate of his end."

Comparison of the versions reinforces my feeling that Clark approached "The Watchful Gods" strongly preoccupied with his desire to make a significant statement about the world. The first draft opens with a discussion of the gods, contains a considerable number of direct abstract statements, and introduces various devices for abstract comment. The revision reveals Clark's awareness of the dangers of giving the story too many of the characteristics of a philosophical treatise, and he reworked the manuscript with the skills that had made the shorter stories successful—rendering experience with accurate detail, selecting and ordering events so that they made the abstract statements for him.

The revision is not, I think, entirely successful. "The Watchful Gods" does become Buck's story. It should be read as a story of Buck's initiation into the world and as a penetrating and often moving look into a 12-year-old's mind. It suggests comparisons with Steinbeck's *Red Pony* stories. It should not be read as an exposition of a philosophical system. Yet it is more than a story of a boy's dreams and problems; the dreams and problems are pressed toward universality by the machinery of the story: the gods and the mythmaking. It interprets the hunt and the shooting as more than an initiation rite, as a religious revelation for Buck, and it alludes to myths and creates myths to broaden this revelation to apply to humanity generally—to suggest that Buck's experience is the recurring experience of society. The multiplicity of themes and the playing with ideas are fascinating, but with the varied intellectual demands on the reader's attention, the novelette produces an effect different from the emotional impact of the closely unified, sharply focused shorter pieces.

Marianne Moore comments that poetry presents for inspection "imaginary gardens with real toads in them." In narrative fiction the acreage of the garden to some extent determines the significance of the work. Great novelists—Dostoevsky, Tolstoy, Faulkner—recreate the universe; the garden becomes a world, and the novel achieves epic proportions. A short story obviously creates a smaller garden; the focus is on the real toads in most of Clark's stories.

"The Watchful Gods" extends the garden from short-story size, approaching a kind of epic significance, but the world created is sometimes too small for the ambitions of the symbolism and the myth and too large for the story. The events of "The Watchful Gods" could have been fitted into the dimensions of the short story, but they were too sparse for a full-scale novel. Clark wanted to explore the implications of the boy's initiation more deeply than a short story would allow, and the long short story or short novel developed.

In many ways the material and purpose of "The Watchful Gods" are suited to the novelette form as it is used in works like Melville's *Billy Budd* or Conrad's *Heart of Darkness*. A novelette can retain the compact structure of a short story but expand the development of themes and characterization. The form allowed Clark to restrict the plot to the boy's adventure on a single day, to observe consistently from the point of view of the boy, and to develop the boy's character and fantasy world and also the broader myths the story generates.

"The Watchful Gods" represents an ambitious scheme. Clark is perhaps attempting something epic in miniature. He expands the garden, and the toads remain real. But through much of the story I feel that he may be trying to extract too much from the incidents. The symbolism and myth become so complex that they sometimes seem remote from the boy's actions or his reverie.

Clark was an extraordinary short story writer, and significant general insights emerged from his economical narration and characterization. "The Watchful Gods" is one of Clark's most interesting works; but in spite of its greater complexity I find it less impressive than many of the short stories.

Notes

1. *Mystery and Manners* (New York: Farrar, Straus & Cudahy, 1969), pp. 67–68.

13

The "Silent" Period

Robert M. Clark and Charlton Laird

Both Clark and Laird have appeared in previous chapters. In this collaboration Clark has done most of the research, Laird most of the writing.

"So did he after all fall victim to the perfectionism that he specifically repudiated in his character Lawrence Black? It is possible. What he had written had been widely misunderstood. . . . I suspect that the dramatization of his difficulty . . . would have made him more self-critical. And yet he was always self-critical; I cannot conceive that mere difficulty would have silenced him or led him to destroy his work.

"What, then? I wish I knew."

As readers may surmise, the subject here is Walter Clark and his "long silence," beginning after *The Watchful Gods* (1950) and lasting the remaining twenty years of his life—twice as long as the Golden Years, the decade after *Ox-Bow* (1940). The writer quoted above is Wallace Stegner, who understands Walter and what he was trying to do surely as well as anyone has or is likely to. And yet he was here asking the wrong question, as were we all. When most of the criticism in this book was being written, we had only what had been printed. During the two decades, 1950–1970, Walter published a few magazine articles and the introduction to a book, a competent little historical essay—a kindness to a friend—but nothing to suggest that the long drouth was over.

At just this time, while the lecturers quoted herein were ask-

ing what seemed to be the pertinent question: "Why did an author so successful as Walter Clark suddenly stop writing?" his
son Robert was cataloguing his father's papers, bringing to light
manuscripts that give us a whole different insight into what
Clark was doing. These documents are numerous and they run
to thousands of pages. Thus for the question, "Why did Clark
stop writing?" the answer now is, "He didn't." In effect, he
stopped publishing, but he did not stop producing. Not that
this new insight leaves us without questions. Instead of asking
why Clark stopped, we have now to ask why he stopped turning
out drafts promising enough so that they seemed to him worth
finishing, a question that may be even more elusive than the
query it supplants.

In 1950, everything looked propitious for Clark. He had
lately gotten a better post at the university. *The Watchful Gods
and Other Stories* was not selling, but collections of short works
seldom sell, and insofar as Clark ever followed a pattern, he had
found one. *The City of Trembling Leaves* was a reworking of several earlier attempts; likewise, a mediocre poem, "Strange
Hunting," had been reworked into a superb novel, *The Track
of the Cat*, which was following the lead of *The Ox-Bow* into
the moving pictures. An unsuccessful short story, called "The
Little Gods," expanded into a novella and published as "The
Watchful Gods," was being moderately well received. Walter
had many more ideas, some completed—badly before he had
learned to write—some abandoned years ago, some in gesta-
tion. Obviously the next step was to pick one of the unfinished
or misdirected pieces and rewrite it, as he had with *The City,
The Cat, The Gods*, and others.

For many years, apparently, Clark had wanted to write an
epic—perhaps *the* epic of the West, such a work as Stegner was
later to provide in *Angle of Repose*. He already had a good first
draft for such a book in a short novel he had called "Water,"
which had all the ingredients, lacking only that Clark had not
yet learned to write. Robert Clark, in his discussion of the
piece, says that "Its prose is often self-consciously 'poetic.' It
suffers from a serious shortage of dialogue and developed
scenes, and from an excess of authorial rumination thinly dis-

guised as interior monologue of the central character." We see this protagonist, Galt Mason, from the time he revolts against grand-parental authority in Maine until he is a beaten old rancher in central Nevada, ca. 1930. Meantime, he has learned about women and small-time crooks, has found out how to survive as a prospector, has married "a big, proud, copper-haired girl with hawk's eyes," has lost one fortune in cattle and another in sheep. Now in his seventies, he is experiencing a kind of redemption, "albeit a dismal one in a reawakened awareness to something larger than himself." The tale was presumably completed before 1938, perhaps by 1936.

Fleshed out, this skeleton could have revealed the whole "boom and bust" cycle that intrigued Clark. He set about turning his dramatic tragedy into an epic, expanding the cast of characters, enriching his theme with subplots, and expunging the introspective passages. The central figure had now become Jason White, a somewhat more engaging figure than the rather bleak Galt, and the novel is linked to Ox-Bow by importing figures like Kinkaid, Farnley, and Drew from that novel. More is made of several sorts of figures who appear, Hispanics, both men and women, and a sardonic but ineffectual newspaper editor. A dedication seems to link the piece to Clark's stay at Indian Springs, 1941–42.

Another long fragment, more than six hundred pages, now called "The Dam," looks as though Clark had been cleaning up his desk and getting a fresh start. The tale is this time not changed in structure but is much tightened in style; it is accompanied by hand-drawn maps of Nevada, drawings of the type of vessel the protagonist was to use in his trip around the horn, and the like. Sometime later there is the start of another draft, incorporating changes already found in the revision above, but breaking off, after about three hundred pages—with Jason still in Maine—possibly because Clark wanted to turn to The City of Trembling Leaves. This is probably the version Clark referred to when he said, in 1945, that a forthcoming novel was "well along." Meanwhile, Clark was interested in shorter pieces, some completed and some not, but none of them published, several of them novellas: "The Queen Is a Powerful Piece" (concerned with the ways a woman can make and break her husband), "Ambrose, the Chess-Playing Poodle" (a satire), "The Angel and the Judge," and a number of short stories show considerable promise.

Whether Clark did much with versions of "The Dam" after 1950 we cannot be sure, but he was engaged with at least three other large projects, incorporating several novels and subsidiary novellas and short stories. Their integration is not very clear, but Robert Clark has worked out a rough chronology, which we have followed here. The extant manuscripts hinge on three novels which bore the working titles "Admission Day," "The Man in the Hole," and "Way Station," presumably worked on in that order, beginning almost immediately after Clark finished with *Gods* in 1950. The first, "Admission Day," is set in Divide City, a community which greatly resembles Virginia City, where Clark was living at the time. One cast of characters is dated 1946, another 1951, and there is reason to believe that the story was worked on as late as 1954. Like *The Cat*, it was keyed to Nevada history, deliberately planned to be revelational of it: the first day suggests the first Nevada period, the roaring boom times; the second day, the intermediate ranching years, relatively calm and socially decent. In the third period, contemporary and recent, the tourist and the land broker are wrecking the Old West.

The second of these sequences of events, one that occupied Clark in various ways for the remainder of his life, was complex in concept, and it did not simplify as Clark worked with it. Superficially, the story recounts the efforts of Jake Christiansen to find a lost pocket of gold in an old mine, and his efforts to escape after he is entombed by a fall induced through indiscreet dynamiting. The seven days that are given over to Jake's attempts, and his reminiscences, parallel the seven days centered on the week of Christ's crucifixion, which again reflects the whole life on earth. It also develops an ideal religion, something of a jumble of Christianity and other cults, oriental and primitive. The experience of being buried alive is traumatic enough so that after Jake finally finds the treasure and is rescued, he gives the treasure to his wife and others and devotes himself to the new religion he has conceived—or at least that may be what happens. Clark conceived several solutions, at least one satiric, in which Jake becomes a legendary messianic figure, because of his supposedly miraculous escape from death, and then forms the basis of a new prosperity for the community for whose ideals Jake now has little but contempt. Clark made at least a couple of dozens of starts and we can only guess how many endings.

How the story appears in one extant manuscript can be seen in Robert Clark's description:

> There are starts on one novel, begun in the early 1950s, about a miner caught in a cave-in at the lower levels of an old mine, which he suspects still has a rich vein somewhere. There are three small spiral notebooks filled with what look to be very rapid writing, very few revisions, very few notes, as if he were going straight through. Then there is another, larger notebook labelled "The Man in the Hole," Number 1, with two or three starts which are about twenty pages long. At the end is an opening paragraph done over and over, getting shorter and shorter. There was also a sheet of paper on which he [Clark] had plotted out parallels between the seven days of Holy Week and the seven days that this man would spend down in the mine. It was worked out in very fine detail, so that virtually every small action of the man could be linked with an incident in the gospel. The conscious analogies that make "The Watchful Gods" seem almost an allegory—even if one doesn't know what the bullet-ridden ears of the rabbit mean, one senses they signify something—were to be even more present here.

The fragments are numerous. They begin with a long sequence of 108 pages, written in Clark's characteristic manner, at tremendous speed, with dashes for punctuation. Thereafter, new versions continued appearing, probably throughout Clark's wanderings and on into the earlier portion of his stay at San Francisco State University. The project was spawning other projected novels, novellas, and short stories. What Clark's sojourning had to do with starts becoming false starts we can only guess, but there is some evidence that as time went on these new starts tended to get shorter. Some are only a few lines or a few pages. The perfectionism, which he recognized in himself, was probably growing in him during this time. Robert Clark has a theory that his father's teaching, especially that at institutes where he talked with contemporary literary figures, tended to make him more self-conscious about his writing.

Meanwhile, Walter was disturbed lest his concern for the allegory behind the story should derange the fiction. He conducted dialogues with himself on the subject, and even left little notes about symbolism and how to control it, admonishing himself, "You know that simplicity and clarity on the level of the actual—both incident and language—are the technical means of that first necessity." This sort of thing appears repeatedly—and so far as I have observed not elsewhere in the surviving manuscripts. "Learn to incorporate an organized (allegorical) symbolism within a natural context," he cautioned. But in "The Man in the Hole" he seems to be planning the story by the organized symbolism, not letting the symbols grow "within a natural context." He reminds himself, "You know that symbolized meanings must be inherent in the real meanings—enlarging them, not saying something else." Clark stayed with "The Man in the Hole" longer, and returned to it more stubbornly than perhaps to any other of his projects, and one may surmise that he treasured the ideas he believed he was writing into that book. I should guess it was one of the manuscripts he expected to return to, once he could "get Alf off his back."

Striking evidence that Clark felt he was in the midst of a life-long exposition of the development—or decay—of the West is provided by the interlocking characters that appear in all the longer pieces that engaged him during the fifties and early sixties. We have seen already that "Admission Day" was to pick up characters from Ox-Bow. Similarly, Jake Christiansen and one Johnny Braggia from "The Man in the Hole" were to have appeared in "Admission Day," and Harold and Gwen Bridges from The Track of the Cat appear in plans for a novel to have been called "Way Station." The central figure in that novel was to have been one Jim Wheeler, a somewhat footloose young man in "Admission Day," and the like. That is, far from feeling that he was finished, Clark was generating stories faster than he could expand them—most of the related fictions mentioned in the writing notes remained in no more than skeleton form.

"Way Station" was presumably started in the early 1950s while Clark was teaching the first time at the University of Nevada in Reno, and probably continued somewhat after his exile began. Whether he continued to work with it after he took up Alf Doten as part of his agreement to return to the university is hard to know, but he did not do much on the novel thereafter. The tale is a continuation of *The Cat*, and, like it, centers in a valley north of Reno, entered from the east by Beckwourth Pass. We see much of the story through Edna Wheeler, whom the younger Clark characterizes as "a non-religious kin to the mother in *The Cat*." She "had reassumed her father's name after her husband ran off to Alaska." She runs the ancestral Wheel-R Ranch; "hard-drinking, hard-talking, and dominating," Edna believes she loves the land and the ranch, as does her daughter Margaret. The flaw in both of them, says a note, is their "possessiveness," and "emotional greed that WVTC's fictional women often mistake for love." We last see her, endeavoring to defend the ranch by trying to shoot down the sheriff. Robert Clark relates the novel to his father's larger plan as follows:

> While *The Cat* covered the closing of the frontier and the festering of pioneer energies, this novel, a generation later, would depict the collapse of the small rancher, his doom speeded by that same historically factual drought of the 1920s, followed by the Depression, that brought catastrophe in "Water," and put an end to the stable community of the old ranch families.

These five major projects—the four novels and the editing of Alf Doten's journals—were the most extensive but not the only subjects to attract Clark during the 1960s and 1970s. Like any normal literary person, he continued to respond to the world around him, scholarship and science tending to prompt him more to satire than to veneration, as in "The Queen Is a Powerful Piece"; but he liked satirical fiction and even looked forward to collecting his humorous pieces into a volume. His life in New England had already generated "The Rapids" and some other pieces, and there is evidence he had more such in mind. He apparently planned other pieces on the Old West. A tale about an old rancher seems not to have been related to any of the cyclical collection that used interlocking casts of characters, and a story about an old Paiute promises to be reminiscent of Joe Sam.

The supposedly "silent" Clark was not an inarticulate Clark and never became that until cancer cut him off, but something did happen to him or was happening, and long before he returned to Nevada he knew it. The commonest guess is that his wandering from one job to another—his occupation with teaching—sapped his creativity. So far as I know, nobody who knows Clark and his work will accept that as a complete explanation, but Walter himself gave it some credence. He knew that I had retired early to give myself more time to write, and he several times raised the question of my experience with retirement, saying that with his home rebuilt, the children graduated, he thought he could afford to retire from teaching and might do it. He attributed some of his trouble to having become a "perfectionist," whatever he meant by that term; he uses it in the long letter to his son, which in this book has been called his "Credo." He told Herb Wilner that his writing now came "too much from the head," and one should notice Clark's tale of the centipede that became helpless when he turned introspective. Robert Clark seems to believe that his father's loss of the ability to finish and polish a major work was rooted more in the material than in anything else, and I have tried to argue that Clark's methods as a writer had something to do with his permeating discontent.

The unpublished manuscripts, then, insofar as they have come to light, give us a relatively clear picture of what Clark was doing, and the way he viewed himself during his so-called silent years. For at least a large part of that time he must have expected that his life and his future would be very much what his present was and his future was expected to become. He was a writer and a teacher, and what such a person expects to do is write and teach: he had every intention of continuing to do both. He had never been a methodical writer; though he obviously tried to keep an orderly desk, he had had to learn that although he could always write, not always did the writing surge within him in a way that he had in mind when he said "it came," "it just flowed." But there had never been a time when everything "just flowed." When he wrote that great third book of *The Cat*, he was doing again what he had already conceived in "Strange Hunting" a decade earlier and had doubtless relived many times since. Why should he not trust that sooner or later his account of Jake Christiansen buried in a collapsing mine would start to "flow" as had the account of Curt hunting a cat? It did not, and there is growing evidence that he knew it should have.

PART III

Walter Clark as a Literary Artist

A resilient writer stimulates generalizations, and Clark was no exception. The critics drawn upon above have wanted to bring order into our thoughts about him, and some of the best general observations available will be found in the essays of observers such as Wallace Stegner, Herbert Wilner, and Robert Heilman, who had ostensibly addressed themselves to more limited subjects. Here we have brought together surveys aimed at broader topics.

Walter Clark, Missoula, Montana, 1954. Photo by Lee Nye. (Special
Collections, Library, University of Nevada, Reno)

14

Walter Clark's "The Pretender": Two Versions

William D. Baines

Clark had trained himself to compose at tremendous speed. That was the way he preferred to write, and sometimes he could. Often we cannot know how the printed draft came to be, but on at least three occasions we seem to have evidence that he wrote brilliantly and almost without effort: in "Hook," in "The Wind and the Snow of Winter," and in the third book of The Track of the Cat. *This evidence is striking enough to have attracted wide attention among critics, so much that we readily forget that Clark, like most human creators, at some time during the sequence between pencil and printing press, had to revise line by line and word by word. Usually we must assume such revision, but occasionally we have the evidence. One of the best examples is provided by a manuscript and the printed version of "The Pretender." A comparative study has been made by William D. Baines, a participant in the seminar held on Clark, and a teacher at Truckee Meadows Community College.*

The compactness of Walter Van Tilburg Clark's "The Pretenders" stands witness to the author's skillful wedding of form and meaning. That this effect was gained in part from an extensive revision of an earlier draft becomes apparent with the recent discovery of an unpublished version.[1] The revision is not typical with Clark, inasmuch as the changes mainly appear as excisions or condensations, whereas in many other known revisions Clark tended to expand rather than contract an earlier treatment. At a minimum, however, a comparison of the two versions limns Clark in at least one writing process.[2]

The story is divided into four parts; the first introduces the setting and the human characters, foreshadows the theme, and suggests the timidity and ineptitude of the protagonist, Jed Southwick. An Indian guide ferries him by boat to a remote and isolated lakeside camp, where Jed is surrounded by "the cries of innumerable water birds" and fantastic rock formations, which to the city man suggest "fortifications" and "citadels," which are "gleaming monstrously."[3] Left alone with his city-bred dog, the New Yorker feels very lonely and apprehensive. A white man (in the various versions sometimes called a trader and sometimes an agent) had warned Jed against going to the far side of the lake alone. He recalls this warning while the clamor of the water birds gives way "to a silence so intense that his ears rang constantly" and he sensed that "every sound was grossly magnified here, and seemed to be made by someone else." He loaded his gun and placed it carefully beside his sleeping bag.

This section has been cut down considerably from the version preserved in the typescript. In the published version, the guide, Joe-Jack, said to be "humorously sardonic," shoved off with scarcely a word. In the typescript, "he considered saying more, but Southwick, out of lassitude, did not ask for the confidence, so the Indian only said, 'Good Bye,' nodded politely, and climbed into the boat."

In a passage omitted from the printed version, Southwick endeavors to reassure himself:

He told himself gladly that he knew now where to go for antelope, how to hide even at what he thought the safest distance, and make no sound within a mile of their great, active ears. In the strange desert, in the bitter sun, patient and canny, he would kill and be proven. He felt in his thoughts, with a joyous swelling of confidence, how the smooth weight of the rifle would lie steady in his hands, how he would, taking all the time in the world, draw his bead from the gray brush across half a mile of scorching white, and hear the abrupt report small in the silences, smell the powder with the taste of his own sweat, and see, when the herd swung and fled, one not swinging, but leaping mortally, and falling back into the dust where they had stood. He became excited at the thought of his calmness and success [typescript, p. 7].

The most extensive condensation concerns Southwick's character and his reason for coming west, which underlie the theme of the story. In the printed version, a paragraph suffices:

Also, when he returned East, having made the trip alone, the only one of his group to have shot antelope or even seen them, he would have new confidence as a hunter. Seeing men like fat Jack Handley, or the immovable Peterson, or easygoing confident Williams, around the fire in their Adirondack Lodge made Southwick feel that he was a pretender. He usually got his buck with the others, nor did they ever ridicule him. Yet, remembering how he handled his rifle, how awkwardly he stalked, how at times his heart closed and his eyes danced when the buck posed in the thin, yellow woods and he could not raise his gun or feel the trigger with his finger, he always felt like a man sitting a little out of the circle. In the circle, in the light, the good hunters sat eating and drinking and talking with passive, humorous faces, and big hands that could not be unsteady. No, he had never been a hunter, but only a man tolerated by the hunters [AM, p. 483].

This has been cut down from a flashback of more than a thousand words in the typescript, which contains many details later excised.[4] Southwick recalls that "sooner or later he would always sink into the certainty that he was pretending, and then he would feel doubly worthless and ridiculous." His shame and sense of inferiority were linked to his hunting, partly because he was so clumsy and inept at it, and partly because his associates tolerated him at best, and at worst made open fun of him. When he had proposed going west to hunt the "hardest-to-get" American game, the pronghorn antelope, and "perhaps later a lion," the "approved hunters" laughed at him, called him "the big-game hunter," and pictured him going native, married to a fat squaw, and reduced to grunts and sign language when he tried to buy ammunition.

Thus, in rewriting, Clark has shortened the introduction, speeded up the story by cutting exposition and background, centered on Southwick by reducing the roles of both Joe-Jack and the trader-agent, and allowed the theme to develop as implicit in Southwick, not mainly a conflict made explicit through flashbacks.

In the second part of the story, Southwick is awakened by "some definite impression demanding wakefulness." He heard voices "chuckle and carry on" in a "conversational" manner, with "somewhat hysterical laughter" until "the mountains, even the shore, became to him an intricate lacework of swiftly casting and purposeful voices." In the printed version, after Southwick's initial fright:

> It came into his mind that these were coyotes, and probably harmless. But the recollection didn't decrease his tension, for too much of him continued to insist upon the need for defense and the difficulty of determining the number, location, and intention of the marauders. Also, never having seen a coyote, he found himself forming an image completely at odds with their reputation, and had several times to diminish the beasts of his brain, only to find them suddenly grown again and taking on improbable attributes of swiftness, savagery, and cunning [AM, pp. 484–85].

In the typescript, this incident plays more on his imagination:

> In his mind he was ringed by creatures like Russian wolves, about which he had read several terrible stories which now returned in detail and with a vividness and reality they had not possessed before. Nor could he help adding a diabolical cunning and organization far beyond the brute pack movements of the wolves. The yapping, howling and chuckling were so clearly talk and so unpleasantly humorous as to make it obvious that he was opposing creatures of an intelligence not markedly different from his own. It did not even occur to him to doubt that there was opposition, on their part as much as on his [typescript, p. 19].

Southwick is now having difficulty distinguishing between dream and thought, and sensing the passage of time. This latter is implied in the published version, but is made explicit in the typescript:

> The fear was worse because of the lapses. He couldn't guess how long they lasted, whether, like dreams, they packed a long period of experience into an instant, or whether, like dreams, they protracted a small thought through a long time. In recollection the lapses seemed so long that he suspected them of being reveries, and suffered an agony of fear at the thought of being jumped while thus distracted. It even seemed likely to him that the coyotes could sense these lapses, and in time would take advantage of one [typescript, p. 12].

Likewise, the trader's warning receives briefer treatment in the printed version than in the typescript. The final text is:

> Foolishly there was filmed on his inner vision, clearly and in a moment of fixity, the bony, morose face of the trader at the Arahoe post, standing behind the counter with a crimson and gray Indian blanket on the wall at his back. The trader was saying, "I wouldn't go over alone if I were you" [AM, p. 484].

This has been rewritten somewhat from a similar unpublished passage:

> Or the white-faced, sour trader in front of the Indian blanket would have just finished saying something, but Southwick could not remember it, but only what he had just said before, "I wouldn't go over alone if I were you," and he wasn't going to say the important thing again [typescript, p. 14].

In another version in the typescript, this scene appears with quite different details:

> Remembering the agent, he remembered also the agent saying, without interest, "I wouldn't go over there alone, if I were you." The agent had not explained, and now Southwick wondered again if there was an actual danger, or just a superstition or the agent's own feeling that the place was queer. The agent had been there for eighteen years, seeing few white men. He might have foolish ideas; or he might know strange facts.

Southwick felt again why it had been impossible to ask the trader
to explain. He had been evidently bored with the idea, whatever
it was, and also regretful that he should have offered the advice
at all [typescript, p. 2].

Thus the trader's warning appears only once in the printed
text, but three times in the typescript. Indisputably this repeti-
tion builds to a cumulative effect, but Clark while cutting for
space, may have been aware also that the scene gains some impact from appearing only once. Dreamlike as the treatment is,
we are inclined to question, and to wonder if Southwick may
not have questioned, whether the warning had ever been given
at all, whether the pretender was not beginning to lose his ability to distinguish between recollection and nightmare.

Another considerable passage was eliminated entirely from
the printed version:

His small, dark-haired wife, over whom he yearned greatly,
was sitting on the back lawn in the late afternoon sun with
their four-year-old daughter beside her, both of them quite
unaware that anything was happening to him. Though he
could see them clearly, they could not see him at all, and these
words went with the pictures, "This will break Madelaine's
heart. Madelaine will never get over it if anything happens to
me; I know it." And then a picture would begin to form of
Madelaine in her grief trying to keep her grief from the child,
but this picture was never finished, and each time began in a
different place, the bedroom, the living room, the lawn still,
a public place, and each time his wife was dressed differently
[typescript, pp. 13–14].

The passage somewhat heightens Southwick's motivation, but
Clark may well have felt he had provided enough of that, and
that the added detail damaged the sense of isolation and disorientation essential to the story.

In the final version of "The Pretender," Southwick's fear
grows from the situation and his reaction to it; much more obvious in the typescript, however, is the inner turmoil the fear
causes. When contrasted with a deleted portion of the typescript, the final paragraph of the second section in the *Atlantic
Monthly* version gives evidence of this:

With difficulty he reloaded his clip, inserted it, and threw the
first cartridge into firing position. Only then did he feel more
secure, and relax enough to realize that part of his clumsiness
in loading had been due to the fact that he was whimpering
almost constantly and breathing in great, tremulous sobs,
though without tears. Thereafter he crouched in his fort, not
as a superior being temporarily at bay, but as a mindless thing
whose instinct demanded that it die squirming and gnawing
[AM, p. 487].

This part, in which Southwick in reality ceases to be "the pretender," implies what the part deleted immediately prior to the
last sentence states:

He knew then that this extreme dread must have continued
since the moment of the empty click, and though he managed
to subdue it now, even his improved position and the nearness
of daylight could not compensate for the knowledge that his
final heroism had been desperation that under a fraudulent
self-command, his body had whimpered and sagged the whole
time. The inner voice of honesty, which had so often derided
him, now announced with incontestable finality that he was
a coward. He banished the voice from consciousness, but only
by complete surrender to its ultimatum [typescript, p. 17].

Another comparison in section three emphasizes the earlier
story's belaboring of this inner conflict:

But as he walked he began gradually to move with more freedom, which restored a fallacious sense of power. His first
starts at the skitterings of lizards wore down to a tolerant expectation. He began to see lizards before they stirred, and,
since there was nothing else to startle him, his confidence increased [AM, p. 488].

The subsequent juggling of this last sentence from midparag-
raph to the position above, coupled with the following deletion, gives a different import and serves as another indicator
of the writer's polishing skill:

In addition, he had slept just enough to bring all his senses
to that keenest point of perception which is more than half
way up the scale between normal dullness and either oblivious
or the erroneous awareness of insanity. He began to see the

lizards before they stirred, and since there was nothing else to startle him, his confidence increased. It was not that he was less certain of cowardice, but that his being refused to consider that accepted fact. Instead it plotted cleverly, not to combat the cowardice, as was his old habit, but to conceal it. In this growing sense of security and smartness, Southwick became so jaunty as to pass willingly beyond the point of contact with his fort, or rather to extend the zone of safety, and even to consider taking up the antelope hunt again, in order to trick his old hunting friends. He would find the dog, go on through the mountains to the antelope desert, and kill his prong-horn. It would be a good joke on those dull, if steady, men. He became convinced that in this new type of specious courage, arising from the admission of cowardice, he had accidentally found the solution of his problem, the real escape from pretence. He was buoyed up by the thought, and walked far along the slopes, on the flint and sand, through the brush, only half looking for the dog, but two or three times calling loudly for it, at which bravado he was elated [typescript, pp. 20–21].

Immediately after this passage, Southwick comes upon his dog, "a test of the reality of the night before" (AM, p. 488), and is shocked when he finds it dead. Then his new-found confidence leaves him; in the final version, a sole paragraph—a single isolated sentence—emphasizes "the pretender's" shock: "His return to the rock castle was nearly a flight" (AM, p. 488). This rhetorical trauma disappears in the typescript because that simple sentence and its import is buried in a paragraph of detracting details of Southwick's retreat to his camp:

His return to the rock castle was nearly a flight. He walked hurriedly, glanced around him frequently, and at times broke into an unsteady trot, which he abandoned only when he stumbled. He was amazed at the false appearances of distances here, the length of time he hurried without appearing to be any nearer the rocks. Several times, and anxiously, he looked out across the lake, now ominously gray, at the long red lights, through horizonal clouds, of a sun very near setting. He was angry that he had not felt the growing coolness, and come to his senses sooner [typescript, p. 21].

This contrast most dramatically illustrates Clark's conscious union of prose and effect.

In the fourth and concluding section of the narrative, Joe-Jack and the agent come to the island to pick up Southwick. The final version focuses on the Easterner and, as earlier in the story, provides very little insight into the makeup or motivation of the other two. However, this is not so clearly the case in the typescript copy; in addition to the already mentioned exclusions regarding these other characters, there appear two more of note. In the *Atlantic Monthly*, the agent asks: "You tellin' me you heard shootin' every night?" (AM, p. 489), to which the Indian answers in the affirmative; the former then speculates that Southwick "was shootin' at coyotes." Included between these two points in the earlier copy is the following:

> "You wouldn't say anything, would you?" the trader said to himself. He shivered in the mist rising from the oily black water, and drew his reefer closer. The trader was a thin-blooded man. The Indian appeared to hear.
>
> "He say in the morning, four days. . . . Now, four days."
>
> "You wouldn't care if he was being killed, would you?" the agent asked, without exasperation. "If he said four days, it'd be four days. No more. No less. God, like the sun and the moon, you are."
>
> The Indian shrugged. After a moment during which he watched the looming of the eastern mountains, which, from his place in the boat, appeared to rise directly from the edge of the water, the trader said, "Sure. Well, what trouble could he get into over there?" Clearly he thought there was none. Yet he amended this a moment later by saying, as if he had remembered something, "Still, every man's his own law; his own trouble, too for that matter."
>
> The Indian made no answer [typescript, pp. 22–23].

Any depth in these two characters beyond that in the published version counters Clark's apparent intent; the less the reader knows about them and the less they appear to know about the situation, the more ominous the story's tone. That the author realized this is readily seen in the following deletion, originally included shortly after the Indian's statement that there were "No coyotes all night" (AM, p. 489):

> "No coyotes other night," the Indian said suddenly.
> "Last night, you mean?" the agent asked, taking the tiller into his hand again, and peering for the indistinguishable shore-line.
> The Indian nodded.
> "Don't your ears sleep? Did he shoot last night?"
> The Indian nodded, but said, "Only few time, near morning." He added, "Same first times; only shoot few, near morning."
> "But the coyotes were singin' then, eh?"
> The Indian nodded, but again amended, "Not when he shoot. All done."
> "He was shootin' after they quit?" The trader was interested now.
> The Indian nodded again.
> The trader once more relapsed onto his tiller. "You should of said something," he said indifferently.
> "He said in the morning, four days," the Indian said.
> "I know," the trader said.

By deleting here, as earlier, references of any import or depth developing the only other humans in the story, Clark has essentially limited their active presence except to basically utilitarian functions, thus focusing all attention, interest, and knowledge on his protagonist, Jed Southwick. As mentioned above, this pruning also excises the crude and obvious foreshadowing present in the earlier manuscript and, in the process, concomitant knowledge outside Southwick of dangerous or malign forces at play. Thus a story dwelling heavily on man's need to prove himself becomes an implicating parody of a rite-of-passage and the turmoil born of both that need and its attendant fear, a chilling study of the effects of fear itself.

Notes

1. The published version appeared in *Atlantic Monthly*, 169 (April 1942) 482–89. The typescript is preserved in Special Collections, The Library, University of Nevada, Reno, as 527/1/8/5. The two will be referred to as AM and typescript, respectively.

2. The revisions may reflect in part the wishes of the publisher. The manuscript is inscribed "19 Albany St., Cazenovia, N.Y." and "Rewrite" on the front page. On the back appears "Pyramid, Nev., July 1937" and Essex, Aug., 1940." Thus we may postulate that the story is to be associated with Clark's visit to Pyramid Lake in the summer of 1937, that the draft was written before *Ox-Bow*, and that the editors of *Atlantic Monthly*, in accepting the story, suggested some tightening. Clark regularly took publishers' suggestions seriously, following them when he could—no doubt the more willingly when he was still relatively inexperienced.

3. Presumably the setting Clark had in mind was the eastern shore of Pyramid Lake, about opposite Suttcliffe, an area that became one of Clark's favorite haunts, but one that had been introduced to him when a boy as an eerie and ominous place, where horrible things could happen. The din of clamoring birds probably came from Anahoe Island, a rookery, and the rock formations are no doubt the Pinnacles at the north end of the lake.

4. Integral text of the flashback:

"Even when he talked as much as the others, he could not forget his agitation and clumsiness, and he felt that this must be indicated by something empty, something pretentious in his talk. It was always possible, of course, that this weakness did not appear to the others. In his failing moments he made use of that hope, but its effect was never enduring. Sooner or later he would always sink into the certainty that he was pretending, and then he would feel doubly worthless and ridiculous. Worst of all, it was at such moments that he felt that he was honest and knew himself, that even if the other men truly believed him to be one of them, they were deceived.

"This state was important, because the doubt frequently began to spread into everything he thought and did, making him yearn to abandon pretense, cease struggling against failure. He would tell himself then, that hunting didn't matter, that in what really mattered in his life hunting was unimportant, like a childhood game; that being a good hunter made no more difference in his life than being a good swimmer would make in the life of a painter. But he could not help recognizing, with self-loathing, that this thought was most likely to occur when he most definitely felt himself a failure. One brief instant of success, like that freak shot over his shoulder at the duck going over the rushes like a bullet in the rainy dawn, made it clear that when he felt most like a good hunter he also felt most like a man capable of anything. In hunting there was more than play for him; to be a good hunter would have a value more than symbolic to him. It would, he felt certain, indicate the attainment of a strength and confidence which would be of value to him in every thought and act of his life.

"He put his food out on a box, fed the dog, and sat down to eat without disturbing these habitual thoughts. All day he had sensed them, the old self-doubt working in his spirit. It had rendered even more dreamlike the natural unreality of this new world of water, white stone, sand tracks through miles of sage, of the white-faced, bearded trader in the post at Arahoe, of riding with the Indian in the small boat on the glassy waters, looking at the hard planes of light on the mountains, the boat making a constant racket and the vast everything else very quiet except just at sun-down, when suddenly the birds, gulls, cormorants, white pelicans, hell-divers, ducks, swarmed up wheeling and squealing and squawking over the stone islands. All day he had sensed the doubts and the unreality, but now he was alone, the thing had been done, and the numbing indecision which had kept him wondering until the last sound of the boat was gone, if he should do this, had departed from him. The vagueness removed, there remained simply the old self-doubt, quite vital and self-inspiring.

"But in spite of it, because he had completed a definite move, Southwick experienced a kind of exultation. It was past recall; for four days at least, he would be entirely alone. He did not believe that it would be possible to make any signal that the Indian or the trader could either see or hear; for his purpose that lake was as effective as an ocean.

"The other men, Handley, Peterson, and Williams, had lightly ridiculed this plan to hunt the hardest-to-get American game, antelope, and perhaps later a mountain lion. They had shown Southwick what they might have thought of a man who had never been out of a city except to shoot ducks on the sound or once every fall to hunt deer in the Adirondacks, going into a country he knew nothing about to hunt antelope and lions he knew nothing about. Over beer and pipes at Steiner's they had called him the big-game hunter, and described amusingly how he would disguise himself to stalk antelope on a thousand miles of sand, and how he would sit for days in the crook of a pine over a canyon, waiting for a lion to appear at the water hole below. He would be unable to leave it at all, they had decided, but would marry a fat squaw and settle in a mud hut in the hills and live by the gun, coming in rarely to purchase ammunition and whiskey by holding up his fingers and grunting. But through all this they had envied him. Before the train had left they admitted it by the way they grinned, but seriously wished him luck. Having killed an antelope, and perhaps a lion, alone in a strange country, it was probable also that he would leave his doubts there. He would no longer be apprehensive and stricken by conflicting ideas when he saw a buck pose in the mere thin, yellow woods. He would be of the circle of approved hunters; he could talk of hunting without seeming even to invent what was the truth" (typescript, pp. 4–6).

15

The Shape of Feeling: Unity of Emotion and Rhetoric in the Work of Walter Clark

Arthur Boardman

Dr. Arthur Boardman, associate professor at the University of Colorado, is both a specialist in American literature and a modern novelist—Captives (New York: Dutton, 1975). His paper below grows from a thesis he wrote for his M.A. degree at the University of Nevada, Reno.

Feeling in the works of Walter Clark exists at two poles, negative and positive; negative feeling is disintegrative, and positive feeling integrative. Though sometimes it is expressed almost explicitly, more often it is expressed implicitly. In implicit form it can become the underlying rhetorical structure of individual works—that is, the indirect expression of feeling can help to shape a given novel or short story.

That the two poles of feeling can be thought of as generally negative and positive seems normal and usual—feelings after all are not neutral, and our feelings about feelings are not neutral. What seems unusual and typical of Clark, though maybe not peculiar to him, is that feeling at the negative pole is disintegrative in that it consists of particular and single emotions,

such as resentment, love, anger, elation. Let us note this carefully: not the kind of emotion, to which we commonly attach
negative or positive values—negative for lust, for example, or
positive for love—but rather the *fact* of the emotion as specific
and single is what is disintegrative.

Feeling at the positive pole is integrative, or to put it as
exactly as I know how, it is integration itself: it *is* wholeness
within the self and with the world—that is, wholeness within
combined with unity without. Just as the feelings at the negative pole can be identified as separate emotions, feeling at the
positive pole, integration, can be analyzed into discrete elements, but the very nature of it is such that the whole is greater
than the sum of the elements making it up.

Clark talks about the disintegrative feeling in an almost
explicit way in a passage in *The City of Trembling Leaves* that
gives an account of the first race between Tim Hazard, the protagonist, and a rival named Red. Tim is envious of Red for his
success with the girl of his own waking and sleeping dreams,
and he has taken up long-distance running out of his envy and
resentment of him, and in order to defeat him. The first time
he is in a race with Red—they are on the same team, it should
be understood, and in a competition with teams from other
high schools—the only feeling he has is one of rivalry with the
other boy. The result before the actual race is that, beside Red,
Tim feels himself hairy and small and awkward and, most significantly, hollow. In the race itself Tim cannot find his proper
running rhythm. Then, when he makes a desperate and foolish
effort to beat Red, who has got far ahead of him, he can only
draw up to him, with his chest laboring and his legs tight, and
eventually feels himself "overcome by despair at inwardly running twice as hard, and yet finding himself falling back."[1] Before and during the race Tim is in the grip of successive emotions—rivalry, anger, and finally despair—the effect of which
manifests itself in the division within him shown in his running
faster mentally but slower physically.

As I have pointed out, the feeling at the negative pole does
not consist only of specific emotions that are conventionally
looked upon with disfavor, like Tim's envy of Red, for in-

stance. The emotion can be one people normally think well of. The romantic love Tim feels for Rachel, still in *The City of Trembling Leaves*, is a good example. Though romantic love, especially in an adolescent, is not looked upon as necessarily the finest of human emotions, it is in general at least tolerated and even moderately approved—or so I interpret the common saying, "All the world loves a lover." Romantic love is of course not disapproved of in *The City*, but as it appears in Tim's feeling for Rachel, it is clearly disintegrative in that it creates division within him. Such division appears in his inability to prevent himself from talking continuously about sports, to her despairing and even excruciating boredom, even though he has told himself before joining her that he must not talk too much and above all that he must not talk about sports, and even though he is aware of the folly of what he is doing *as* he is doing it.[2] Later, when Tim has become a young man, he realizes that he was foolish during all the years that he loved Rachel, for he "had never really expected to have her . . . had never believed that he would either quell or fulfill that yearning."[3] The recognition that the desire was without the substance of true expectation is the recognition of the division within himself, the disintegrative effect of his adolescent love.

In the examples I have given, the treatment of feeling is explicit, or about as close to explicit as one can reasonably expect to find in a piece of fiction. In the next example feeling is expressed far more indirectly, and thus it is a good one to use in order to begin to show how feeling, or the expression of it, can become a part of the rhetorical structure of a work. The short story entitled "The Rapids" tells how a city dweller, probably of sedentary occupation, who is out in the country for a day or a weekend, spends an adventurous and magnificent afternoon riding an old, abandoned boat down some rather tame rapids.[4] The specific emotion the man feels is elation: "The man . . . was immensely elated."[5] Because of the sympathy the protagonist arouses in the reader—this poor devil of an account executive or junior partner is having a wonderful and boyish time for once; he would seem to be at play in the very best sense of that term—because the activity occupying him is one that

brings him closer to nature and also allows him to assert himself, and because the emotion he experiences is elation—for all
these reasons the story may seem an unpromising one in which
to find feeling at the negative pole, disintegrative feeling. It
may seem odd, also, to speak of elation as disintegrative, yet
the text indicates that it is, and in fact much of the theme or
point of the story resides in its being so. The protagonist enters
into his adventure on the basis of an illusion: on looking down
at himself while he splashes in the pool of water where he finds
the boat, he sees himself, because of the refracting effect of the
water, as a "more powerful and formidable man" than he is.[6]
And though the play with the boat produces the elation with
which the reader sympathizes, it also makes the man ridiculous,
for he behaves in a childish fashion. The fact comes out near
the close of the story, and the way it comes out illustrates how
feeling and rhetoric can come together.

From the beginning of "The Rapids," the narrative point of
view has been of the kind called by critics, rather unhelpfully,
omniscient—that is, it has been the voice of an all-seeing author who can describe setting, character, and action and can
also report what characters feel and think—and the tone has
been at once judicial and slightly amused. When a large cloud
appears in the afternoon sky, the man's reaction is reported
thus: "The man felt this cloud to be a recognition of the dimen-
sion of his undertaking, and gazed at it with stern exultation."
Abruptly, after this indication that elation is becoming or has
already turned into foolish pride, there is a shift of focus to a
woman, presumably the man's wife, who appears, stares incred-
ulously and in irritation at the man, and exclaims to herself
over his behavior. Immediately the focus shifts again, with the
effect of presenting the scene as any witness, including of
course the woman, might see it:

> The man was just launching out. . . . He was standing upright
> in the orange boat, the bamboo pole held aloft like a spear. . . .
> his mouth could be seen to open tremendously and repeatedly.
> He waved his left arm in accompaniment. Faintly, even over
> the wind and the rush of the falls, the woman could hear the
> words. "Sailing, sailing," roared the man in the boat. He

shook his spear. "Sailing, sailing," he roared, until the boat
stumbled and knocked him to his knees. Even then his mouth
opened and closed in the same way.[7]

This man is divided from himself, in the sense that he is almost
beside himself. Or, to put it another way, his present—the adventure in the boat—and his past—his daily life—have no relationship to each other. The disintegrative effect of the feeling
of elation in the man is communicated by a rhetorical device
that *reflects* disintegration, the abrupt and radical shifts in focus
from the man's exultation, first to the woman's reaction, and
then to an almost pictorial report of what the man looks like
as he rides his boat. Paradoxically, by the use here of a technique the essense of which is discontinuity Clark achieves
unity of form and content.

Another example of feeling that is disintegrative and of the
expression of that feeling should suffice to make my point about
such feeling clear. It comes from *The Track of the Cat*, and it
concerns Curt on his long and at last fatal trek in the mountains, beginning as a hunt for the mountain lion that killed his
brother but becoming soon an escape from a mountain lion
created by his own imagination. Even though Curt begins the
hunt in order to avenge his brother's death, he also feels some
fear from the beginning, a fear that becomes progressively
greater until it turns into the panic that kills him. Clark shows
the disintegrative effects of the fear by having Curt *talk* to himself, the talk consisting of admonishments to keep alert and to
think. Thus, a kind of internal debate between some part of
Curt's reason and the generally inarticulate and confused rest
of him occurs more and more frequently as the fear grows, the
debate expressing the fear and in its very existence the disintegration that accompanies it, for a man talking to himself is on
the way to being two rather than one.

The culmination comes with the panic, when Curt, running
heedlessly and hysterically, hears "someone . . . making tremulous, unceasing whimpers of terror," and then the (imaginary)
panther "panting and making little nervous, whining noises
closer and closer," and finally "a wild, long scream going down
with him" as he falls to his death over a cliff.[8] All of these

noises, the reader knows, come from Curt himself. Curt never
realizes that they do. And at no point does Clark explicitly attribute them to him. There is Curt's consciousness, and there
are the noises, presented separately and without connection in
an elegant stylistic embodiment of the disconnected compo-
nents that Curt has now become.

In the grip of a single, overwhelming feeling Curt falls to his
death; yet negative, disintegrative emotion can lead to wholeness. The possibility is illustrated in the material with which
I shall begin to try to define the feeling at the positive end of
the pole, the feeling that is integration itself. Let us return to
The City of Trembling Leaves and to the track meet, where we
left Tim Hazard losing a race while "inwardly running twice as
hard," very much in the grip of specific and thus disintegrative
emotion. Tim loses the race, going then so far toward breaking
down that his collapse becomes physical, and he almost faints.
He has to rest, fortunately, for he must run in a second race
in a little while, and he recovers in a physical sense but his feeling remains essentially the same: when he lines up for the second race he feels "a steady determination to outrun Red." And
Clark goes on with, "That was practically all he was thinking
about." There is one difference between the way Tim feels now
and the way he felt before the first race: he no longer feels nervous. Still, for the first three laps of the race, he cannot get his
usual rhythm, he runs in irritation, and he runs stiffly and with
a stride that jars him every time his foot strikes the ground. He
feels himself battling the wind, which makes "his eyes water
and his lungs labor." He even despairs "of ever getting right."

Then quite suddenly he *does* get right:

> When the turn put the wind onto his shoulder instead of
> against his chest this little knotting of the inner runner
> slipped straight. He thought . . . that if he couldn't run joy-
> ously, then he must at least run evenly. He concentrated on
> evenness, and gradually the tension passed from him. A kind
> of golden anger of triumph poured into him. Second wind it
> is generally called, and it is made up as much of smoothness,
> of getting the inner and outer runner together, as it is of at-

taining an oxygen balance. Joyously he thought, several times,
rapidly and in the tempo of his running. "Now I've got you."[9]

The "you" is Red, and he does indeed have him. Let me immediately add, however, that now the winning or losing of the
race becomes not merely incidental or unimportant but absolutely irrelevant, to the character and to us as readers, for Tim
in having his inner and outer selves together has arrived at integration.

Let us analyze the feeling so far as we have seen it—and we
have not yet seen the whole—in order to see what it consists
of. In the given instance, and not all instances are or need be
exactly the same, it consists on the material or physical level
of that oxygen balance we call second wind. Put in a general
way that would apply to other instances as well, it consists of
that state of physiological equilibrium achieved when the
human body functions perfectly in human terms—that is,
when it works well. On the level of personal identity it consists
of the balance or perhaps more properly the blending of the
spiritual and the physical elements of the self, what Clark calls
in the passage I quoted "getting the inner and outer runner together"—put another way yet, a blending into a whole of the
intellectual, emotional, and physiological elements making up
the individual human being.

We have not yet, I repeat, seen the whole of the feeling of
wholeness, and before we try to we must see more exactly how
it comes about, at least in the particular instance, because that
has a bearing on the whole. I noted earlier that Tim's getting
right happens suddenly: the "little knotting of the inner runner
slipped straight," Clark tells us, "and gradually the tension
passed from him." This happens quite quickly—as Tim runs
about half a lap on the track—but it does not just happen. For
Clark also tells us that the unknotting of the knot occurs "when
the turn [in the track] put the wind onto his shoulder instead
of against his chest. . . ." The feeling of integration has various
roots, so to say, one of them being physical sensation (feeling).
Explicitly the relationship between the two seems temporal:
when Tim rounds the turn and feels the wind with instead of

against him, the feeling of integration begins to develop. Implicitly the relationship is causal: for, considered dispassionately and abstractly, the difference between running with the
wind and running against it, unless we are to imagine a hur-
ricane, is of no importance, is just a matter for chronometers.
But subjectively and experientially considered, the difference
is enormous: it is the difference between battle and harmony.
Thus *because* Tim enters into a harmony with the world outside
himself, he starts on the way to achieving the feeling that is
wholeness or integration.

Now we are ready to go further in our analysis of the feeling
of integration, in order to understand what else it consists of
besides physiological and spiritual balance. It consists also of
harmony or unity with the external, the harmony that starts
the feeling of wholeness for Tim. As it develops, Tim becomes
filled with the knowledge of it, as Clark emphasizes after he has
had Tim think that he has got Red. First, "He increased his
pace, and it was no trouble to do this." We have here a brief
reminder of the physical and spiritual balance. Then, "The
spring sunshine was wonderful. He had forgotten about the sun
. . . and now it burst open around him." Because Tim now per-
ceives the sun, he can enter into relationship with it, whereas
before, enclosed as it were in his single emotion, he could
forget it. Clark now further emphasizes the harmony with the
external: "He rode before the wind. It was wonderful too." And
a few lines later, "Even the head wind pleased him now; it was
great to breast the head wind."

In the new feeling the single feeling of rivalry with the other
boy is dismissed: "He wanted to laugh at Red, this futile battler
out of the past. . . . He didn't really pay any attention to
Red."[10] The change is radical, and it is radical in another sense
as well, which will help us to see integration more fully. In contrast to the singleness of the negative feeling, whether rivalry
or love or elation, the positive feeling is composed of *several*
elements, as is implied by one of the terms I have used for it,
"integration." Along with the elements of physical well-being,
adjustment of the physical and the spiritual, and harmony with
the world outside the self, specifically the world of nature, there

is the element—perhaps "characteristic" would be the better word—of multiplicity. Tim in the last part of the race experiences a variety of feelings all more or less at the same time, which coalesce into the wholeness we have seen.

The feeling is not always of such short duration as it is for Tim Hazard in the race, and it is not always so dramatically rapid in its coming on: in the instance I have discussed it comes on in the last lap of a one-mile race. In the short story entitled "The Indian Well," the feeling of wholeness as existing and as developing occupies approximately the first two-thirds of the story. [11] Interestingly, inasmuch as the verdant area watered by the well of the title is not inhabited by humans as the story opens, the feeling is there at first without human participation, except that implied by the omniscient but after all human narrator and by the "presence" of the reader—of us, that is, the narrator's audience and thus indirectly the witnesses of the events narrated. The place of the story is one in which multiplicity—shown in the various species of life there—can exist in contrast to the single force of the sun, which otherwise dominates the region: the desert near or perhaps of Death Valley. The cause is the Indian well, representing well-being itself and giving it to those drinking from it. The feeling of wholeness there is completed by the harmony of living—vegetable, animal, and mineral (Clark actually speaks of the "thinking cliffs")—which the opening of the story evokes.

Into this harmony and wholeness come a prospector and his burro. With the taking of water, the man and the burro begin the processes of recuperation and of integration that go on quite gradually, and show themselves in the health of the two, the cheerfulness at work and play of the man, Jim Suttler, and most notably in his fitting, in time and without essential disturbance, into the harmony of the life of the Indian well. It is in retrospect—an important word to keep in mind—that we most clearly see that wholeness has been achieved, for when a change comes, disrupting the harmony or wholeness and imposing at least for a time disintegration, the shocking difference forces us to awareness of what has been lost.

Ostensibly the change comes from an external agent, a

mountain lion that invades the little oasis and kills Jenny, Suttler's burro. In fact, however, the change comes from the man's
reaction to the loss. The mountain lion, Clark makes it plain,
has killed because driven by the physical need of hunger, and
has killed dispassionately and not under the domination of
some specific emotion. In contrast, Suttler reacts to finding the
dead burro with a passion of hatred that becomes a
monomaniacal desire for vengeance. The single emotion
brings with it disintegration not only for Suttler but also for the
whole life of the Indian well: "There was a difference in his
smell after that day which prevented even the rabbits from
coming into the meadow. . . ."[12] As for Suttler:

> . . . he did not miss a watch. He learned to go to sleep at sun-
> down, wake within a few minutes of midnight, go up to his
> post [a niche in a cliff], and become at once clear-headed and
> watchful. He talked to himself in the mine and the cabin, but
> never in the niche. . . . All winter he did not remove his
> clothes, bathe, shave, cut his hair or sing. He worked the dead
> mine only to be busy, and became thin again, with sunken
> eyes which yet were not the eyes he had come with the spring
> before.[13]

The dramatic contrast between the Jim Suttler completely
given over to vengeful passion and the Jim Suttler of before
helps to show the last characteristic of integration: that it is dynamic, that it is process. Jim Suttler gripped by hatred is stat-
ic—he seems frozen into a given attitude (not forever, for he
does come out of it)—whereas Jim Suttler before the death of
Jenny the burro is dynamic in that he *grows* into the wholeness
of the Indian well. With the change, retrospectively we can see
that the first and larger part of the story showed wholeness
being achieved, constantly. Not that we cannot see the process
as it occurs, only that looking back from the perspective of the
change, we see it emphasized and dramatized. Thus the story
suggests that wholeness is becoming, and if we look further
back now—to Tim Hazard—we can see that for the hero of *The
City of Trembling Leaves* too the feeling of wholeness involves
process, the drawing together continuously of the multiplicity

of elements composing it. In Tim too we can see that if wholeness is true being, true being is becoming.

"The Indian Well" illustrates how the feeling of integration can be reflected in the rhetoric of a work, and it illustrates it by a technique calling in part for the retrospection I have taken pains to emphasize—retrospection focusing the reader's attention on the characteristics of process and multiplicity that are parts of integration. The technique is deceptively simple and unobtrusive—so much so as scarcely to seem rhetoric, yet of course it is. In "The Indian Well" the rhetoric of the feeling of integration consists of the statement of particulars followed by the crucial shift in focus that comes with the change in the story.

As I have said, Clark devotes approximately the first two-thirds of the story to the establishment of the feeling of wholeness through the description of the life of the oasis and of Suttler's harmonious entry into it. The shift coming with the change underlines the fact that, if the theme has heretofore been wholeness, it has been developed through the statement of the details of multiplicity, for the focus of the first two-thirds of the story includes *everything*—everything that is, around the Indian well: the cliffs, the bubbling water, the cliff swallows, Jim Suttler, the bats, the coyotes, the lizards, the previous passersby in the form of the graffiti they left, the brush, the singing insects, Jenny, the aspen trees, the rabbits—these things *and* the way they feel *and* the way they interact. In other words, the evocation of the feeling of integration comes about by the process of listing the particular and concrete elements making it up, but without ever explicitly stating what it is that gets made up.

"The Indian Well," which serves to show the possible integration between the feeling of integration and form in Clark's work, also illustrates how feeling, positive and negative, can be reflected in the basic structure of a work as a whole. The shift in focus after the first two-thirds of the story is to the action of the work, taking up all but a page of the remaining third, and consisting of the description of the mountain lion's arrival at the oasis and his killing the burro, and most importantly of the description of Jim Suttler in the grip of his vengeful mania, the period when he watches for and eventually kills the mountain lion, skins it, and buries the pelt in the same grave in which he has earlier buried Jenny. The shift is from the all-inclusive view of the life of the Indian well to a narrow and exclusive focus on action, concentrating mainly, and finally only, on the lone man eaten up by his desire to kill. It is perhaps not fanciful to call this portion of the story claustrophobic—tense with excitement, as I suppose claustrophobia may be, and devoid of all else save intense narrowness. We have moved from the rhetoric of multiplicity and integration—the statement of many particulars—to that of single emotion—here the unfolding of a single action that is the physical expression of the emotion. The disintegrative effect is marked simply and poignantly by the absence of wholeness, which was so much present before.

In the last page of the story there is a return to the broad focus and to the feeling of integration. Having sated his vengeance, Jim Suttler seems to come back to himself. He sleeps through the night for the first time since the violent death of the burro, he repeats a cleansing ritual he celebrated the year before on arrival, he sings and dances to spring, and then he leaves, "a starved but revived and volatile spirit." Then, Clark tells us, "The disturbed life of the spring resumed." The rabbits love in the willows, the rats play again in the abandoned cabin, a roadrunner takes up once more its normal hunting rounds, the antelope return, the aspen leaves make a "tiny music of shadows."[14] Singleness is no more, and wholeness again *becomes*. Clark re-creates it by the same process, much reduced in length, that he used earlier: the statement of particulars. Thus the story ends essentially where it began, emotionally, thematically, and rhetorically—essentially but not entirely, for the end includes Jim Suttler as a part of the past—and the correspondence in "The Indian Well" between feeling and structure is exact.

To say that such a structure exists in all of Clark's work would be to insist on a kind of humorless consistency on his part that I for one should not like to attribute to him. Writers, like other people, are freer than the theories we make about them. It would be particularly unwise, further, to posit the correspondence about the larger works, for novels are usually too complex to allow the application to them of a single principle in an exclusive way. Not many novels, I think, have a single structural principle. With this caution, however, I will risk the argument, briefly and in closing, that two of Clark's novels— *The Ox-Bow Incident* and *The Track of the Cat*—do have a structure in which *one* principle is the parallel to feeling.

The Ox-Bow Incident opens with the evocation of the feeling of integration. But most of that novel does *not* evoke that feeling: in fact, the very opposite. The characters making up the mob that chases and eventually hangs in error three innocent men are in the grip of various single feelings, the disintegrative effects of which are visible in them individually and in the society of which they form a part. At the end of the novel, however, with the crime committed, the mob disabused of its error and dispersed into its shamed parts, and the leader who has tried to prevent the lynching—Arthur Davies—in a state of moral and physical collapse, then there is at least the hint or prophecy of a return to integration. The narrator, Art Croft, is recovering from a wound suffered during the chase. He and Gil, his friend, both feel a longing to leave the town and get back on the range. The spring, which lapsed back into winter during the chase and lynching, returns. Art hears in the distance the calls of meadowlarks. The mood is of a very guarded optimism, implying wholeness not achieved but achievable, and the evocation of the possibility is a kind of resolution.

The Track of the Cat contains almost none of the feeling of integration—none at all, really, for it appears only in the form of memory in the first section of the novel and in the form of a latent possibility in the second and in the fourth, which is also the last. So far as feeling is concerned, the work is a study of single emotions and their disintegrative effect. I have already spoken of the disintegrative effect of fear on Curt Bridges, who psychically becomes at least two men in the moments before his death. Because Curt dominates the third section of the novel, that section in terms of feeling focuses primarily on fear, though with some brief looks at lust and rage (Curt's is not an attractive personality), conveying the disintegrative effect of the single emotions largely by means of Curt's talking to himself, but also by means of dreams. The second section is a preparation for the third, again of course in terms of feeling, concentrating on the single emotions of the other members of the Bridges family: the mother's narrow religiosity alternating with her feeling of guilt about her treatment of the dead Arthur, the father's resentment of the present, the sister's hysterical sorrow at the death of her brother, and the youngest brother's, Harold's, love for Gwen Williams.

The effect appears clearly in the individuals—most tellingly in the father, who spends most of the time in an alcoholic near stupor that makes him think he is in the past. It appears also in the divisive tension between the members of the family, revealed for example in the father's and mother's mutual contempt and in Harold's inability to make a comforting gesture toward his mother despite his wish to. The essential difference between this section and the third, Curt's, is that the point of view is Harold's, and in Harold is the latent possibility, utterly out of the question for Curt, of experiencing the feeling of wholeness.

That is established in the first section, told mainly from the point of view of Arthur, whom the mountain lion kills at the end of the section. The section opens with a reporting of the feeling of uneasiness, which almost immediately becomes fear expressed in a dream Arthur has. As I mentioned but did not explain in connection with Curt, a dream can be used as a rhetorical device to imply disintegration, for a dream divides the dreamer from his waking self, and Clark stresses the division by putting Arthur's and the other characters' dreams in italics. Arthur wakes up and immediately Clark gives a strong hint that he is a character capable of experiencing integration, for he has him touch the wall next to his bed and smile, and then he explains, "It was an old test with him, this touching something real."[15] Clearly, this is a man who enters into relationship with the external world, thus experiencing at least part of integration. The hint is confirmed explicitly just before he is killed, in a memory brought to his mind by the sight of a particular high rock, on which he has often sat and looked at a tremendous and varied view, with the effect of achieving for a time a sense of integration.

That the same general capability exists, not much developed yet, in Harold, Clark has suggested from the beginning by showing the sympathy and understanding existing between the two brothers, despite the great difference in their age (Harold being younger by some twenty years). Clark reemphasizes the sympathy and at the same time unmistakably implies the younger brother's crucial likeness to the elder by having Arthur conclude his reflection with the thought that he must tell Harold to bring Gwen, his fiancée, to the rock so that they too can look out from it. [16]

The fact of Harold's character having significant resemblance to Arthur's is not forgotten in the second section of the novel. In the fourth and final section, then, in which Harold is again the central figure and which begins like the first with fear and a dream—only this time it is Harold dreaming—the fact that Harold's is the main consciousness in itself suggests a contrast in feeling with the previous section, which was Curt's. The contrast is reinforced immediately by the lessening of tension between Harold and his fiancée Gwen (there will be integration there, certainly), and between Harold and his mother as he agrees to go look for Curt. The final hint of the possibilities in Harold and in and for the future comes just before the end, when the young man, having killed the mountain lion and found the corpse of Curt, suddenly realizes that he has now become the de facto head of the family and that the fact can make an "enormous difference."[17] On a concrete level there can now be no barrier to his marriage with Gwen; on a more general level there can now be an attitude very different from Curt's dominating the ranch. Possibilities, in short, are open to new life and new feeling.

Although the lessening of tensions at the beginning of the section is very evident, and although the fact of the "enormous difference" is stated overtly, the possibilities of new feeling have been *there* all along, embodied in the simple presence of

Harold. It is easy to forget that a character is a structural principle, a rhetorical device, like any other specific element in a literary work. Because of the spiritual kinship Clark establishes at the outset of the novel between Harold and Arthur, Harold can function as the connection between the experience of the feeling of integration which has been Arthur's and the possibility of it in the future. Like the wall, the something real Arthur touches when he wakes, reminding him of his connection with the real world, Harold is the rhetorical something real implicitly maintaining in the second and final sections of the novel the connection to the reality of wholeness.

The way Harold functions, so far as feeling is concerned, brings me to a point I have been skirting for some time. The parallels we have seen between feeling and form—implying their oneness, ultimately—imply another kind of integration, one involving the author and the reader. That integration occurs even in connection with feeling that is disintegrative. It is the author, of course, who has given feeling expression in a form that in a sense is one with it: the disintegrative feeling of fear, for instance, in Curt's divided consciousness, or the feeling of wholeness in a statement of particulars coupled with a contrast or summation—but it is we the readers who respond to the form. We perceive and experience separation in Curt; we look back to the multiplicity of particulars, and perceive and experience wholeness. As we do, we share briefly and modestly in the shaping of feeling; it is then our privilege to be for the moment one with the spirit of the artist, Walter Clark.

Notes

1. *The City of Trembling Leaves* (New York: Random House, 1945), pp. 188–90.
2. Ibid., pp. 233–37.
3. Ibid., p. 395.
4. *The Watchful Gods and Other Stories* (New York: Random House, 1950), pp. 51–64.
5. Ibid., p. 60.
6. Ibid., p. 56.
7. Ibid., pp. 61–62, *passim.*

8. *The Track of the Cat* (New York: Random House, 1949), pp. 364–66, *passim*.

9. *The City*, pp. 192–94.

10. Ibid., pp. 194.

11. *The Watchful Gods*, pp. 123–48.

12. Ibid., p. 145.

13. Ibid., p. 146.

14. Ibid., p. 148.

15. *The Track of the Cat*, p. 6.

16. Ibid., p. 80.

17. Ibid., p. 403.

16

On the "Voice" of Walter Clark

Robert M. Clark

In this dead land, like a vast relief model, the only allegiance was to the sun [opening, "The Indian Well"].

Growing tough and dry again as the summer advanced, inured to the family of the farmer, whom he saw daily, stooping and scraping with sticks in the ugly open rows of their fields, where no lovely grass rustled and no life stirred save the shameless gulls, which waited at the heels of the workers, gobbling the worms and grubs they turned up, Hook became nearly content with his shard of life ["Hook," in *The Watchful Gods*, p. 23].

He had expected a lot of orange windows close together on the other side of the canyon. Instead there were only a few scattered lights across the darkness, and they were white. They made no communal glow upon the steep slope, but gave out only single, white needles of light, which pierced the darkness secretly and lonesomely, as if nothing could ever pass from one house to another over there ["The Wind and the Snow of Winter," in *The Watchful Gods*, p. 46].

Harold could see the ranch, still tiny with distance, and already in the shadow of the mountain. Once in a while it showed clearly, so he could see even the smoke lining out from the chimney of the house, but more often it grew faint or even disappeared behind the running snow [conclusion, *The Track of the Cat*].

My father was one of those writers with a distinctive style, writers who, like Faulkner, Hemingway, or James, could be readily named in a literary parlor game if the players were presented with such representative passages as I have here provided. They do represent, I believe, that particular and peculiar "voice" that is Walter Van Tilburg Clark's, and I will try to elaborate some on the qualities of that voice, and on the separate elements the combination of which makes the voice distinctive.

The success of Dad's writing is more closely related to style—style in the sense of the selection of a particular word, to this syntactical arrangement and not another—than is true for many prose writers, who depend more upon character or situation. Such precision of diction and arrangement is more commonly a concern of poetry than of prose, and of lyric poetry, with its emphasis on expression of individual feeling. I am sure many of you were pleased to hear Dr. Boardman, in the preceding lecture, put his emphasis on feeling, on emotional impact, and lead us away from our previous rummagings among ideas, themes, symbols, and archetypes.

Dr. Laird has remarked that, try as we might in these lectures and discussions, we keep coming back to literary in-house talk, ransacking symbols for their ultimate meaning, while somehow those things about Dad's writing that we most admire and enjoy escaped unmentioned. Ed Hancock made an effort the other night to grasp them, saying that memorable images were what we carried away and treasured. And Mrs. [Ellen] Thompson, by now one of the veterans of these lectures, made a gentle but forceful rebuke after one of our dissections when she recalled the gathering of university people and their legal champions for a late picnic and strategy session during the President Stout days around a campfire in the ruins of the old mill up on American Flat, behind Gold Hill. She compared the quality she took from Dad's writing with the moment when a large moon rose free from the hills to the east, and there was an immediate, spontaneous quiet among that group of talkative and talking people, and a silence filled with pale and flickering light and a lot of shadows. It was a silence and a situation charged with meaning, but with no need to analyze and no desire to find an abstract paraphrase for the moment. The feeling was real, and contained the meaning.

Perhaps we should let it go at that, and go home. But the literary commentator feels duty bound to comment. It is a happy moment for the commentator who feels thus duty bound to try to explain at least why something moves him when he first has his own emotional reaction to a piece of writing and then, going back to see what happened, discovers what he felt was what the writer wanted him to feel. That lets him talk about the writing some more. And this is very often the case with me and my father's writing. For Dad was, I think, despite the philosophical or religious nature of his themes, despite his technical sophistication, and despite his symbolism, principally an emotive writer.

Ed Hancock reminded us that one of the maxims Dad gave to beginning writers was to render emotion, not idea. Dad was much taken, I think, from at least his undergraduate days here at Nevada, with a book on epistemology by James Harvey Robinson, quite well known in its time, *The Mind in the Making*. It might be termed an intellectual history admirably suited for the doggedly disillusioned, young "lost generation" of the 1920s. It may have been from Robinson that he took a notion I should have to call a conviction, that our ideas were nothing but a rationalization of our feelings anyway. And if, indeed, Jungian principles of psychology can be detected in his work, as Dr. Westbrook certainly detected them, I suspect it is because Dad's efforts to render his dreams, reveries, and feelings happened to illustrate the Jungian thesis. His writings are more a testimonial to the truths of the psychological system than any embodiment of Jungian precepts he first considered in the abstract, and for which he then sought to find a story.

Because I knew Dad mainly as the college teacher, being very rational in his analyses of Henry James, I tended to assume this same analytical rationality had been at work all along in the fiction. Now I think I was wrong. Dad was not only an emotive writer, whose principal aim was to move the reader, but an emotional one. Charles Dickens is said to have wept when writing the passage where little Nell expires, and to have laughed uproariously and immodestly when doing a funny scene. Truman Capote, on the other hand, once remarked that, before he actually started to put a story on paper, he had exhausted the emotion the material raised in him, and then aimed at re-creating it in cool detachment. Dad was closer to the Dickens side. Not that I recall, from the Washoe Valley when he was working on The Cat or from Virginia City when he was struggling with the novels that would not come, any tears dribbling onto the page on the kitchen table, or raucous laughter or fierce swearing from the study. Maybe some occasional swearing. With Dad we should put it in terms not of noise, but of motion. He has told us that in The City. We watch Tim Hazard in the honeymoon cabin at Lake Tahoe, starting, angrily scratching it out, starting again, wadding up the failures, sometimes sitting for hours, staring, with pencil poised, then going along almost faster than pencil or mind could move.

It does not work out perfectly, of course, but well enough to be significant. Where Dad had trouble, when he was in the scratching-out mode, the reader and the critic are apt to have trouble—the ranch house scenes in The Cat, most of the second "book" of The City. When he wrote relatively quickly and easily, he gets the most applause—the long hunt sequence in The Cat, "The Indian Well," "The Wind and the Snow of Winter," "Hook."

We need not pause to consider the degree of the conscious or unconscious involved here. We can borrow Dad's term and say, in those good stretches for his writing, it is "balance" and let that go. It is interesting, however, that these stories and passages that "nearly wrote themselves," as he put it, are frequently found to be quite complicated rhetorically. They might strike us as being the end result of a great deal of calculation and rewriting, when they were not.

We are looking here, I suppose, at that extra something beyond the honed talent that we can recognize as his particular genius, and can admire, but not talk very clearly about. All I would suggest is that, to be at his best, Dad needed to find material that sustained some original feeling that compelled him to write, the feeling generated by the particular image that was so often the source for his fiction.

That may seem a truism about almost any writer at his best. If there is a difference worth mentioning, it is that the material had to quite literally sustain the very feeling in Dad that he was trying to put across to the reader, or be able to re-create it once more, in the man himself, when he returned to work on a longer story or novel. Moreover, this feeling is relatively un-complicated and consistent. He evokes from the reader a re-sponse that is quite intense, and quite narrow—if I may picture our emotional possibilities more neatly than they actually are, and suggest that emotions can be worked on like separate veins of ore, following one along quite separately from all the others.

The importance of this sustained, single vein of feeling is why, in my opinion, he was a better short story writer than a novelist. The short story allows this simplification and inten-sification of emotion as the novel does not. The Ox-Bow and The Track of the Cat are more successful as wholes than is The City of Trembling Leaves precisely because they are more like short stories. What we remember from The City are isolated chapters of more or less short story length, quite complete in themselves, and built around a single emotional note, though they are meant to be part of the total structure. I suppose Dad hoped the "symphonic" structure would be a means of melding the separate emotional notes into a harmonious whole, but it does not seem to have succeeded for very many readers.

Let me take Ox-Bow to try to make myself more clear. Most readers must find the book uneven, virtually breaking in two. The first part is the three sections culminating with the lynch-ing. The second is the two sections that contain mostly ex-changes between Davies and Art Croft, with the Tetley sui-

cides off-stage. These last two sections are certainly crucial to
the book's structure. They are there to change the incident
from unfortunate mistake to tragedy. But just as certainly our
responses to the two parts are quite different.

This difference has been explained in terms of structure. The
first three sections are directed so economically toward the
lynching that the book loses its structural focus when the men
are hanged, and has to start over again. We might explain the
difference in emotional terms as well. A kind of deliberately
restrained anger lies behind the effectiveness of the first three
sections. I am saying that this is not just what I feel when I read
that part; I am claiming that is what Dad felt too, that his apprehension of the gathering injustice first produced, and then
sustained, that tone, made up from hundreds of little details
and devices, that succeeds then in making me a bit angry each
time I read it, although I know full well the ending and that
my anger will not do any good. There are breaks, pauses, in this
tone. Little jokes. Tension and release. But what we call the
mounting suspense is very much the steady pressure of the author's restrained anger. The pressure is released at the hanging,
and the story has to look for a new emotional center. It does
not quite find one. The intellectual debate does not lend itself
to that kind of steady emotional intensification.

I would even venture to say that the obtrusiveness of
symbolism that has sometimes been noted occurs just where
the emotion involved in the story is fragmented, confused,
or complex in conception, as it must be in "The Watchful
Gods," where the complexity of Buck's emotions is the point,
or as it must needs be in scenes involving several characters,
each bringing their own emotional temperament and needs
to a scene, as in many of the ranch house exchanges in
The Track of the Cat. These are the moments we are allowed
to be too conscious of a stairway leading up into darkness
in the corner, by patterns of black and white. This does
not happen in such scenes as Arthur's funeral. There we
have a variety of reactions from a variety of characters, but

they are all variations on the same central emotion, grief for something very valuable that is irrevocably gone, and that is the emotion evoked in me too. The one character incapable of expressing some version of that emotion—the father—is not in the grave scene. I am sure the patterns of symbolism are at work there, as they are through the hunt sequence, but they do their job as Dad wished them to do, surreptitiously, working on our feelings.

Here I am talking about symbols again. But any talk of Dad's style, especially the style as it appears in passages I take to represent his distinctive voice, does involve us once more with symbols, and leads me to try to explore a little further Dr. Gorrell's distinction between the natural symbol that was in, and the artificial symbol that seems to intrude on, the story. As Dr. Gorrell points out, part of the difficulty with "symbol" as a literary term is that we tend to think that symbol means something that should be paraphrasable into abstract, discursive terms. If the black cat is a symbol, then a lecturer ought to be able to say the cat is death, or evil, or the cosmic conscience, or the embodiment of an aspect of Curt Bridges's collective consciousness. Symbol can occupy the whole, huge gap between allegory, where a ditch means the Slough of Despond, and a ditch that is nothing more nor less than a ditch.

In Dad's writing, feeling and symbol have something to do with one another, a relationship that is perhaps best revealed in a couple of small memo sheets with notes for a class lecture on symbols in literature. If one sets out to chart types of symbolism, one could conceivably locate hundreds of gradations between the Slough of Despond and the ditch. Dad, however, limited himself to three.

First, he cited natural symbol, where something just takes on added importance automatically, from the nature of the English language itself, and from our habits of mind. Such symbolism is close to what we mean by a representative thing or character. Mike Braneen, just by being alone in the story, represents all of a kind, the single, wandering prospector, and his decay "symbolizes" the passing of that kind. Or we can go up through gradations. His decay taken with the decay of Gold Rock symbolizes the passing of an era as well as of a breed.

Secondly, Dad listed the verbal symbol, where language pushes a comparison not necessarily there. Metaphor is one of the most obvious such verbal devices. A famous example is color in Stephen Crane's *The Red Badge of Courage* where, near the close of the book, we find the setting sun "pasted" like a "red wafer" in the sky. Now the sky probably was red. If he had said just that—the sky was red—we would probably still extend its suggestiveness, given that we have just come through a horrendous Civil War battle, to be a reflection of spilled blood. With "wafer" the sun is demeaned by comparison with a trivial object, and "pasted" suggests some sort of unsympathetic Aristotelian First Mover up there, one with a certain sense of aptness, not to say irony, who pastes the red sun there as his cryptic comment on the human activity. Such verbal symbolism is very important in Dad's style. I will just mention here the story "Hook," where color, particularly of the hawk's eyes, functions this way, and is in turn part of a metaphor running all through the story that suggests there is a similarity between fire and the main quality of hawk life.

The third form, Dad said, and one that combines the first two, is the "objective correlative." T. S. Eliot established that term in our critical vocabulary, and said it was the only way of expressing emotion in the form of art. He defined it as "a set of objects, a situation, a chain of events which shall be the formula of that particular emotion, such that when the external facts, which must terminate in sensory experience, are given, the emotion is immediately evoked."[1] This is part of the now familiar and widely accepted modern dogma that literature should be "concrete," not abstract, should "show," not "tell," all of which Dad subscribed to in his creative writing teaching. But Dad has here equated "means of communicating feeling" with "symbol" as Eliot did not, and as most of us who have used the word during these discussions have not. We have usually talked of symbol as a means of suggesting ideas, of extending intellectual meaning. Ideas can evoke emotion, of course, but Dad's emphasis here is significant. Symbol is the means of expressing his feeling and, when things are in balance, of evoking the same feeling in the reader. And we should remember that, under Dad's categories, the objective correlative includes both the actual object and the verbal extensions the writer may employ in presenting that object.

We should keep this in mind because it suggests that natural symbolism in Dad's writing is not likely to be the associations that "ditch" may suggest by itself, which are likely to be quite different to different readers, but "ditch" with a special verbal presentation that will not try to make the ditch stand for the Slough of Despond, but will try to re-create in the reader the feelings that the image of the ditch aroused in Dad. The ditch is going to be an objective correlative that reinforces, or slightly modulates or varies, but essentially reinforces a dominant feeling in the scene or story.

This dominant feeling comes across to us as tone. Tone and voice are both a bit slippery as terms, and I should try to come to somewhat closer grips with them at this point. Tone can be defined as both the author's attitude toward his or her material and readers—condescending, naive, sardonic, and so forth—and the "mood" of the piece—sad, exuberant, eerie, and so forth. The two operate hand in hand, of course. If one needs to distinguish between them, one could say that it is specific rhetorical devices such as alliteration, or metaphor, that most influence the mood, whereas broader elements of structure, such as viewpoint and arrangement, are our best clues to the authorial attitude. Some elements, obviously, such as diction, the selection among available words, are crucial to both. And everything I have been saying up to this point certainly suggests that these two types of tone are very closely related in the Clark "voice"; Dad is seldom as "neutral" an author as many, even most, contemporary writers of fiction.

Voice, I should say, subsumes tone. An authorial voice might still be recognizable through a variety of tones, all marked by recurring syntactical arrangements, images, diction, and rhetorical features. In Dad's case, one can quickly distinguish at least two major tones. One we might call the serious, although it might also be tabbed the lyrical, and the other the satirical. This is the difference between "Hook" and "The Ascent of Aeriel Goodbody" or those "moral fables" in *The City of Trembling Leaves*. I think these two would turn out to have quite a bit in common, including tone in the sense of authorial attitude, although quite different in tone in the sense of the prevailing mood. They would not be as quickly recognized as typical, however, and my selections have all been drawn from the general category of the serious, so the point is moot.

The selections are also noticeably devoid of dialogue. Some writer's "voices" are so prevalent that they pervade the conversation of supposedly separate characters within their works. Thus we say a Jamesian character "sounds like James." This could not be said of Dad's characters, except perhaps sometimes in *The City* when Tim Hazard is philosophizing. It is in the narrative and descriptive passages that we catch the Clark voice. Certainly it is one of Dad's strengths that these two aspects of his prose are so often neatly interconnected. The reader is made to "see" as the story is moved along in time and through events. His dialogue, I should say, is in general simply functional, and designed to sound realistic, the way such a person would talk. His characters do have a tendency to bring out the worst in each other when they converse. This may be something of a theme in itself, a recurring illustration of the axiom we get in *The City* where the narrator claims each of us is made less than what we are at our best by the presence of others. *Ox-Bow* certainly dramatizes that notion. But it may also be Dad's drive for simplification of emotion in the prose that makes characters, in dialogue, so often emphasize a single trait, take their party line in the politics of that work. Curt's invariable scoffing and bullying in the earlier scenes of *The Track of the Cat* is a fine example. Only later, when Curt is alone on the hunt, do we get a sense that he has some variety and complexity to him.

Now, at last, to something about the passages. I must admit that I have worked deductively here. I picked the passages by ear, before I worried about their possible common denominators, and I was relieved to discover that they do indeed share some things, if not always as neatly as I might wish.

The first thing I call attention to, and the opening of "The Indian Well" presents it in a particularly pure form, is the peculiar viewpoint that operates in much of Dad's fiction. The viewpoint in that sentence is detached several removes from even the normal omniscient narrator of fiction. We might call it "cosmic," or borrow "geologic" from the Prelude to *The City*. If there are any literary echoes here, they might be Stephen Crane, in such openings of stories as "The Blue Hotel" or "The Open Boat." Maybe some Thomas Hardy too. At any rate, it provides us with an unspecified, though huge, Presence, perhaps a fatalistic force overseeing all things, but also one that helps disguise and, I think, control the preacher and teacher. There is a moral fierceness in Dad, and a strong yearning for moral simplicity, which Crane did not have.

Detached but unspecified, this narrator can be a fairly subtle manipulator when it combines with a figure in a story to become ostensibly the character's viewpoint as reported by the author. This is a crucial element in both the passage from "Hook" and from "The Wind and the Snow of Winter." This viewpoint, in turn, is a prerequisite for two other striking and interconnected characteristics of these passages. They both exhibit a formality of diction, doubly surprising when we recall the central figures are an old prospector and a hawk, presented in fairly lengthy and grammatically complex sentences, and an overall "poetic" quality, often called Dad's lyricism. Such words as "shard" are part of the poetic impression, of course, but the main source is the metaphoric implications of most of the sentences. A variety of devices contribute. Animate verbs credited to inanimate objects, factually inaccurate but figuratively accurate adjectives, similes, all help direct the reader's emotional reaction along the desired lines as a sparser prose could not do.

"Hook," for instance, achieves an amazing feat inasmuch as

it makes a hawklike attitude acceptable, even sympathetic, even to those of us who might consider ourselves doves. The tone of the passage is something like controlled scorn, with the arrogance from which scorn usually issues. The diction is particularly loaded. If we took it to be the author stigmatizing the farmers with "stooping and scraping," contrasting their "ugly" fields with "lovely" grass while castigating the gulls as "shameless" and reinforcing the accusation by having them "gobble," not eat, "worms and grubs," we should dismiss it as invidious propaganda, the Raptor's Society on a rampage. Because it is the hawk, we tend not only to go along with, but to accept, without much reflection, the hawk's evaluation. At least temporarily, we accept the contempt as just, and feel the emotion that a propagandistic argument can engender, all the stronger for being one-sided.

Actually, if we look a bit more closely, it is not quite the hawk thinking, either. If one had to imagine a hawk thinking, would you have him observing that "no lovely grass rustled"? I think of hawks as being more practical than esthetic. Yet nowhere does the hawk specifically think in these esthetic terms. That "lovely" is thought for him in a subordinate clause, but it is also one of the subtle ways we are made to take the hawk's side. It is part of Hook's dignity, his being true to a high ideal, that he makes such distinctions, and is shamed when he cannot stick to them. It is also an argument for wild grass, and against plowed fields.

Although the opening sentence alone is not sufficient to prove the point, "The Indian Well" also is dominated by a kind of restrained scorn for humankind and its works, a scorn heightened, rather than lessened, just as it is in "Hook," when a man—in both cases using a gun—defeats a wild creature that deserves better. Both stories, in their basic conceptions, run the risk of being too simply ecological messages, too simplistic condemnations of human interference with nature. They are saved, in good part, by that peculiar viewpoint that allows the author to interfere, but not speak directly.

Turning to the passage from "The Wind and the Snow of Winter," we find it to be virtually the story in microcosm, in theme as well as in the emotional response it extracts. We get, in effect, a compact lesson in the contrasting symbolic meanings of orange and white, of lamps with flames as opposed to electric lights. Once again, as in "Hook," the meanings are directed for us. Once again we are disarmed because these are presumably the old prospector's reactions to orange and white, although clearly not in words that Braneen, even if he were less confused about past and present, would be able to use. The poetic, unspecified narrator has emerged again to describe the old orange lights as a "communal glow," the newer electric lights as "needles," and to make the extension for the readers that they might easily not make for themselves if left with only the contrast between orange and white lights, about the lonesomeness and separateness of latter-day civilization. Given the circumstances the story establishes, one cannot really say this is Dad making a comment on a failing of contemporary civilization. One suspects he is, but the extension of the only partly "natural" symbols of the different kinds of light is necessary to evoke the sought-for response, a sadness for good things gone, even in those who might have no interest in mining towns in the desert, old or new.

With the ending of *The Track of the Cat*, the viewpoint is much more the standard omniscient narrator, over the shoulder of a chosen character. The diction is less formal, the rhetorical devices less pronounced, restricted mainly to that favorite verbal construction of a main verb plus an adverbial modifier, in "lining out," and the faint but characteristic blurring of an animate subject with its inanimate object. The whole passage is Harold's visual perception of the ranch house in the distance. In the second sentence, the ranch house becomes an active subject. The "showed" and "grew" are not so removed from ordinary usage as to be obtrusively animistic, but they do give an impression of something external to Harold's perception, and even to his thoughts. The "it" begins to have a life of its own, and the image of the ranch house in the snow becomes, by easy extension, an image or emblem of Harold's uncertain future. The lines are surprisingly packed with suggestions for the conclusion of quite a long novel.

Even this last paragraph, though it holds out the promise of some sort of future, strikes me as somewhat melancholy with its "distance," "shadow," "faint," and the partially obscuring snow, which also concludes "The Wind and the Snow of Winter." All my selections, if I may invoke the entire story of "The Indian Well" that follows the first sentence, suggest this is a recurring mood in Dad's fiction. The voice seems often to be evoking sympathy for something good that is irrevocably gone, or glimpsed but not quite graspable. Often the good is some kind of innocence and youthful strength, which enjoyed a corresponding freedom.

My neat equation of emotion felt by the author being passed on to the reader needs some modification here. The end result, especially in the serious or lyrical pieces, may be melancholy, but often, I suspect, the pieces were fueled by anger. Not always, of course. We have Dad's testimony that many of his stories started with a simple description, landscapes without stories. The landscapes are frequently rendered from nostalgia, as were stories based on his own youth. Here an authorial melancholy is passed on directly, sometimes even against the author's intent. *The City of Trembling Leaves*, though meant to close on a kind of triumphant arrival of Tim Hazard at maturity as man and composer, is one of the most melancholy books I know.

But once characters are introduced into the landscape, especially characters who are not autobiographical, they are likely as not characters toward whom the author is not very sympathetic. I recall Herb Wilner's remark that he sensed a lot of anger in Dad. I believe there was—an anger a good deal deeper than the flash-point temper. He was angry at the general course of human activity. And a good part of Dad's strategy as a writer had to be to channel the anger, somehow control it, or it would too much damage the story. It is liable to come too close to the surface, for instance, when he tries to use a viewpoint figure that is too autobiographical, and yet not the central actor. I think of the first-person narrator of "The Buck in the Hills," and the "Walt Clark" of *The City* who denies Helen Black, once she is in Beverly Hills, almost all the quick perceptiveness she

had shown earlier, and describes her as the worst kind of af-
fluent, insensitive suburbanite. He shielded his stories against
the anger either with the satirical extravagances of the moral
fables, or with a viewpoint that could provide a controlling
channel. Hook is an angry bird, whereas "The Indian Well" is
given detachment by a point of view so far removed that it en-
velopes the human element in the calmly recurring cycles of
the well. Dad's fiction often seems a means of relieving the
anger, which is transformed by the mechanics and the duration
of the story to anger spent, muted to melancholy by the distance—the silence of the moonrise, in Mrs. Thompson's story,
that calms the frenzied human activity.

This is all very impressionistic, to be sure. To give at least
the melancholy some corroboration, let me quote Dad as he is
quoted in a short poem by William Stafford, "Something Walter Clark Said." Stafford visited the University of Nevada to
lecture at one of the teacher's institutes Dad was working with
in the mid-1960s, and I am sure the poem recalls an actual comment when the two of them were talking, probably over a
boilermaker on the porch of the place west of Reno that looked
eastward across the city to the desert mountains:

> "Things end that were good;
> the big picture is always sad."[2]

Notes

1. Quoted in William Flint Thrall and Addison Hibbard, *A
Handbook to Literature*, revised by C. Hugh Holman (New York:
Odyssey, 1960), p. 326.
2. *Concerning Poetry*, 1/1 (Spring 1968) 56.

PART IV

Two Biographical Accounts of Walter Clark

Brief notices of Clark appear many places, but no extended biography has been published, and presumably none has been written. Following are two basic documents for such a biography: the first (chapter 17) is by Walter Clark; the second (chapter 18) was prepared by his son Robert for this volume.

Walter Clark, Reno, Nevada, 1966. (Special Collections, Library, University of Nevada, Reno)

17

Autobiographical Information

Walter Clark

*Walter Clark's statement calls for explanation. Everybody who be-
comes well known is pestered by young people who have been required by their teachers to write letters to famous personages, pro-
pounding questions that would require a hefty volume to answer.
Many writers ignore such impositions, but Clark could not do that.
Instead he prepared "Biographical Information" (here called "Autobiographical Information"), answering briefly the questions he was
most frequently asked, had copies made of it, and sent one to who-
ever asked. It is very uneven. It starts as Clark might have talked,
in chatty, gently humorous vein, with plenty of fact and few excursions. As he proceeds, however, Clark's love of serious discussion
takes over, and he becomes both more expansive and more philosophic. Almost suddenly he brings the whole to a close—one can
imagine that he was getting tired and the time was getting late. Thus
the statement contains little of what one would like to know about
Clark's most productive years, or those subsequent times when he
was writing but producing little that he considered publishable. The
piece provides, however, a glimpse of Clark as he saw himself shortly
after he had begun the Doten period.*

Born Aug. 3, 1909, in log cabin (now gone) in woods out-
side of small farming community of East Orland,
Maine, first child of Dr. Walter Ernest Clark (see earlier *Who's
Who*) teacher and economist, and Euphemia Abrams Clark,

musician. Three other children, Euphemia, David, and Miriam. Lived three years in apartment on St. Nicholas Ave., New York City (father teaching Econ. at City College—then head of dept.) with summers in the cabin in Maine. Then five years on farm in West Nyack, N.Y., twenty miles up Hudson from the city. Hated the city (still hate cities; too many people elbowing other people in too little space, with nothing else alive except in a zoo or on a leash, which is not really being alive) except for walks in the parks, the Christmas displays in the big department stores (I was still a believer) and the fire-engines going by at night. They were still horse-drawn engines, three big dapple-grays abreast, sparks flying from their hooves and the tires on the cobblestones, and from the chimney of the pumper, and a spotted Dalmatian running under the rear axle. Magnificent. Loved the Maine country and seashore and the farm. Lots of space and sky and weather, all sorts of things growing, wild and in gardens (had one of my own to ruin from the time I was five) and fields, and all sorts of living things domestic and wild, from tadpoles in the cow pond to a huge, red bull. The deep interest in all kinds of life which I developed then has never left me. On farm, too, by way of my mother's piano, my father['s] fine storytelling and reading aloud to us, King Arthur, Robin Hood, Indian and frontier tales, Greek, Roman, and Nordic gods and heroes, the Bible, much else, and the kind interest of a neighbor who was a painter, developed the love of reading and writing, music and art which have also continued. My first painting I can remember, a very wet and mingled water-color of the first football game I ever saw, which had excited me a great deal. My first poem I cannot remember, but have been told it was a quatrain about a pair of rubbers. Unfortunately for posterity, both masterpieces have been lost. Also wrote many very adventurous and very short short-stories, even serials of a distinctly cliff-hanging variety, all of which were "published" in a very local weekly paper, The Clark News, to which I also contributed poems and illustrations.

When I was eight my family moved to Reno, Nevada, where my father became president of the University of Nevada (1917–1937). Went through grammar school at the Orvis Ring

School (named after a pioneer Nevada educator) where the principal and my eighth-grade teacher was an eagle-eyed, durable, devoted, strict, and knowing old lady by the name of Libby C. Booth, who had come across the plains in a covered wagon when she was only sixteen, and fought off Indians beside the body of her new, young husband, whom they had killed. (A Reno school and school street are now named after her.) She also made a great many lasting impressions on me, both pleasant and uncomfortable. (The uncomfortable ones were richly deserved. Example: Two hours doing algebra on the blackboards every afternoon while the rest of the gang were playing football, when I was the *first team* left half-back, weight 89 lbs. with a helmet on, and the punter and passer.) Also learned to play the violin, more or less, during that time, generally with the neighborhood gang playing football or baseball on the lawn outside while I was doing finger exercises. At the Orvis Ring, and in Reno High School, I ran through a succession of some twenty or twenty-five deathless loves, only a couple of whom ever knew about it. The knowledge did not seem to make them happy. In high school, in such spare time as romance left me, I also played tennis and basketball, took part in dramatics publications, and debating, and finally, in my junior year, even began to make good grades in subjects other than English and art, where everything just naturally went happily. Also began writing a good deal of verse and drew colored chalk cartoons on the blackboards all over school for the political campaigns (Andy Gump was elected president by an overwhelming majority during my senior year, and we had to hold the election all over again, with Andy, rather arbitrarily, stricken from the ticket), dances, plays, and games. Also, during these school years, much time climbing and camping in the Sierras, and hiking and camping in the big, fenceless (quite a few fences, worse luck, in parts of it now) desert country east of Reno, and a great deal of ocean swimming with my brother off the beaches (beautifully empty and clean then; we swam as often without suits as with suits on; now they're crowded and littered and built up; in fact you have to peer between garbage cans to even see the beaches and surf we knew, and then the most of what you see is beach umbrellas and hotdog wrappers) of Southern California. Also a good deal of hunting and fishing; I quit for keeps before I was twenty. Learned then, and still believe, that living creatures are a great deal more beautiful than dead ones, and that only real physical need, as among the animals themselves, justifies killing. Began to hunt with my eyes only, and have been doing it with great pleasure ever since. Don't even like cameras. They get one so busy with the gadget itself that he doesn't really see what he should be looking at. Look and remember; look and remember, that's the thing.

Earned my social spending money during the high school years as a student janitor. Also helped out sometimes (the amount of help is questionable) driving horses and cutting cattle on some of the ranches in the region. Worked in Southern California a year between high school and college to make part of my college expenses—a variety of odd jobs, mostly very oddly done too, house painting (got lead poisoning and was put on a diet of bread and milk and pills for six months), gardening, feeding the fish in an aquarium, truck driving, and acting as assistant to the assistant linoleum layer for a hardware company. Then through the University of Nevada to B.A. and M.A. degree in English, but with almost as much study in philosophy and psychology. Also more basketball, tennis, dramatics, and publications, and a great deal more writing, still mostly poetry. First publication in a professional sense, a few scattered poems. Also more dating. Met the girl I would marry, Barbara Frances Morse, daughter of a Presbyterian minister in Pennsylvania. While taking the M.A. also did my first teaching (it's been my chief means to the bread and butter ever since, and also an occupation I respect so much and am so fond of that it's kept me from doing anything like as much writing as I should have; Who's Who lists me as teacher first and writer second, and it's quite correct), practice teaching at Reno High School and a couple of frosh comp courses at the University. Scared green at first, of course, but so happy when things went right, which they did once in a while, that I was hooked for life. Also acted as an assistant director in dramatics and a student coach in tennis. By the time I had finished at Nevada, obviously, my direction was set for life. Not that I haven't found things interesting since. On the contrary, I've kept busy constantly (only complaint, sometimes too infernally busy in too many directions at once, to do enough of just lying on my back, staring at the sky and ruminating, something I firmly believe everybody, but especially, perhaps, teachers and writers, should do often) and enjoyed myself enormously. But the rest has been pretty much a continuation, in different ways and places, of the various things I've already suggested, teaching, writing, sports, art, and music (though mostly just as looker and listener), hiking and camping, outdoor life in general, when I could get it in, and socializing. My favorite diversion, by long odds, socializing, just sitting around with a beer or more in all kinds of places talking to all kinds of people about all kinds of things. (It's a professional necessity for a writer too, but it's no good to him if he takes it that way, watching people and listening to them, making mental notes and saying to himself, "This I must remember." He'll never get to know people in the ways that matter most if he treats them as specimens. Nobody likes to be a specimen. The thing is to be really a part of whatever is going on, without a thought about "using" it. The memory will keep what matters.) I've added a few interests, chess for the fun of it, history, particularly western history as told by those who were personally involved in it, by way of journals, memoirs, letters, newspaper pieces, etc. (Much history, as written by professional historians, bores me to death. Most of them write so badly that they can't bring anything alive for the reader, and most of them try to cover too much also, and the more you try to cover, the less you can bring it alive.) Indian lore, geology, mining, and ranching methods, not professionally, but as necessary knowledge for stories I still hope to write. And time and experience have brought me some new convictions and concerns and prejudices, and strengthened some old ones and rubbed out some others, just as they will for anyone. I believe, for instance, that the two most important concerns of the human race now, all of it everywhere, must be birth control and natural conservation, the preservation and even, where possible, the restoration, of other forms of life and of all natural resources. Unless we make big gains in those realms, and make them promptly, too, we won't last long enough to let our concern about anything else matter much. I detest racial, religious, and class or occupational prejudice, but I detest them on both sides. One cannot help but feel more sympathy, of course, for the people who have been having the hardest times in life, the minorities (though by the time we get done adding up all the minorities in the U.S., just for instance, Negroes, Jews, Indians, Chinese, Catholics, Buddhists, farmers, college graduates, labor union members, etc., etc.—even writers, for that matter—it seems to me it's something less than easy to tell just who the big, bad wolf majority is; there are a great many kinds of division, and all sides of all of them seem to me bad when they get hostile, greedy, or so concerned with their own interests that they can't even recognize anybody else's rights or problems), which have really endured abuse and lack of opportunity, but I have no more use for the haters among minority groups than for the haters in any larger group. Hate means division, and all division, from that between two people who can't get along to that between nations, is evil. In an atomic age it is also the seedbed of doom. I also believe that education, both formal and informal, is the only thing which can really lead to a large enough recognition and practice in all three of these huge, basic, all-inclusive necessities of survival, voluntary birth control, natural conservation, and the reduction of divisions, to matter, so I also believe that equal opportunity in education is the most important of all equalities. But I am afraid, very much afraid, that it will be too slow an instrument to these necessary understandings and practices, unless a great many more people are brought to recognize its importance, starting with its importance to them, very rapidly, and to seek it much more broadly, to seek it primarily as a means to understanding, not merely as a means to make a living, above all not as a means to getting the jump on anybody else. I haven't been across yet, of course, so I can't speak from first-hand experience, and I've never talked with anybody who has been, either, but I very much doubt that the dead take any

interest in wealth or prominence, or in race, religion, class, occupation, or nationality either, for that matter. I also believe
that this absolutely necessary mutual understanding and toler-
ance must begin at the beginning, with the efforts of individuals to understand and tolerate all kinds of other individuals, to
voluntarily, that is, strive to reduce the ignorance, hate, and
power of division in themselves. There is no other way in
which the larger unifications can ever be brought into trustwor-
thy being. Which, at least, brings it all down to the level where
everybody can really do something about it every day. Which
might be summed up the way James Lowell once summed it up
when he tried to make clear to a largely aristocratic, skeptical,
and somewhat condescending Oxford audience, why the best
hope of humanity (hope, not actuality, then, or even, unfortu
nately, now) lay in a democratic way of life. "Democracy," he
said, "means not 'I'm as good as you are,' but 'You're as good
as I am.' " And such beliefs, convictions, feelings, are, of
course, however he may choose to put them, what matters most
about a writer. Which is why I doubt that I'll ever write a longer
autobiography than this, or help anybody else to write much
about me at length, either. My personal life doesn't matter
much to anybody but me and those closest to me, and besides,
I've already tried to say, as well as I could, and much more fully
than I could here, what has mattered most to me, that could
also matter to somebody else, in my stories, and hope to keep
on doing so for a while more. Not that any of them are directly
autobiographical, but all of them, like all of any storyteller's
writings, have drawn upon my own experience—how could
they help it?—and all of them have been, in different ways, efforts to dramatize, give life to, the beliefs, convictions, ideas,
and feelings that have mattered to me. The *Ox-Bow*, for instance, was an effort to create an experience that would make
the reader feel deeply what I felt about the forms of justice as
safeguards for the realities of justice, and to present the kinds
of human prejudices and divisions which destroy justice. (The
preface to the *Life* edition says as much about my intention
there as I dared to say. Something must be left to the reader
to find for himself, or there won't be any experience.) *The*

City—though it is not by any means autobiographical—will show you a good deal of the world I grew up in. *The Cat* embodies much of what I have been talking about here in the matters of natural conservation, the destructive powers of prejudice, and the self-destructive powers of conceit, self-righteousness, and violence. Each of the short stories will give you another glimpse of some part of me and my world. "The Watchful Gods," "The Buck in the Hills," and "The Fish Who Could Close His Eyes," for example, all show different aspects of what I feel about man's relation to other creatures. And "The Portable Phonograph" says something of what I feel about the suicidal potential of man's selfishness and division, only the more so because its little drama is played out among men of the sort who ought, above all others, to know better. And, so far as my work is concerned, both teaching and writing, I have said, however humorously and exaggeratedly, enough of what I feel and believe in those realms in a long half-story, half-article, entitled "Where Is the Little Man Inside?" . . . In short, what matters about the rest of my life to anyone but me was already on its way when I finished at the University of Nevada, and can be found in other things I have already written, so the rest can be told briefly. 1932–34, further graduate work in American lit. and Greek classical drama, poetry, and philosophy, with part-time teaching and a great deal more writing, at U. of Vermont. Married during this time, and during this time also found the subjects I most wanted to write about drawing me out of poetry and into fiction. Lived for a year with my wife in an old farmhouse outside of Essex, New York, writing constantly and for long hours, but publishing only a few poems. We had very little money, but a fine life nevertheless. It was the depth of the depression then, so nothing cost very much either. We stored away a whole side of beef for the winter, for instance, which cost us, the best of steaks and roasts included, only seven cents a pound. Taught a summer session at City College in New York, where my father had taught, to build up the kitty a little. Then moved to the lovely, old (from Dutch colonial days) village of Cazenovia in the Finger Lakes region of New York. There taught high school English, coached tennis and basketball and directed dramatics for ten years. There also our two children Barbara and Robert were born, and there too I wrote the first works which won any important attention, *Ox-Bow*, and "Hook," a long story about a hawk drawn from memories of my California summers, and most of the rest of my published short stories. We took a year off on the earnings of the *Ox-Bow*, and lived in a kind of artists' and writers' colony on the old Indian Springs Ranch in the desert north of Las Vegas, Nevada, where I wrote the first half of *The City*. Finished it in Cazenovia. Then, in 1945, when it was published, moved to Rye, N.Y., as head of high school English Department and tennis coach, but forced to resign at mid-year by complete physical exhaustion and, apparently (though I didn't discover that until much later) a touch of TB, brought on by working too long school hours at Cazenovia, classes all day, other activities almost every evening, writing into the small hours of the morning, with too much coffee and too many cigarettes to keep me going. In Taos, New Mexico, on the Lujan ranch for a year, exploring that magnificent valley, the Sangre de Christo (Blood of Christ) mountains east of it, the San Juan forest and mountains west of it, the long, deep gorge of the Rio Grande, and the little Spanish villages and Indian pueblos along it, while I recovered some energy and interest in life. Then three years on the old, pioneer Lewers ranch in Washoe Valley, Nevada (named after the Indian tribe, particularly fine basketmakers, who were living there when the white man came), where I wrote *The Cat* and the greater part of "The Watchful Gods," besides a lot of things which I threw away, and my first articles and reviews. So we were back in the country where I'd grown up, and which I loved most. (It has been "home" to our children ever since, too.) We haven't been far from it for any length of time since. We have lived five years in our favorite town, the famous old mining town of Virginia City, where I again taught English and coached basketball in the high school, three years in Missoula, Montana (and there in some of the handsomest country in all the west), where I taught at the state university, and five years in Marin County, north of the Golden Gate, while I taught creative writing at San

Francisco State College. . . . The rest has been professional excursions during those years, a trip to Colgate University in the spring of 1957, where they were kind enough to award me an honorary degree of Doctor of Letters, a year as visiting lecturer in the Writers' Workshop at U. of Iowa, a term at the Stanford Writers' Workshop, a year as fellow in writing at the Center for Advanced Studies at Wesleyan University, in Connecticut, a tour as Rockefeller Foundation Lecturer in writing to Reed College, U. of Washington and U. of Oregon, and shorter visits for lectures or as a teacher in summer writers' conferences, to a great many other colleges and universities, including Utah, Wyoming, California, Southern California, Illinois, Missouri, and Arkansas. Also numerous talks about literature and writing and teaching before various professional groups, teachers, librarians, writers, and a good many radio and TV appearances of the same sort.

Now we hope we have finished our circling, though doubtless we will make many excursions. I am back at the University of Nevada, from which I started my teaching-and-writing wanderings more than thirty years ago, as Writer-in-Residence, which means, at present, that I am drawing a narrative "life" of one Alfred Doten, California '49er and rancher, a Nevada silver miner and long-time Comstock editor, out of his almost unbelievable journals (79 of them, missing not twenty days between March, 1849, when he left his native Plymouth, Mass., to sail around Cape Horn, to Nov. 1903, when he died in Carson City, Nevada) and thousands of manuscripts, newspaper clippings, letters, and pictures which he kept with them, and after that I will, probably for several years, be editing a full set of the journals and papers themselves—both books to be published by the University Press. While I'm at it we live in the center of an old ranch on a hill west of Reno, with all our beloved mountains and deserts and old mining towns within easy reach, and I hope, when the first Doten book is finished, and I get into the editing, to find time to do a little teaching again too, and to get back to writing another novel or story of my own. I have several, in fact too many, in mind, all dealing, by way of ranches and mining towns, with various happenings, ideas, and beliefs about which I still have strong feelings.

18

Chronology

Robert M. Clark

Robert Clark used his own recollection in preparing this chronology, along with documents in the possession of the family and conversations with surviving members of the family and friends, especially the artist Robert Caples, who was long Clark's closest companion.

Born August 3, 1909, at parents' summer cabin on Toddy Pond, near East Orland, Maine. First of four children. Father, Walter Ernest Clark, born in Ohio, 1873, son of a former schoolteacher who had become a Methodist minister, dying of yellow fever in 1878, leaving the family very poor. Dr. Clark put himself through school, a B.A. and M.A. at Ohio Wesleyan, and a doctorate at Columbia (1903). Taught economics at the City College of New York, becoming head of the Political Science Department, authored and collaborated on several textbooks. Mother, Euphemia Murray Abrams, born 1882, daughter of a prosperous Hartford, Connecticut, physician. She graduated from Cornell, studied piano and composition at Columbia, and did social work in New York City before the marriage in June 1908.

1909–1912. Lives in apartment on St. Nicholas Avenue during the school year, summers in Maine.

1912–1917. At West Nyack, New York, in large, onetime farmhouse near the Hudson. In the fall of 1917, his father accepts position as president, University of Nevada, and moves family to Reno. WVTC lives in the President's House on the southeast corner of the campus bluff through all his local schooling, Dr. Clark serving as president until 1938.

1917–1926. Attends Orvis Ring Grammar School and Reno High School, one year younger than most of his classmates because of skipped grade in elementary school. Plays varsity basketball, takes three years of R.O.T.C., becoming one of four cadet captains, in debate club, student dramatics, business manager for the yearbook in his senior year, tennis team. Family spends summers in La Jolla, California, near the Scripps Institute of Oceanography, where WVTC and his younger brother occasionally work at odd jobs.

1926–1927. Lives with maternal aunt in El Centro, California. Works for uncle, owner of the Imperial Valley Hardware Co., as truckdriver, warehouseman. Discovers Edwin Arlington Robinson, begins to write narrative poetry, solidifies distaste for business world, large and small, accompanies other employees on brief visits to Mexican border towns.

1927–1932. Attends the University of Nevada, earning B.A. in May 1931, M.A. in December 1931. Majors in English, with strong minor in philosophy, more than required French literature. An A– average, elected to honorary scholastic fraternity Phi Kappa Phi, 1930. Plays freshman basketball, but knee trouble keeps him from making the varsity. Ranks fifth in state in tennis, takes part in two student dramatic productions, writes satirical pieces for the college humor magazine and poems for the senior yearbook, but spends much of his free time on poetry. Publishes individual poems in collegiate magazines and anthologies. In the fall of 1928 meets Barbara Frances Morse (b. 1906), daughter of a retired Presbyterian minister and biblical scholar, from Troy, Pennsylvania. She had transferred from Oberlin College for her senior year because of sinus trouble. In the summer of 1929, takes camping tour of country with college friend, visiting Barbara in Missoula, Montana, where she was attending summer school. Attends Stanford University, summer quarter, 1930, contemplating that school for graduate work, and makes first acquaintance with the poetry of Robinson Jeffers. Narrative poem "Christmas Comes to Hjalsen," with cover illustration, used by family as Christmas card. In 1931, gets permission to write predominately creative Master's thesis, completes "Sword Singer," a narrative poem version of the Tristram legend, during the summer at La Jolla. After receiving M.A., spends Spring semester 1932 taking courses, including student teaching at Reno High School, to satisfy requirements for a Nevada secondary school credential. Summer with mother, brother, and sisters at Carmel, California. Meets Robinson Jeffers on visit to Tor House. *Ten Women in Gale's House and Shorter Poems* published at father's expense. Overhauls poetry notebooks, throwing away, by his own estimate, some four hundred poems.

1932–1934. Teaching assistant at the University of Vermont while doing further graduate work. Makes up courses in Anglo-Saxon and Chaucer, reading for examinations in American and English literature and Greek philosophers and tragedians, writing a laudatory critical thesis on Robinson Jeffers for an M.A. with honors, June 1934. Numerous short poems published in the college literary magazine. Spends summer of 1933 with his mother, other Clark children, at the same cabin in Maine where he was born. Marries Barbara Morse, October 14, her father performing the ceremony at his home in Elmira, New York. After brief honeymoon at a borrowed cabin in the Adirondack mountains, Barbara returns to Elmira while WVTC continues to rent a room in a professor's house in Burlington. In November first "national" publication with two poems in *Poetry*.

1934–1935. The recently married couple spends part of the summer following graduation from Vermont with the Clarks in Maine, part with Morses at their family summer home outside the village of Essex, New York, on Lake Champlain. Contemplates going to Columbia for doctorate. The couple decides instead to stay on at the Essex house, despite lack of electricity, running water, or furnace, on money saved from the assistantship. Publishes another poem in *Poetry* in September, and one in *American Poetry Journal* in February 1935. Makes first sustained efforts at fiction, trying to develop novels from narrative poems. Writes short first version of *The Track of the Cat*, without any female characters, and discards it. Works on a novel with a proletarian slant involving a tailor, Todd Jenkins, crushed by depression circumstances. May have submitted first short stories for publication, with no success. In the early summer of 1935 WVTC goes to Blauvelt, New York, near his old West Nyack home, to visit with mother, sister, and brother, who is attending medical school in New York City. Living with the family at Blauvelt, teaches his first literature courses from June to August for a summer session job at CCNY arranged by his father, as family continues to doubt his practicality. Barbara joins him in July. They visit Maine with the Clarks, return to Essex, planning another winter devoted to writing. In the fall Barbara's brother-in-law, superintendent of an experimental centralized grammar school-high school in the small, central New York town of Cazenovia, offers WVTC a half-time English-teaching job to begin the following January. Moves to Cazenovia in November.

1936–1941. Teaching at Cazenovia, classes ranging from "slow" seventh-graders to postgraduate courses for college-bound students. The half-time job quickly becomes full-time, with a heavy load of extracurricular duties, including producing, directing, and participating in student dramatic productions, coaching the basketball team for three years, coaching and playing basketball with the local town team. Social life mainly with other members of the faculty.

Poetry becomes occasional, although as late as 1941 WVTC contemplates putting together a publishable volume. Writes on school vacations, weekends, and late at night. After boarding for several months, couple moves into a summer cabin on the East Lake Road, bordering Cazenovia Lake, later into the larger, but still small and low-ceilinged old farmhouse on the same property, within walking distance of the school. Spends summer of 1936 in Essex. During this period probably completes "Water," the only pre-*Ox-Bow* novel extant. It is rejected, with compliments, by publishers. At some point it is submitted to a novel contest, winning second prize, and an inquiry from an agent that leads to the submission of *The Ox-Bow Incident.* In the summer of 1937 WVTC travels west by car with his brother and a cousin, touring the southwest, visiting in La Jolla, stopping to check a college teaching possibility at Santa Barbara, then visiting at his family's home on the Nevada campus into August. Works on short stories, including "The Pretender," which uses Pyramid Lake, north of Reno, as setting. Much of the Lawrence Black material in the second section of *The City of Trembling Leaves* is based on experiences during this sojourn in Reno, during which WVTC saw a good deal of his painter friend Robert Caples, Black's prototype. The two friends go camping at Pyramid, and make a stay of several days in Virginia City, the much-dwindled mining camp some twenty-five miles southeast of Reno in desert mountains. The return east made via the northwest, includes Yellowstone Park, and WVTC arrives at Essex just before the birth of his daughter, September 1, in a Plattsburgh, New York, hospital. Begins *The Ox-Bow Incident*, probably during the following Christmas vacation, completing the first draft over Easter vacation, 1938. Summer at Essex, which provided the setting for "The Rapids." Writing in the "tower," the smallest and topmost room of a three-storied octagonal front on the late-Victorian house, WVTC works most of the summer on an early version of *The City of Trembling Leaves*, but burns it. The *Ox-Bow* accepted by Random House that December, but WVTC made further revisions, probably during the summer of 1939. Moves family to apartment on ground floor of a large house at 19 Albany, Cazenovia's main street. Son born, October 22. Before publication of *The Ox-Bow* in October 1940, sells "Hook" to *Atlantic Monthly* (July). The good reviews and quick success of *The Ox-Bow* after its publication in October 1940 bring a run on stories already written. In October the *Atlantic* buys "The Pretender," and the *Saturday Evening Post* "Trial at Arms," the $450 payment equalling the advance on the novel. In November he sells "Between Joseph and God" to the *New Yorker*, and in December another story, "Prestige," to the *Post*. A burst of writing and rewriting short stories follows, with "The Rapids," "Why Don't You Look Where You're Going," "The Portable Phonograph," and "The Anonymous" all accepted for publication in various magazines before the fall of 1941. He would have one story included in each volume of the O. Henry prize stories from 1941 through 1945.

1941–1942. Spends summer at Essex except for a brief time

with his brother and wife at Martha's Vineyard, Massachusetts, where the eager but inexperienced sailors swamp a large, borrowed sailboat. In the fall of 1941 starts a year's leave of absence from Cazenovia school, and moves family to Indian Springs, Nevada, in the desert north of Las Vegas, at the invitation of Caples, whose wealthy second wife had bought a onetime ranch and converted it into an art colony, providing housing, evening dinners at a main house, and even living expenses in exchange for a percentage of the profit that would theoretically ensue from the labors of the assortment of resident artists, mainly painters and sculptors, though WVTC insists upon paying his own expenses. Works first on a satirical novel based on Little America, a motel-resort complex on U.S. 40 in Wyoming, and on book of poems. Starts *The City of Trembling Leaves* again. Also writes "The Rise and the Passing of Bar," "A Letter to the Living," and "The Ascent of Aeriel Goodbody." In March 1942, the movie (and television) rights to *The Ox-Bow* are sold to Twentieth Century-Fox, bringing WVTC $5,265. After a visit to Reno, returns to Cazenovia in late August 1942.

1942–1945. Family lives at 31 Fenner Street, Cazenovia. Teaching load is increased as faculty reduced by the war. Summer at Essex. Tries to reactivate a reserve commission granted after high school R.O.T.C., but is turned down because of bad knees. Works mainly on *The City*, completing the book in 1944, with considerable time spent trying to shorten the book at the publisher's request. Writes "The Indian Well" during the winter of 1942, "The Buck in the Hills" shortly after and, in late 1944, "The Wind and the Snow of Winter," which wins the O. Henry short story prize for 1945. Contemplates enlisting as late as 1944, but is dissuaded by a recruiter who tells him he would be assigned to stateside training camps anyway. Submits typescripts of all his short stories for a possible volume, but Random House apparently vetoes this idea after *The City of Trembling Leaves* is published in May 1945, with mixed reviews and poor sales. After finishing the major work on *The City*, WVTC starts a rewrite of "Water," and continues it through some six hundred manuscript pages before abandoning it. In August 1945, sells "The Fish Who Could Close His Eyes" to *Tomorrow*.

1945-1946. In the summer moves to Rye, New York, when the Cazenovia superintendent moves to that district and asks him to head the English Department at Rye High School. Near a physical collapse, his weight reduced from his normal 175–190 range to 140 pounds, and disliking the region, resigns after the first term, and accepts an invitation, apparently from Mable Dodge Luhan, who may have seen a coming D. H. Lawrence in the author of *The City,* to occupy an adobe house and studio on her property in Taos, New Mexico, but insists on paying rent. In Taos from February to September. Recuperates health, helps fight local flood and more distant forest fire, attends as invited spectator at seancelike ceremonials for D. H. Lawrence at the Luhan house, where he meets Frieda Lawrence, and, with fewer reservations, accepts invitations from Tony Luhan, chief of the Taos Pueblo, to observe some pueblo ceremonial dances usually closed to whites. Makes acquaintance of a large number of area artists, including Frank Waters, plays the ghost of Kit Carson for a local little theater, but with health, social activities, and Mrs. Luhan's growing eccentricities, such as notes pushed under the kitchen door at 6 A.M. with domestic orders, gets no writing done. In late summer travels with wife to Nevada and rents house on the former Lewers ranch, at the foot of the timbered Sierra foothills in Washoe Valley, between Reno and Carson City. Family moves there in September.

1946-1949. On Lewers ranch. Probably in the last months of 1946 writes the first version of "The Watchful Gods." Active in the Carson City Chess Club as well as the Reno Tennis Club, through the first six months of 1947 completes two novellas involving chess, his only longer fiction to use an academic background, "The Queen Is a Powerful Piece," followed by the satirical "Ambrose, the Chess-Playing Poodle." "Ambrose" he carries through a final typescript and submits to Random House, but abandons efforts to publish it when Saxe Commins, his regular editor, advises against it. In 1947 becomes a stockholder in a magazine established by an association of writers, in which he publishes a small nonfictional blurb about turtles and for which he works on a short story developed from City material, "Willis and the Holy Water," which he completes in manuscript but does not rework, perhaps because of starting on The Track of the Cat, begun the end of 1947 or the start of 1948. He finishes typescript revisions for The Cat by December of that year, despite time off in the summer for teaching his first writers' conferences at the University of Kansas, then at Stanford.

Spends the following summer at University of Utah. Besides this first acquaintance with the academic-literary world and various well-known writers, such as Allen Tate, William Carlos Williams, and Irwin Shaw, begins, during this period, to receive requests and to write articles and reviews, starting with an advance review for the Book Find Club of A. B. Guthrie, Jr.'s The Big Sky in 1947. The Track of the Cat published in June 1949, with generally favorable reviews. Takes trip with family to visit Cazenovia and wife's family members summering at the Essex house.

1949–1954. At the end of the summer, moves to Virginia City, first renting the large and deteriorating former Chollar Mining Office, then, planning a permanent residence, for the first time buys a house, on Stewart Street, into which the family moves in the summer of 1950. In January 1950, completes rewriting of "The Watchful Gods." Random House, following the good success of The Cat, which briefly made several bestseller lists, agrees to a volume of selected short stories to be published with the new novella. WVTC originally plans to include "Between Joseph and God," "Prestige," "A Letter to the Living," and "The Ascent of Aeriel Goodbody" as well as those finally published. Makes minor textual changes in all the earlier stories, working on carbon typescripts of the originals. The Watchful Gods and Other Stories published in September 1950, getting very little attention and small sales. In June of 1950 works the Utah Writers' Conference again, followed in July by another at Wyoming, cut short by his first stay in a hospital, for removal of an infected tooth. From September 1950 to June 1951 teaches half-time, at $200 a month, at Virginia City High School, which had been without an English teacher for several years. Starts chess club, helps build the town's first tennis court, and coaches the basketball team of six players. Enjoys the active and varied social life of the town, centered in the saloons along the main street and composed of people with a great variety of backgrounds and occupations. For the 1951–52 school year teaches in the Writers' Workshop, University of Iowa, living in boardinghouses while the family remains in Virginia City, to which he returns for Christmas vacation. Declines offer to remain at Iowa. In June 1952, at Universities of Omaha, Missouri, and Arkansas Writers' Conferences in succession. In the fall of 1952 accepts half-time position with the English Department of the University of Nevada, in Reno, teaching freshman composition and American literature. In April 1953, speaks at Reed, Washington, and Oregon as Rockefeller Lecturer. June 1953, resigns from Nevada as protest during a faculty-administration struggle over policy brought to a head by the arbitrary firing of a biology professor by the university president, backed by the regents. In July and August teaches at the Montana Writers' Conference in Missoula, and accepts a teaching position there for the fall and winter quarters, living alone in an apartment at Fort Missoula, a moribund army post. Spring quarter teaches as visiting lecturer in the creative writing program at Stanford, and financial pinch relieved somewhat by sale of the movie rights to *The Track of the Cat* ($6,075). In the summer of 1954 gives up hope that Nevada situation will work out, accepts regular position at Montana, sells Virginia City house, and moves with family to Missoula.

Throughout this period, WVTC works on a variety of fiction. Probably in 1950, starts on "Admission Day," a novel based on contemporary Virginia City, but soon turns to "The Man in the Hole," a more heavily symbolic conception, which he works on while in Iowa City. In early 1951, perhaps to be helpful, Random House asks him to do a book on Virginia City and the Comstock Lode for their Landmark series of historical nonfiction for teenagers. When work on the novel bogs down, WVTC attempts the Landmark book, which he returns to off and on for the next ten years. Also starts an article on Nevada requested by *Holiday*, and in the summer or fall of 1952 starts on a novella "The Angel and the Judge." Nothing is completed, and the only publications are two book reviews, an unsigned historical sketch of Virginia City for a tourist pamphlet, and a piece for the *Western Review* defending creative writing as a valuable college course.

1954–1956. In Missoula, Montana, where buys house at 212 Hastings in the university quarter, is associate professor of English and chairman for the developing creative writing program. Gives numerous talks at regional teachers' conferences. In July 1955, teaches a summer session in the creative writing section at San Francisco State College. Father dies, after prolonged illness, in Reno, 1955. Daughter marries, and moves to Sparks, Nevada. In July 1956, WVTC takes part in the Montana Writers' Conference, and meets William Faulkner, but dislikes increasing intradepartmental wranglings and, hoping that a strictly creative teaching load will leave more time for his own writing, accepts full-time position at San Francisco State.

During the Montana period works on "Way Station," the last novel he would attempt, envisioned, like the other two, as one of a sequence of related novels centered in Nevada and chronicling its history from settlement to the present. Despite failure to publish new fiction, his literary reputation grows, and other books besides *The Ox-Bow* begin to be reprinted in paperback. The spring of 1956 is enlivened by an ingenious plagiarism in a pulp western called *Ramrod*, author unknown, which appeared to dovetail material from *The Ox-Bow Incident* and one of Luke Short's westerns.

1956–1962. At San Francisco State as teacher in and, for the final three years, director of a mushrooming creative writing program. Lives in Mill Valley, renting first at 43 Molino, then 552 Northern. Becomes increasingly involved in literary side business—talking at luncheons, writers' clubs, teacher's associations, universities, judging fiction contests, writing recommendations for grants and fellowships and blurbs on advance copies of novels, book reviews, and testifying, as one of the literary authorities for the defense, in the controversial censorship trial of *Howl* in 1957, but continues to work on his own writing, especially "Way Station," during summers, and rejects publisher's propositions for textbooks in creative writing. In March 1957, flies to New York for appearance on "The American Scene," NBC Television (in conjunction with the airing of an animated version of "Hook"). Spends two months of the summer of 1957 alone in Virginia City and starts several short stories. Travels east with wife in June 1958, to receive an honorary doctorate from Colgate and visit in nearby Cazenovia. In July 1959, gives talk to San Francisco State semantics conference, which he expands into a long article during the fall of 1962 for publication in *Chrysalis*. Though he had rejected offers from Texas and Illinois to head creative writing departments at higher salaries and less workload, and would never apply for a fellowship himself, he accepts, for the academic year 1960–61, a resident grant from the Center for Advanced Studies at Wesleyan University, he and wife living at 4 Hubor Manor in Middletown, Connecticut. There makes one last attempt at the Landmark book, and when that and efforts at fiction fail, volunteers to teach a creative writing class. On return to the Bay Area lives at 121 Hawthorn in Larkspur, another town in suburban Marin County, and resumes duties as director of creative writing at San Francisco State. Mother dies, 1961.

1962–1968. In January 1962, accepts an 18-month contract, to begin in the summer, with the University of Nevada, Reno, to prepare a biography for the Nevada centennial (1964), based on the journals of Alfred Doten, a "49er" and newspaperman on the Comstock Lode in Nevada, the university having recently acquired the extensive Doten journals (purchased jointly by the state legislature and the Fleischmann Foundation). WVTC and wife move to Reno in the summer, living in a house built and owned by his brother on a bluff above the Truckee River west of the city. Finds an unsought reputation growing as an authority on Western Americana as well as western literature and creative-writing teaching, and writes prefaces for several western books, including his own *The Ox-Bow Incident*. Plans for the Doten book expand to a scheme for using all the journals, covering from 1849 to 1903, instead of just those pertinent to Nevada. Lack of other materials besides Doten's diaries and newspaper writings confound the biographical aim, however, and only one article for the *Nevada Highways and Parks* magazine is done in time for the centennial year. Abandons the biography, accepts an extended contract and the title of writer-in-residence, and works at editing the journals themselves. Begins, in the fall of 1964, to teach creative-writing courses half-time at the University. In June and July 1964 does writers' conferences at Utah and Montana, and in the fall travels to Oklahoma to make a talk on Doten to the annual meeting of the Western History Association, but turns down most conferences and invitations to lecture. The summers of 1965 through 1967, teaches as part of the staff at Nevada's NDEA Institute in English. In June 1967 is interviewed and filmed at home as part of an educational movie on Robinson Jeffers. He gives several readings of stories for local groups, but does not work on any new fiction.

1968–1971. The rebuilding of a house bought in Virginia City, the same he had rented in 1957, is completed, and WVTC and wife move into it during the summer of 1968. WVTC continues to teach creative writing half-time at the university, with plans for an expanded program, and works on the Doten editing. He finishes the preface for *Lady in Boomtown*, Mrs. Hugh Brown's reminiscences about Tonopah, Nevada, his last publication. In the fall of 1968, an operation discovers prostate cancer, but is apparently successful. Nevada awards him an honorary doctorate in June 1969. Wife Barbara increasingly ill during that summer with what also turns out to be cancer; she dies November 12, 1969. WVTC continues to teach, edit, and give talks locally. A second operation in January 1971, reveals cancer, now in the lymph system. Clark resigns from the university in June. He remains at home, increasingly bedridden and in pain, but refusing morphine until November 1. Dies in St. Mary's Hospital, Reno, November 10, 1971, at age 62. Buried beside wife in Masonic cemetery in Virginia City.

Index

288

INDEX

Briaski, Jacob, 152. See also City of
Trembling Leaves, The
Bridges, Arthur, 65, 103, 182,
185, 244, 245–246. See also
Track of the Cat, The
Bridges, Curt, 44, 59, 66–67, 82,
108, 112, 184, 185, 235–236,
243–246. See also Track of the
Cat, The
Bridges, Gwen Williams, 66, 185,
212, 244, 245. See also Track of
the Cat, The
Bridges, Harold, 67, 182–183,
185, 244–246. See also Track of
the Cat, The
Bridges, Mrs., 66, 139, 244. See
also Track of the Cat, The
Bridges family, 60, 65–67, 243–
246. See also Track of the Cat,
The
Brooks, Cleanth, Jr., 52
Buck, 13, 108, 111, 115, 193,
196, 204. See also "Watchful
Gods, The"
"Buck in the Hills, The," 116,
191, 272

camping, 267
cancer, 9, 286
Caples, Robert, 124, 161, 162,
165, 173, 275, 279, 280
Capote, Truman, 251
career, shortness of, 69
Carmel, California, 63, 154, 158,
166
"Carolyn Plays Chopin," 146
Carpenter, Kenneth, J., 145
Carr, Peter, 109. See also "Anony-
mous, The"
Carson, Kit, 197, 198, 203
Carson City, Nevada, 75
Carter, Gil, 74, 85–87, 104, 243.
See also Ox-Bow Incident, The
Cather, Willa, 59, 61
cats: 183; black cats, 182. See also
Track of the Cat, The
Cazenovia, New York, 6, 7, 68,
165, 272, 278
celebration, life-giving, 131, 139

Cervantes, Miguel de, 75
character flaw, 98, 213
characterization, 39, 47–49, 66,
75, 123–125, 155, 169, 182–
186, 205, 243–246, 257, 261–
262
chess, 269
Christ, 210
Christiansen, Jake, 210, 212, 215
Christmas Comes to Hjalsen, 126,
145, 180
Chrysalis Review, 21, 23, 25
Church, Dr. J. E., 3
City College (New York, New
York), 272
City of Trembling Leaves, The, 6,
11, 13, 16, 19, 26, 28, 47, 50,
55, 62, 64, 66, 100, 118, 129–
130, 134, 146, 147–180, 188,
193, 208–209, 232–233, 236,
240, 246, 251, 252, 257, 258,
261, 272, 273, 279, 280
civilization, 58, 61–69, 99, 107,
113, 115, 183
civilized rationalizations, 108, 110
Clark, Barbara, 273. See also
Salmon, Barbara Clark
Clark, Barbara Frances Morse, 6,
9, 55, 268, 276, 286
Clark, David, 266
Clark, Euphemia, 266
Clark, Euphemia Abrams, 5, 159,
266
Clark, Miriam, 266
Clark, Robert Morse, 7, 76, 77,
145, 161, 163, 170, 179, 208–
215, 273, 275–286
Clark, Walter Ernest, 4, 26, 58,
265
"Clark, Walt" (fictional), 149,
159, 164, 261
claustrophobic, 91, 242
clear spring, 14
Clemens, Samuel, 3. See also
Twain, Mark
climbing, 267
Colgate University, 274, 285
Commins, Saxe, 281
communication, 107